D1084413

The Foreign Policy of
Col. McCormick's
Tribune

1929–1941

The Foreign Policy of

SHE DREADS A RETURN OF HIS OLD WEAKNESS

Col. McCormick's

Tribune

1929–1941

JEROME E. EDWARDS

UNIVERSITY OF NEVADA PRESS
RENO, NEVADA 1971

PN4899
C4
+76

071
E26

University of Nevada Press, Reno, Nevada 89507
©University of Nevada Press 1971. All rights reserved.
Library of Congress Catalog Card Number 79–156760
Printed in the United States of America
Designed by William H. Snyder
ISBN 0–87417–031–1

ℭONTENTS

Preface

During the presidential administrations of Herbert Hoover and Franklin Roosevelt, the *Chicago Tribune* was indisputably the leading isolationist organ in the Midwest, if not in the United States. It was the only consistently anti-Roosevelt daily possessing a large foreign staff of its own, therefore having independent sources of information. It also had more news space at its disposal than any other isolationist paper since it was one of the most prosperous publishing ventures in the country. Furthermore, from 1939 to 1941, crucial years in this study, the *Tribune* was the only morning newspaper in the nation's second city.

The publisher of the *Tribune* was a remarkable man, Robert R. McCormick (or the Colonel as he liked to be called), one of the most controversial figures in twentieth-century journalism. Rarely has any one person so deeply imprinted his own personality and views on a major metropolitan daily. This writer, therefore, has followed the assumption that the *Tribune* editorial page represents the opinions of McCormick. This, then, is the study of an individual and his reaction to American foreign policy as much as the study of a newspaper.

In approaching this subject, one cannot write about foreign policy attitudes alone. The vehemence of McCormick's opposition to Roosevelt's foreign policy, especially from 1939 to 1941, was heightened by, and perhaps was an outgrowth of, his previous strong opposition to Roosevelt's domestic policy. As early as 1936, a poll of ninety-three Washington correspondents ascertained that this group considered the *Chicago Tribune* and the Hearst chain the "least fair and reliable American newspapers."[1] This vote was prompted by the *Tribune*'s handling of domestic, rather than foreign, policy issues. Thus it will be necessary to study in some detail how McCormick's violent antipathy to the New Deal may have influenced his attitude toward world affairs.

The year 1941 was chosen as the terminal date for this study since Pearl Harbor obviously marks a watershed in American foreign policy. The Hoover administration was included in order to examine the consistency of the *Tribune*'s views under both a Republican and a Democratic president.

The Colonel's private papers were not available. For some reason the *Tribune* has sat tight on these papers, not even using them for what could be a friendly house biography. Luckily the Colonel was a fluent, blunt man, whose colorful editorials and speeches provide by themselves valuable information. Perhaps because of the unavailability of his papers, McCormick has received surprisingly little scholarly study, and the field has been left to his enemies. The biographies in Wayne Andrews's *Battle for Chicago* and John Tebbel's *An American Dynasty* were influenced too strongly by the passions of the time to depict McCormick as anything more than a complete simpleton. George Seldes in various books went even further in branding McCormick a fascist. The most complete biography to appear to date is Frank C. Waldrop's recently published *McCormick of Chicago,* but it lacks documentation. Moreover, Waldrop lacks respect for his subject and avoids a critical evaluation of the *Tribune*'s stand on political affairs. Accordingly there is a need today for a close examination of the newspaper's political ideas and an evaluation of its influence among anti-New Deal circles.

I am deeply grateful to Walter Johnson of the University of Hawaii, Richard C. Wade of the University of Chicago, and Michael J. Brodhead and Wilbur S. Shepperson of the University of Nevada for their insights and criticism of the manuscript. In the research process, most helpful were Herman Kogan, the late Senator Everett Dirksen, Maryland McCormick, Leon Stolz, Charles Cleveland,

William Strand, Chesly Manly, and Willard Edwards among many. Especially valuable were the comments of Walter Trohan, chief of the *Tribune*'s Washington Bureau. The library staffs of the University of Chicago, the Chicago Historical Society, the *Chicago Tribune* reference library, and the Newberry library gave me many helpful leads. Finally, appreciation must be extended to the Desert Research Institute of the University of Nevada for awarding a research grant which made possible summer travel and accelerated the completion of the manuscript.

NOTES

1.   Leo C. Rosten, *The Washington Correspondents* (New York: Harcourt, Brace and Company, 1937), p. 357.

Colonel McCormick

Robert R. McCormick was born to the purple. His father, Robert Sanderson McCormick (1849–1919) was a distinguished diplomat who served successively as ambassador to Austria-Hungary, Russia, and France. By most testimony, he was a charming but ineffectual man. His mother, Katherine Van Etta Medill, was the daughter of Joseph Medill, publisher of the *Chicago Tribune* from 1855 to 1899. She was a strongly dominant woman who held the family purse strings, her husband having lost his money playing the commodity markets. McCormick's oldest brother, Joseph Medill (1877–1925), later a United States Senator from Illinois, was his mother's favorite. Robert, born in 1880, was somewhat the ugly duckling of the family and ignored by his mother. Interestingly, in his memoirs McCormick has almost nothing to say about either parent and he saw rather little of them. The bonds of affection did not appear particularly close.[1]

Robert attended an English school, Ludgrove, in Middlesex, in the same neighborhood where so many battles of the English Civil War had been fought. He remembered with amusement in his later years how his brother and he were so afraid of becoming Anglified that they spent a major portion of their time reading *Tom Sawyer* and *Huckleberry Finn*. The more he traveled and the more cosmopolitan he became, the stronger his attachment was to the United States. His simple, uncritical patriotism never left him.[2]

McCormick's early life was insulated from the American masses. He had plenty of time for leisurely pursuits and never had to worry about financial affairs. Thus he enjoyed an active, outdoor life and became an expert rifle shot and sportsman. He rode as a cowboy, a roper, at polo, hawking, and fox hunting. While at Yale, he spent one summer hunting in Idaho and another on a sea trip to Hudson Bay.[3]

He attended Groton, graduating in 1899, two classes ahead of Franklin Roosevelt. Groton was one of the most exclusive of the eastern prep schools, and fully 90 percent of Groton youths came from families in the social register. Under the remarkable leadership of its headmaster, Endicott Peabody, the boys were subjected to a rigid schedule—7:30 breakfast, chapel at 8:15, six classes a day, full athletic program, and grace before all meals. Peabody urged his boys to enter a life of service. He once wrote, "If some Groton boys do not enter political life and do something for our land it won't be because they have not been urged," and Groton was to produce public figures of the caliber of Franklin Roosevelt, Averill Harriman, Dean Acheson, Sumner Welles, and Joseph C. Grew among many. In the style of the times, the orientation of the instruction was tilted toward the classical along with modern foreign languages and religion. Much to McCormick's later dismay there was nothing taught about the United States.[4]

From Groton he decided to attend Yale. Yale had a certain atmosphere bordering on smugness which attracted many. This attitude was expressed well in a contemporary book about the university: "Yale is one of the brotherhood of colleges. Some will have it that she is particularly the national institution of America; but this is not the place for claims. It is enough to say that she is one of those whom God has called to light and lead a people."[5]

Yale catered to a narrow social group; the great majority of his college mates had no need of working to support their way through college. Republicans outnumbered Democrats four to one, and even McCormick believed that the weak point of the class of 1903 was its conservatism. Religiously the members of the class belonged to elite Protestant denominations; overwhelmingly they were Episcopalians, Congregationalists, or Presbyterians. By contrast there were only 18 Catholics, 9 Methodists, and 5 Jews in a graduating class of 318.[6]

McCormick started at Yale the first year of Arthur Twining Hadley's revolutionary tenure as president, when the elective system was adopted. Before his accession, Yale's curriculum, unlike Harvard's, was completely circumscribed. As the leading historian of Yale has indicated:

> These men who would later become professors of English or economics or theology, librarians or book collectors, deans or college presidents, engineers, patrons of science, lawyers, governors, or statesmen, all prepared for their variant careers with almost identical studies. The simple reason was: they had to.[7]

The members of the class of 1903, as freshmen, were required to follow a definite, required curriculum consisting of Greek, Latin, mathematics, a modern language, and English. As juniors and seniors, however, the elective system held sway with history and English by far the most popular majors.[8]

McCormick's years at Yale do not appear to have left a deep intellectual imprint upon him although in his *Memoirs* the Colonel stated that he had listened to lectures in economics by Professor William Graham Sumner, "so I was well grounded in that vital topic." His second wife has remarked, however, that she had never known her husband to speak of any professor from his college days. The intellectual influence, if any, was probably minimal. What most interested him in his college years was the social life, the sports, and debating. "Patriotism was high at Yale," he later recalled. "We sang all the national songs, the Civil War songs, and the Spanish-American War songs." His attachment was to his class, not his studies. In 1909 he wrote, "I have no definite plans for the future other than to attend all reunions of the class," and he almost never missed a class reunion! Sentimentally he noted in his later years, "We were like the gods of mythology, blessed with eternal youth." It was unfortunate that graduation had to interrupt such an idyllic existence.[9]

His decision to attend Northwestern Law School was not based on the school's academic standing:

> My father thought that, as I had been away from home so long,
> I should go to law school in Chicago and become acquainted in
> the community where I would practice.
>
> A number of my friends took a year to go around the world.
> Some other friends advised me to do this, saying that otherwise
> I would have to wait until I was forty, when I would be too old
> to have any fun. Decision on both of these questions was largely
> determined by my desire to play polo [which he could do in
> Chicago].[10]

Although his life had been insulated his vistas began to broaden
after his graduation from law school. McCormick's father had been
in the public service for many years, and whether out of a sense
of duty or, more likely, of ambition, the son ran in 1904, with the
powerful backing of Fred A. Busse, for a seat on the Chicago City
Council. His ward, the 21st, was on the Near North Side, the
population primarily American born, most of the foreign born having immigrated from Northern Europe, especially from Germany,
Ireland, and Sweden. McCormick, with the help of the Municipal
Voters' League, won handily.[11]

Once McCormick entered politics, the direction of his life sharply
changed. He became committed to a lifetime of public service. As
an aristocrat, he had to learn how to deal with politicians, how to
meet the people. As he wrote his Yale classmates in 1906:

> As to my life since graduating from college, which had been
> neither so interesting nor so successful as you seem to think,
> if you were to say that I have felt obliged to spend ninety per
> cent of my time in saloons and the remaining ten per cent in
> bar-rooms, you would about have it correct.[12]

McCormick was a hard-working alderman, had an almost perfect
attendance record at council meetings, and was far more active than
his colleagues from the 21st ward in insisting on local improvements.
In general his record may be characterized as moderately progressive. As a member of the Local Transportation Committee he came
in sharp conflict with Democratic Mayor Edward F. Dunne. Dunne
wanted all surface transportation franchises to be taken over and
operated by the city; McCormick believed Dunne was entirely

unrealistic, that the franchises should be left in private hands but with stringent control. Certainly McCormick's record was not conservative; he favored most of the reforms of his day. Since he was wealthy he naturally favored private enterprise, but he was willing to admit the need for public regulation.[13]

The city council provided narrow range for McCormick's ambitions, and in 1905 he ran for president of the Chicago Sanitary District. He narrowly defeated his opponent by eight thousand votes, carrying nineteen out of the thirty-five Chicago wards. During the campaign he had envisioned the day when the district would go out of business, but in fact during his four year tenure of office its powers increased. He extended the Chicago Sanitary Canal by connecting the North Branch of the Chicago River with Lake Michigan. He urged the state and federal governments to build a deep waterway through to the Gulf of Mexico, argued for the necessity of a Calumet canal (which was subsequently built), erected additional dam facilities, and added to the electric generators situated in Lockport. All this while cutting the total budget! At the end of his tenure of office he boasted that every department had a standard of efficiency which would "challenge comparison with any privately conducted business."[14]

Ironically, McCormick, in later years so critical of "socialistic" dam and hydroelectric projects, proved himself an efficient administrator of one of the chief public utilities in the nation. Its profitable electric generating business was in direct competition with Insull's Commonwealth Edison Company, and this forced the Insull interests to reduce drastically their prices in many areas. McCormick was very much aware of the irony of his operating a public utility in direct competition against private interests:

> It may not be without interest to note that the Trustees, among whom are men whose public records show them conservative, embarked upon action more radical than any that radical politicians have dared suggest, to find them conducting matters in a way almost socialistic. At the same time it must be borne in mind that this was done, not as a political propaganda, nor with a desire to range class against class, but that it was undertaken as a necessity to preserve the public interest.[15]

He was proud of his political realism and flexibility, often comparing his efficient administration with that of Mayor Dunne whom he characterized as an impractical visionary. In a comparison designed to show the need for political flexibility, McCormick made his point well:

> The man who will be for no canal unless it is for a given size has no more intelligence than the man who would be opposed to any but a four-track railroad to connect two towns whose only method of communication is a mountain trail. Railroads are always laid out single track and increased as the traffic provides money for their increase.[16]

For a brief period it appeared that a distinguished political career was in the making. Many thought of him as a possible candidate for mayor in the 1911 election, a post he evidently desired. But the political career went awry when McCormick was defeated for reelection as president of the Sanitary District in 1910. He was the victim of a general Democratic landslide, but he was never to run for public office again.[17]

He maintained his progressivism and enthusiastically supported Theodore Roosevelt in 1912, although on the local level backing most Republican candidates. McCormick contended that some reforms were necessary but that Roosevelt was no radical experimenter. The Progressive party "simply proposed to equip the train with a sand box, automatic air brakes, and other safety appliances which have been evolved in the world's workshop of politics." To McCormick the Bull Moose movement meant an "honest government" type of progressivism, for after all it had been William Howard Taft who had upset the will of the people and stolen the nomination. The Colonel, during the Progressive era, was by no means narrowly conservative but supported many of the reforms of the day.[18]

Although he lacked previous newspaper experience, family connections enabled him to become president of the *Chicago Tribune* in 1911. When his uncle Robert W. Patterson died in 1910, Victor Lawson, the publisher of the *Chicago Daily News* and the *Record-Herald,* had attempted to buy the *Tribune* in order to amalgamate it with the faltering *Record-Herald.* Lawson, in McCormick's estimation, was the greatest all-round publisher who ever lived, "with perhaps one fatal flaw—his penuriousness." Lawson had proposed to buy the *Tribune* for ten times the annual earnings, which had amounted to $814,000 in 1909. The opposition of McCormick and his cousin Joseph W. Patterson prevented this sale. When James Keeley, the managing editor, resigned from the paper in 1914, Patterson and McCormick gained undisputed editorial control. Later, McCormick's mother sought to have his brother Medill brought back into the *Tribune* management. This move was successfully blocked by the other stockholders who were pleased with the McCormick-Patterson regime and, as the Colonel noted with satisfaction, "did not want to see it disturbed." After 1919, when Patterson left to found and direct the amazingly successful *New York Daily News,* McCormick remained in sole command of the *Tribune.*[19]

World War I distracted the nation's interest from domestic politics. McCormick desired a much more adventurous role for himself than merely being the publisher of a major metropolitan newspaper. He traveled to Russia in 1915 to observe how the war was going on the eastern front, and this led in turn to a deep interest in military affairs. He was allowed to travel freely since his father was well remembered in St. Petersburg. To give him prestige for the occasion, Governor Edward Dunne of Illinois appointed McCormick a national guard colonel, an aide on his staff.[20]

McCormick was stirred by what he witnessed in Russia. The trip proved to be an important, even a determining milestone in McCormick's life; no longer did he wish to be simply a lawyer or even a newspaperman. In his words, "My Russian experiences changed my point of view, and as I put it to Joe Patterson, I was determined to live a great life, an adventurous life, which I have done ever since." He became fascinated by the subject of personal courage, and was tormented that he might disgrace himself if ever brought before a firing line. The memory of the trip bit deeply into his consciousness.

> And here I am home again at my desk, where the first thing I see each morning is yesterday's balance sheet, same as it used to be before, and I have written a book, not phrasing it as a

wise man should with a single eye to sales, but with no higher aim than to serve my country, and as I look over the daily balance sheets I know this is stupid and will not pay.

But I have tasted of the wine of death, and its flavor will be forever in my throat. The great debauch, which periodically affects mankind, will come to us again, as it has come before, and when it comes I know that a million men must fall, while we are striving to learn in the stress of war, with the best men gone, the lesson that so easily could have been taught in peace.

If my book serves to minimize the crime of unpreparedness, what matter a few kopeks more or less.[21]

In June, 1917, McCormick reported for military service as a commissioned major. The memory of World War I always fascinated McCormick and he even named his country estate Cantigney—after the only battle in which he took part. Although one critic claims that "war to him was a round of parties" he appears to have done his duties competently and well. He was honorably discharged from the army as a colonel, December, 1918.[22]

The World War gave McCormick a taste for military history which was never to be quenched. He later wrote a knowledgeable treatise on Grant's battle tactics and in hundreds of speeches addressed himself to military history. The subject became almost an obsession. When his first wife (whom he had married in 1915) died in 1939 she was buried with full military honors, only the second time in the United States that a military funeral had been accorded a woman. When McCormick died, by his request he was buried in his World War I uniform while the rifles of soldiers from his old outfit delivered a final salute. The funeral theme was "Onward Christian Soldiers."[23]

Why did this man, so in love with the mechanics and tactics of war, turn so violently against it? Various explanations have been offered by men who knew him well. One *Tribune* reporter told this writer that Churchill's World War I memoirs helped change McCormick's mind. The Colonel was deeply impressed by the British statesman's speculations as to whether it would have been best, after all, if the United States had never entered the war and the European powers had sought a negotiated settlement. Walter Trohan's explanation has more authority from the Colonel himself. Trohan declared that McCormick had told him he would have become a Brigadier General if the war had not ended so soon. McCormick's *Memoirs* state how disappointed he was that the armistice arrived when it did. Later McCormick, in analyzing his reasons, concluded that he was falling too much in love with war. He was frightened by his own fascination for the subject. If he could become so ambitious and self-seeking that he was sorry the fighting had ended precisely when it did, what was the effect of war on others? He was never afterward to support American involvement in any way although he continued to denounce vehemently those leaders who failed to support a large military establishment. Perhaps a more basic reason, however, was that McCormick came to distrust completely the leaders of the United States, and feared that involvement in a war would destroy the "American way of life."[24]

Although his editorial page was tigerish in battle, McCormick personally was shy and modest. He discouraged familiarity. Even such a foe as George Seldes (who had worked several years for the *Tribune*) described McCormick as "modest, friendly, easy to get along with and apparently one of the few press lords who had escaped the Napoleon-Northcliffe power obsession." All evidence indicates that he was an unusually kind man. Many observers testified to his diffidence, and Seldes believed that the Colonel suffered from a deep inferiority complex. He certainly realized that he was not the most clever of men. Some five weeks before his death he was talking to his minister about his brother, the late Medill McCormick. "A brilliant man," he said. Then he looked into the fire and added, "I was never brilliant." Both Trohan and Seldes believed that his personal shyness developed from the fact that his mother had always favored Medill.[25]

One reason he avoided close personal contacts was that he believed they could place him in a position where favors would be asked of him as a publisher. James O'Donnell Bennett, one of McCormick's most famous reporters, testified that "society people" bored the Colonel because they tried to tell him how to run the *Tribune*. In fact he was fond of remarking that he belonged not to "society" but to the middle class. Although he had inherited great wealth, he despised others who had become rich by the same method. Doubtless he forgave his own inheritance since he had, by his own exertions, risen above his wealth to become a prominent public figure. He felt one had to work for a living, and in the final analysis was too consumed by his work, too tired for a social life.[26]

His shyness evaporated whenever he put his thoughts into print. The *Tribune* under McCormick had the reputation of being the most pugnacious major newspaper in the United States. Joseph Martin, the Republican House leader, remembered McCormick as a "man who was hard, not to say practically impossible to argue with," and who would have been far more effective if he had been a bit more temperate. Arthur Vandenburg, who after 1945 was the recipient of some of the *Chicago Tribune*'s most ill-natured barbs, was sensitive to the newspaper's failure to realize that its opponents might possibly be acting in good faith. Once, after being called a "Judas" in a *Tribune* editorial, the senator wondered if he were progressing or not, as earlier he had been a "Benedict Arnold." McCormick was a sternly patriotic man who denied the patriotism of those who disagreed with him, an important reason he made so many enemies.[27]

Walter Trohan noted that the Colonel was one of the most complex persons he had ever known. It was hard to be indifferent toward him, and he could not tolerate being ignored.[28] Despite his personal shyness, he did not lack a sense of self-importance which at times made him obtuse as to his effect on others. His radio speeches, delivered weekly for the fifteen years prior to his death, were monumentally dull, but perhaps out of vanity he insisted on inflicting them upon his listeners. A letter he wrote in February, 1942, points up some of his egotism:

Dear Mr. Sawyer,

Thank you for your very temperate letter.

What the most powerful propaganda organization in the world has misled you into believing was a campaign of hatred, has really been a constructive campaign without which this country would be lost.

You do not know it, but the fact is that I introduced the ROTC into the schools; that I introduced machine guns into the army; that I introduced mechanization; that I introduced automatic rifles; that I was the first ground officer to go up in the air and observe artillery fire. Now I have succeeded in mak-

ing that the regular practice in the army. I was the first to advocate an alliance with Canada. I forced the acquiring of the bases
in the Atlantic Ocean.

On the other hand, I was unsuccessful in obtaining the fortification of Guam; in preventing the division of the navy into two
oceans. I was unable to persuade the navy and the administration that airplanes could destroy battleships. I did get the
marines out of Shanghai, but was unsuccessful in trying to get
the army out of the Philippines.

Campaigns such as I have carried on inevitably meet resistance, and great persistence is necessary to achieve results. The
opposition resorts to such tactics as charging me with hatred
and so forth, but in view of the accomplishment, I can bear up
under it.[29]

He was fond of using the personal pronoun. He told a senate
committee in February, 1941, for example, that the United States
had little to fear from the Germans. "The Germans are not so
tough," he declared, "I have been up against them and there is no
use being scared of them." When one unfriendly senator asked him
what he would do if Hitler defeated England and took her bases in
the western hemisphere, he replied complacently, "I would not let
him do it."[30]

The Colonel's work was his whole life; he had little time or taste
for art. Once he went to see "Hamlet" with his chauffeur. The two
were late for the perfomance and had to stumble to reach their seats.
The curtain had already risen and the stage was dark as Horatio
awaited the appearance of the ghost. When the ghost appeared, the
audience was startled to hear McCormick's booming voice cry out,
"Come on, Bill, let's go. I saw this play in college." His taste in
architecture was provincial. He once declared that the Museum of
Science and Industry was "the most beautiful classical structure in
the world," that the Baha'i Temple "transcended" the Taj Mahal,
and that the Chicago business district contained several skyscrapers
"more beautiful than can be found elsewhere." His taste in music
and literature was conventional and heavily weighted toward the
patriotic, military, and sentimental. In a book he compiled shortly
before his death, entitled *Gems of Literature and Song,* representative selections included "Patrick Henry Speech, Lincoln's Farewell

Address, Grant's Terms to Buckner, The Declaration of Independence, It's a Long Way to Tipperary, the Lord's Prayer, Onward Christian Soldiers, In Flanders Fields the Poppies Blow, Oh Give Me a Home Where the Buffalo Roam, and Drink to Me Only with Thine Eyes."[31]

Perhaps most important to his thought was his deep belief and pride in the American experience. McCormick's greatest heroes in American history were those who, like Lincoln and Grant, rose from a lowly station in life—thus demonstrating the opportunities inherent in the free enterprise system. He always insisted that the American Revolution had a greater meaning than being a mere struggle for independence, that it was in fact a democratic revolution and the single most important event in world history. He considered this idea at length in one of his books.

> A reading of the histories and the constitutions of Europe did not take long and revealed the fact that everything good in those constitutions stemmed from the American Revolution, Constitution, and Bill of Rights, and that the same was true of the countries in this hemisphere, and of what little good has come into Asia.
>
> If you read this volume, you will notice, I hope, that it does not contain any of that self-abasement with which most American histories tell of their own and other countries. . . .
>
> The American Revolution was the turning point in the history of the world. There had been political philosophers before the American but they did not get beyond essay writing. There had been revolts against oppression, but they had ended in failure. Royal and aristocratic might have everywhere prevailed.[32]

Walter Trohan declared that McCormick would read the Declaration of Independence as if it were the "Lord's Prayer." Joseph Martin recollected how the two once went to the Links Club in New York. "As he [McCormick] walked through the club he glared at portraits of princes, dukes, lords, and assorted royalty. 'Where's Lincoln?' he asked crossly. 'I don't see George Washington either.' "[33]

McCormick steadfastly lived up to his pledge of 1915 to live an adventurous life. Even when an old man, he never lost his enthusiasm or his boyish sense of romance. His taste for adventure, desire to do great things, and unquenchable search for knowledge remained undimmed. Like a little boy, the Colonel loved to send his foreign correspondents on mysterious and romantic errands, and he constantly flew about the world himself in his private airplane in quest for a good story.

In his lust for adventure and romance, he always remained an overgrown boy; thus his heroes were those men a little larger than real life—people like Theodore Roosevelt, Winston Churchill, and particularly Douglas MacArthur. He strongly supported Thomas E. Dewey for the Republican nomination in 1940 for little discernible reason except that Dewey had political appeal for him—he was the clean-cut district attorney who had defeated the forces of gangdom and almost vanquished the New York Democracy. And the Colonel soon found that the best way he could express himself was in opposition. His thirst for romantic adventure could never be satisfied by merely supporting governmental policies; rather it had to be satisfied by constantly slugging it out with the "crooks" and "wicked men" in power. McCormick had, perhaps, inflated notions of his importance, as he liked to view himself as the chief of an army battling the iniquitous forces of the New Deal. He liked to "head the fire brigade, to shoot it out with the crooks, to lead the parade." With his power and money, he could live up to this boyish dream-world.[34]

Yet, these romantic yearnings did not blind him to life's realities. The Colonel was a tough-minded newspaper executive who knew what he wanted and exactly how to obtain it. Few major papers in the history of journalism have been so completely the extension of one man's personality. He was one of the greatest of the group of men, Joseph Pulitzer, William Randolph Hearst, Edward Scripps, and Joseph Patterson, who knew precisely how to impress their wills upon a large newspaper enterprise. They were not to be replaced by the succeeding generation.

NOTES

1.   Interview with Mrs. Robert McCormick, July 25, 1967; Walter Trohan, "My Life with the Colonel," *Journal of the Illinois State Historical Society,* LII (Winter, 1959), 479; George Seldes, *Tell the Truth and Run* (New York: Greenberg, 1953), pp. 80–81. For biographies of his father and brother see Dumas Malone (ed.) *Dictionary of American Biography,* XI (New York: Charles Scribner's Sons, 1933), 609, 612. The best brief biographies of McCormick can be found in *Current Biography, Who's News and Why, 1942* (New York: The H. W. Wilson Company, 1942), pp. 545–48; *Chicago Tribune,* April 2, 1955; *New York Times,* April 2, 1955. The best extended biography is Frank C. Waldrop, *McCormick of Chicago, an Unconventional Portrait of a Controversial Figure* (Englewood Cliffs, N.J.: Prentice-Hall, Inc., 1966). For an interesting picture of his father as ambassador see Thomas Bentley Mott, *Twenty Years as Military Attaché* (New York: Oxford University Press, 1937), p. 125.

2.   Interview with Walter Trohan on December 30, 1964; Robert R. McCormick, *Memoirs, Broadcast over WGN, WGNB and the Mutual Broadcasting System* (unpublished MS., Chicago Tribune Library, latest revision, July 22, 1954), p. 10.

3.   *Ibid.,* pp. 35, 42–43.

4.   Interview with Mrs. McCormick; Frank D. Ashburn, *Peabody of Groton* (New York: Coward McCann, Inc., 1944), pp. 72, 96; Frank Freidel, *Franklin D. Roosevelt,* I (Boston: Little, Brown and Company, 1952), 35–41.

5.   Lewis Sheldon Welch and Walter Camp, *Yale; Her Campus, Class-Rooms, and Athletics* (Boston: L. C. Page and Company, 1899), p. xix.

6.   Yale University, Class of 1903, *Class Book, 1903* (n.p., 1903), pp. 87, 207, 211, 216.

7.   George Wilson Pierson, *Yale College, An Educational History 1871–1921* (New Haven: Yale University Press, 1952), p. 76.

8.   Yale University, Class of 1903, *Class Book, 1903,* pp. 184–85.

9.   Interview with Walter Trohan; interview with Mrs. McCormick; McCormick, *Memoirs,* pp. 38–39, 41, 63.

10.   *Ibid.,* p. 67.

11.   *Ibid.,* p. 73; Chicago Daily News, *The Daily News Almanac and Year-Book,* 1905, p. 357. The vote was McCormick, 4,153, George H. Sheahan (Dem.), 3,571, 3 other candidates, 558. Also see *Daily News Almanac and Year-Book,* 1906, pp. 440–43.

12. Yale University, Class of 1903, *History of the Class of 1903* II (trennial, Yale University, 1906), 183.

13. See, e.g., Chicago, *City Council Proceedings, 1905–1906,* pp. 1154–55, 1208, 1661, 2639.

14. *Chicago Record-Herald,* October 19, 1905, p. 5, col. 1 (hereafter written 5:1); Chicago Sanitary District, *Proceedings of the Sanitary District of Chicago,* 1908, p. 59; *Proceedings,* 1910, p. 1459; *Daily News Almanac and Year-Book,* 1906.

15. Chicago Sanitary District, *Proceedings,* 1910, pp. 95, 1464; *Proceedings,* 1906, p. 11929; Interview with Charles Cleveland, July 1, 1967.

16. Chicago Sanitary District, *Proceedings,* 1910, p. 85.

17. *Daily News Almanac and Year-Book,* 1911, p. 401; *Chicago Record-Herald,* September 1, 1909, 6:7.

18. *Chicago Tribune,* October 21, 1912, 10:1–2; October 22, 1912, 6:2; *Chicago Record-Herald,* October 30, 1912, 5:4; Yale University, Class of 1903, *History of the Class of 1903—Decennial,* IV (Yale University, 1913), 179–180.

19. McCormick, *Memoirs,* pp. 185–6, 188, 192. See also James Weber Linn, *James Keeley, Newspaperman* (Indianapolis: the Bobbs-Merrill Company, 1937), pp. 185–192; Charles H. Dennis, *Victor Lawson, His Time and His Work* (Chicago: The University of Chicago Press, 1935), p. 310; Waldrop, pp. 92–96.

20. See the editorials reprinted in *The War Record of the Chicago Tribune, Submitted to the People of Illinois, Indiana, Iowa, Wisconsin and Michigan . . . Compiled by Henry Ford* (n.p., n.d.). For *Tribune* policy before the war Warren Gard Jenkins, "The Foreign Policy of the Chicago Tribune, 1914–1917: A Program of National Self-Interest" (unpublished Ph.D. dissertation, University of Wisconsin, 1943) is useful; *Chicago Tribune,* March 20, 1918, p. 8; McCormick, *Memoirs,* pp. 92–93, 125; Joseph Medill Patterson, *The Notebook of a Neutral* (New York: Duffield and Company, 1916).

21. Robert R. McCormick, *With the Russian Army: Being the Experiences of a National Guardsman* (New York: The Macmillan Company, 1915), pp. 30, 252–53.

22. The Union for Democratic Action [Elmer Gertz], *The People vs. the Chicago Tribune* (n.p.: 1942), p. 11; Waldrop, pp. 170–173.

23. *The Trib,* XXI (August, 1939), 4. (*The Trib* was the newspaper's house organ.)

24. Elmer Gertz, "Eccentric Titan: McCormick of the Tribune," *The Nation,* CLXXX (April 30, 1955), 362–64; interview with Chesly Manly, June 14, 1965; interview with Walter Trohan; Trohan, *Journal*

of the Illinois State Historical Society, LII, 491; McCormick, *Memoirs,* p. 177.

25.   George Seldes, *Lords of the Press* (New York: Blue Ribbon Books, 1941), p. 41; Trohan, *Journal of the Illinois State Historical Society,* LII, 479; John T. McCutcheon, *Drawn from Memory* (Indianapolis: The Bobbs-Merrill Company, Inc., 1950), p. 290; John Bartlow Martin, "Colonel McCormick of the Tribune," *Harper's Magazine,* CLXXXIX (October, 1944), 404; interview with a *Tribune* executive, July 14, 1965, name withheld by request; interview with Mrs. Maryland McCormick; Seldes, *Tell the Truth and Run,* pp. 81–82; *Chicago Tribune,* April 5, 1955, 6:3.

26.   Interview with Mrs. McCormick; Jack Alexander, "The Duke of Chicago," *Saturday Evening Post,* CCXIV (July 19, 1941), 74; *New York Times,* April 2, 1955, 13:3; *Chicago Tribune,* April 2, 1955, 5:4; Trohan, *Journal of the Illinois State Historical Society,* LII, 485–86.

27.   Joseph Martin, *My First Fifty Years in Politics* (New York: McGraw-Hill Book Company, Inc., 1960), pp. 132–33; Arthur H. Vandenburg, Jr., *The Private Papers of Senator Vandenburg* (Boston: Houghton Mifflin Company, 1952), p. 308.

28.   Trohan, *Journal of the Illinois State Historical Society,* LII, 479, 481–82, 485.

29.   *Chicago Daily News,* March 19, 1942, quoted in John Tebbel, *An American Dynasty* (Garden City, N.Y.: Doubleday & Company, Inc., 1947), pp. 222–23; Robert Lasch, "Chicago Patriot, The World's Greatest Newspaper," *Atlantic Monthly,* CLXIX (June, 1942), 692.

30.   *Chicago Tribune,* February 7, 1941, 6:1; the hearings are also reproduced in *Hearings before the Committee on Foreign Relations, United States Senate, Seventy-Seventh Congress First Session on S. 275 A Bill Further to Promote the Defense of the United States and for Other Purposes, Part 2, February 4 to February 10, 1941* (Washington, D.C.: Government Printing Office, 1941), pp. 447–490.

31.   Trohan, *Journal of the Illinois State Historical Society,* LII, 487; Robert R. McCormick, *Memoirs,* p. 17; Maryland and Robert R. McCormick, *Gems of Literature and Song* (Chicago: The Tribune Company, 1953).

32.   Robert R. McCormick, *The American Revolution and Its Influence on World Civilization* (Chicago: The Tribune Company, 1945), Foreword.

33.   Interview with Walter Trohan; Joseph Martin, *My First Fifty Years,* p. 132.

34.   Elmer Gertz, "Chicago's Adult Delinquent: the *Tribune,*" *Public Opinion Quarterly,* VIII (Fall, 1944), 415–424.

2

"The World's Greatest Newspaper"

Robert R. McCormick was a remarkable publisher and had absolute control of the *Tribune*. This can be demonstrated by noting how closely the paper's editorial page correlates with McCormick's speeches. Or one can take the word of the men who worked under him. Walter Trohan states flatly that "Colonel McCormick was the policy," and Frank Hughes, a reporter on the *Tribune* staff, adds that McCormick was always in tight control of the newspaper's foreign-policy editorials. Nothing of significance in the *Tribune* escaped his supervising eye although his particular interests were the editorial page and the staff of foreign correspondents. Before World War II he handled his large foreign staff directly.[1]

At the editorial conferences held every morning he was undisputed master. However, McCormick was not a tyrant; one could argue with him in a gentlemanly fashion, for he never wished to be surrounded by yes-men, but the ultimate decisions were his. At these conferences, usually attended by six or seven editorial writers and cartoonists, he proved to be easy and approachable. This did not entirely disguise an iron will. Often he would personally pass out news assignments, and in his forty-four years as an executive on the newspaper, he dispatched thousands of notes to managing and city editors "in his own atrocious handwriting."[2]

To many the *Tribune* appeared to be merely an extension of his personality. Not only was he supreme on the editorial page and in news-gathering operations, he was a master of the technical aspects of publishing. A pioneer in the use of color, McCormick was deeply interested in the latest advances in mechanical equipment and type, and he personally saw to it that the newspaper acquired the best equipment no matter what the expense. As Elmer Gertz, a critic, wrote, "He is a first-rate executive, a businessman who counts the cost when he should, and forgets it when he should."[3]

McCormick was an unflagging publicist for those ideas in which he believed. A newspaper was more to him than a mere commercial enterprise, it was a way to disseminate his opinions, although not the only way. While in control of the *Tribune* he wrote, lectured, traveled, and, as mentioned previously, had his own radio program. Marlen Pew wrote in 1933 that McCormick was the representative of a particularly vigorous journalism:

> The most agile publisher in America is Col. R. R. McCormick. . . . I heard him speak at the Inland Daily Press Association in Chicago on Wednesday, Oct. 18. On the following Saturday, he set out by plane, visiting St. Louis, Oklahoma City, and points in Texas, Arizona, New Mexico, California and Utah. On October 28 he arrived in New York to speak at the John Peter Zenger celebration and at the Columbia school of Journalism. Col. McCormick has been a skillful and enthusiastic birdman for many years.[4]

Because he so vigorously expressed his views, the Colonel became one of the most controversial men of his time. Much nonsense has been written about him. Wayne Andrews wrote that McCormick "made no secret of his interest in the German experiment in racial purity," which was a vicious fiction. Courtenay Barber, Jr., a leading Chicago critic, in 1943 compared McCormick with Goebbels. Other writers such as Michael Sayers, John Carlson, and George Seldes suggested that he was a fascist. Stephen Becker, the biographer of Marshall Field III, wrote that McCormick "would have relished a corporate state and a place on its board."[5]

His critics often accused him of being a cynic because of the *Tribune*'s coloring of the news to fit its publisher's views. Yet the "coloring" resulted not from cynicism but from apparently sincere motives. "Profits," he once remarked, "are not a true measure of a newspaper's worth." He sincerely believed the *Tribune* was the "world's greatest paper" precisely because it refused to curry favor from organized pressure groups, and often, in fact, went out of its way to curry their disfavor. It took a high degree of tenacity and resolution to stand by one's editorial guns on issues which threatened to alienate thousands of readers. Because of this sincerity, McCormick was not afraid of being called unobjective. "Put your editorial protest against a wicked deed in with your record of it," his newspaper approvingly quoted Charles M. Sheldon, "not in a detached editorial six pages distant." Doubtless it would have been to the *Tribune*'s advantage if its publisher had been a bit more circumspect in its criticisms of the New Deal. If McCormick had not attacked the Roosevelt administration so vociferously in the years 1939–1941, Marshall Field probably would not have invested money to found the opposition *Sun*. It was because of the rigidity of McCormick's opinions and the violence with which he expressed them that he was confronted with major newspaper opposition after December 4, 1941, opposition which in time would prove serious.[6]

The *Chicago Tribune,* or the "World's Greatest Newspaper," as it called itself, was, from the standpoint of circulation and influence, easily the leading midwestern paper during the period under study. Although dominated by one man, it had one of the most brilliant staffs on the contemporary journalistic scene. McCormick chose his men well.

Edward Scott Beck, the managing editor of the *Tribune* from 1910 to 1937, was characterized by one of his reporters as a "man of education and natural refinement, . . . conservative, tactful, mild-mannered, conscientious; he took his job more seriously than any other man I have ever known." Tiffany Blake, an intimate friend of Charles Dawes, was the chief editorial writer from 1908 to 1939 and was followed in that post by Clifford Raymond. Dawes once highly praised Blake for having one "of the most interesting and cultured minds and from his conversation I always take away something worth while of knowledge." But within the *Tribune* organization Raymond was considered as somewhat the star of the department and McCormick always believed he was the best editorial writer in the country. McCormick rarely wrote editorials himself although his words often got into the paper, since the men worked closely together and knew each other's thoughts.[7]

McCormick believed that editorial policy was arrived at by something resembling a democratic process.

> Six days a week there is an editorial conference lasting from one to three hours. The decision to take sides on a new question or one which has assumed new aspects is taken after much consideration and debate and when the accuracy of the view seems established. An editorial page, therefore, has the benefit of a large amount of information hardly to be found elsewhere.[8]

The cartoonists were less anonymous. McCormick led in pioneering techniques of pictorial representation, and always lavishly made use of cartoons, emblazoning them on the front page, because he believed they presented their political messages much more quickly than did editorials. Consequently cartoons were of major importance in disseminating *Tribune* doctrines. One student of the newspaper went so far as to write that from 1939 to 1941 cartoons were used much more heavily for "isolationist" propaganda than were editorials. During that period only one in four *Tribune* editorials was "isolationist;" half the cartoons were.[9]

Throughout the years from 1929 to 1941 the *Tribune* employed the services of Carey Orr and John T. McCutcheon. Joseph Parrish joined the staff in 1936. Orr and Parrish came to the *Tribune* by way of the *Nashville Tennessean;* McCutcheon came from the old *Chicago Record-Herald.*[10]

Carey Orr never deviated from the dicta of the editorial page. Born in 1890, he joined the *Tribune* in 1917. Once in an interview he warned prospective cartoonists against too vindictive cartooning. "The American public is growing more and more kindly and is getting smarter," he declared. "People today know that a person is not all bad, no matter how terrible he may be portrayed." Ironically, he never followed his own advice. There was no cartoonist more vindictive than Orr. An indifferent draftsman, his cartoons usually portrayed battles between good and evil, and he was venomous in his depiction of evil. Parrish, who also came from Tennessee, was born in 1906. Unlike Orr he was a superb draftsman, but he too never deviated from the *Tribune* editorial viewpoint.[11]

John McCutcheon was an incomparably greater, more subtle artist and one of the most beloved cartoonists of his generation. Dawes once wrote, "Of all the friends I have ever had I think John had the kindliest ways and the most sympathizing heart." Winner of the 1931 Pulitzer Prize in cartooning, he was of immense value to the *Tribune*, a fact which McCormick duly appreciated. For instance, although McCutcheon was ill for the greater part of 1932, the newspaper continued to pay him at his normal rate of $50,000 a year. He was gentler in his methods than Orr and Parrish. Born and raised in Indiana (he was the brother of the novelist, George Barr McCutcheon), he drew cartoons that often nostalgically reflected his rural heritage. A letter from S. E. Thomason, the publisher of the Democratic *Daily Times*, congratulated him for never being "mean or nasty." Because of these qualities McCutcheon could be enormously effective.[12]

Unlike Orr and Parrish, McCutcheon felt free to take viewpoints independent of the *Tribune*'s editorial position. When the newspaper was in its most militaristic phase, before Franklin Roosevelt became president, McCutcheon would often draw cartoons expressing antiwar sentiments. Until 1937, McCutcheon refused to attack Roosevelt. Nor did he ever draw anything opposing prohibition although the *Tribune* was violently antipathetic to the "noble experiment." Explaining his independence, the cartoonist later wrote in his autobiography that "I was never a prohibitionist . . . [nor was I] wholly supporting F.D.R.'s program. I simply felt that both experiments should be given a chance." Despite these differences of opinion, McCormick invariably ran McCutcheon's cartoons on the front page.[13]

Nevertheless McCutcheon was deeply suspicious of Europe and everything European and after Roosevelt's 1937 "Quarantine Speech" in Chicago, he opposed the administration with all the talent at his disposal—which was considerable. "From being a fairly friendly partisan," he wrote, "I changed in that moment to profound opposition. I believed beyond a doubt—and I said so in my cartoons in every way that I could think of—that the President intended by every means in his power, to seek to involve the United States in war."

In a 1933 interview, McCutcheon contended that a good cartoonist was one who sought to bring about the reforms he favored "by means of satire and ridicule rather than by using a bludgeon." For the most part he lived up to this dictum and therein rested much of his greatness.[14]

The members of the Washington Bureau during the period under study were its chief reporter, Arthur Sears Henning (assistant Washington correspondent, 1909–1914, and head of the bureau, 1914–1949), and, under him, Chesly Manly (after 1934), Willard Edwards (after 1935), and Walter Trohan (after 1934). The Colonel thought very highly of the Washington Bureau and believed its head held a position second only to the president's in importance. He was peculiarly dependent upon the bureau for his contacts in Washington, since McCormick personally was not the type who on his own would visit senators and government officials. Henning therefore was in great measure the Colonel's personal representative in Washington. Henning was a gentleman, a courteous, kindly reporter who could write a pretty mean story when he had to.

At times during the Roosevelt years, the bureau was in a difficult position because of its intransigent opposition to the New Deal. Relations with other reporters in Washington sometimes became a bit sticky and since all the *Tribune* representatives were devoted conservatives, friendly arguments often ensued. Despite this, Walter Trohan and Willard Edwards at least were able to get along with Democratic party officials, and Trohan became particularly close to James Farley. Franklin Roosevelt often joked with the *Tribune* reporters about the Colonel; at one time when the newspaper was printing huge ads asserting how "undominated" it was, the president stopped a press conference to ask the *Tribune* reporters to rise, and said, "I just want to see what an undominated reporter looks like."[15]

McCormick also built up one of the nation's finest staffs of foreign reporters. This in turn enormously enhanced the influence of the newspaper, since the resources of its large foreign service gave it access to independent sources of information. The service was a comparatively new organization in 1939. Immediately after the Spanish American War, with the upsurge of public interest in foreign affairs, the *Tribune* established staff correspondents in London,

Paris, Rome, Berlin, and Vienna. These bureaus soon languished and from 1900 to World War I the newspaper had few journalistic achievements to its credit in foreign fields. After World War I the story was different. McCormick was interested in establishing a permanent corps of reporters abroad and he asked Floyd Gibbons to build up a foreign service. Within a few years, the *Tribune* was receiving news stories from Europe and Asia from such talented reporters as George Seldes, William Shirer, Vincent Sheean, Frazier Hunt, David Darrah, John Powell, and Larry Rue.[16]

By 1930 the *Tribune* was one of only seven newspapers having a special foreign service. These included the *Christian Science Monitor,* four New York dailies (the *Times,* the *Herald Tribune,* the *World,* and the *Evening Post*), and two Chicago newspapers (the *Daily News* and the *Tribune*). The *Tribune* asserted in 1928 that it had nearly thirty correspondents, mostly stringers, scattered among twenty-two offices. In 1939 the newspaper had eight correspondents, all in Europe, who were writing under their own bylines. That compared with eight for the *Chicago Daily News,* eight for the *New York Herald Tribune,* and forty for the *New York Times.* Explaining this failure to increase the corps in a period of heightening international tensions was the expense of keeping up such a service. Although information is difficult to obtain, it was estimated in 1930 that the *Chicago Daily News* with a foreign staff of similar size was spending one thousand dollars a day for its service; in 1940 the *New York Times* allocated over a million dollars for news from abroad. Reporting the 1931 incident between China and Japan cost the *Tribune* from eighteen to thirty cents a word for press rate transmission alone.[17]

Lines of communication were all-important. A reporter had to make sure that the home office would be able to receive his story in as rapid and efficient a manner as possible. Cable rates were sufficiently expensive so that almost all cabled messages were severely skeletonized and had to be deciphered in Chicago. Normally the *Chicago Tribune* cable desk received from four to eight thousand words in cables each night from its own correspondents alone. Increasingly many of the dispatches were radioed instead of cabled to Chicago. As early as 1920, the *Tribune* was receiving news by wireless direct from Bordeaux, France.[18]

The *Tribune's* foreign service was not directly competitive with the Associated or United Press, but rather attempted to be supplementary. The latter two agencies were interested in reporting facts, whereas a foreign correspondent searched for the meaning behind the facts; he was more of an editorialist. As John Gunther put it, "Not only the facts count for him, but opinion." To get this background material, a reporter had to rely upon local newspapers and personal friendships. The more contacts he maintained in government circles, the more valuable he was to the home organization.[19]

The *Tribune* had a surprisingly youthful foreign staff. Edmond Taylor, a typical example, joined the *Chicago Tribune* foreign news service in 1930 at the age of twenty-one and was appointed head of the important Paris office by 1933. Jay Allen, William Shirer, and William Barber among others had been born after the turn of the century. Thus, the *Tribune* foreign news service looked for and developed young reporters. Another characteristic of the corps was that many of the foreign news representatives for the newspaper began their careers with the *Paris Tribune,* which was owned and operated by the *Chicago Tribune* from its founding in July, 1917, until its demise in November, 1934. David Darrah, who was managing editor of the *Paris Tribune* at the age of twenty-five, became Rome correspondent for the home *Tribune*. Edmond Taylor likewise moved from the *Paris Tribune* to become head of the *Chicago Tribune's* Paris bureau.[20]

The Colonel concentrated his attention on Europe. Until John Powell was fired in 1937, the newspaper had a first-class correspondent covering Far Eastern affairs, but he was not replaced. According to Walter Trohan, McCormick liked to play with his correspondents as if they were pieces in a gigantic chess game. He believed in mobility. Having established the basic bureaus—London, Paris, Rome, and Berlin—he would send correspondents to investigate conditions elsewhere whenever a crisis arose.[21]

The *Tribune* had a reputation for having the most conservative of all the foreign news services. It was the only major American newspaper with a large foreign staff which did not support a liberal international foreign policy. (This was one of its chief values to the isolationist movement.) Yet most of its correspondents enjoyed full freedom to write as they wished. For example, Sigrid Schultz, the correspondent in Berlin, was deeply anti-Nazi and often disagreed with McCormick, but there was no attempt to coerce her into conforming to the newspaper's policies. According to Miss Schultz, the *Tribune* was never guilty of distorting her reports. Jay Allen enthusiastically favored the loyalist side in the Spanish Civil War and wrote dispatches emphasizing that bias—yet the *Tribune* played up his stories. Edmond Taylor worked for the newspaper for ten years, yet he described himself (privately) as "under the influence of Wilsonian, to say nothing of Rooseveltian, ideology." In his diary on August 2, 1939, while still in the *Tribune*'s employ, Taylor expressed the feeling that Europe's one great hope was America and Roosevelt. Eventually relations soured between him and the home office and he quit, but Taylor later declared that McCormick had been an extremely considerate employer and no pressure had ever been put on him. John Powell in China agreed that no coercion was ever used to force reporters to follow the editorial policy set in Chicago. *Tribune* correspondents for the most part were individualistic, independent young people, or as one historian has called them, "high flying young falcons." In most respects the corps was first-rate. Evidence shows that reporters respected and liked Colonel McCormick. A few (like Shirer, Taylor, and Seldes) attacked *Tribune* policies after they quit, but for the most part they refrained from attacking the Colonel personally.[22]

McCormick was not interested in detailed background stories— what he wanted in a foreign news story was the exclusive interview, the dashing exploit, exposés, scoops, something to make big headlines. Wars fascinated him. The Chinese-Russian "war" of 1929–1930 was covered in its entirety by only two correspondents, representatives of the *Chicago Daily News* and the *Chicago Tribune*. This led the surprised German Consul in Harbin to inquire why Chicago should seem so interested in the Manchurian war. A Canadian editor replied that Chicago correspondents felt entirely at home in any war. McCormick once mysteriously instructed one of his foreign reporters, Alex Small, at the time of the Munich Conference: "Wars always start at dawn. Be there at dawn."[23]

The *Tribune* congratulated itself most for exploits such as the ten-thousand-mile airplane flight of Larry Rue to cover the revolt against King Aman Cullah of Afganistan in 1929, Floyd Gibbons' voyage on the Laconia when it sank in February, 1917 (the ship was chosen purposefully in the hope that it might be sunk), Jay Allen's brush with death in the Spanish Civil War, Frederick Smith's airplane flight to Berlin in 1918 which made him the first American newspaperman to enter that city after the armistice, the publishing of the Treaty of Versailles as a world scoop, and Floyd Gibbons and Larry Rue's trip into the heart of famine-swept Russia in 1923. These were the stories over which the *Tribune* gloated the most, for they were colorful and adventurous. Yet they were not always the stories which most broadened a reader's understanding of complex issues.[24]

With this able staff McCormick was able to command the intense loyalty which grows out of respect. It also worked the other way. To McCormick every man he had on his staff was the best man available. In one speech, for example, delivered in the closing months of the Hoover administration, McCormick solemnly told the *Tribune* advertising department that Arthur Sears Henning was undoubtedly "the best informed man on political affairs in America." He evaluated Philip Kinsley's articles on the Far East with extravagant, but sincere praise: "I have no hesitation in saying to you that *every one* who has read all of Kinsley's articles in the last eleven months knows more about conditions in the Pacific Ocean and in the lands bordering it than *any one* who has not read those articles." In his memoirs the Colonel noted with pride that when he took over the newspaper's management, the *Tribune* had the best business manager, the best Sunday editor, and the best circulation manager in America. He never took credit for himself when it more properly belonged to his staff. Consequently there was a genuine spirit in the organization, a pride even among those who did not entirely share the Colonel's political views. To work for the *Tribune* was one of the most prestigious jobs in journalism.[25]

He was not only generous in his praise, but also in the salaries he paid. This was why very few people quit the newspaper after the founding of the *Sun*. One employee noted in later years how, "like a benevolent Ebenezer Scrooge he was the author of our feasts, and mighty good eating it was too." To take a sample year, in 1936 $765,000 was given *Tribune* employees in bonuses. The company was paternalistic toward its workers, even offering mortgages to employees on easy terms through the Medill Building and Loan Association, and providing free insurance. In addition every *Tribune* employee was given a free dental checkup twice a year.[26]

Management and ownership of the *Chicago Tribune* were not synonymous. McCormick was the sole manager of the *Tribune* throughout this period but he owned only 13.625 percent of the stock. In 1939 ownership of the Tribune Company (which also published the *Washington Times-Herald* and the *New York Daily News* and operated pulp mills in Canada) consisted of two-thousand shares divided as follows:

Medill Trust	1,050 shares
R. R. McCormick	10 shares
Eleanor Patterson	10 shares
Lloyd Family	500 shares
Cowles Family	305 shares
J. M. Howels Family	100 shares
John E. Kohler Family	10 shares
Elias Colber Descendants	5 shares
George P. Upton Descendants	10 shares

The Medill Trust with 52.5 percent of the shares thus controlled the company. The four members of the trust were McCormick, Joseph Patterson, Ruth Hanna McCormick (Medill McCormick's widow and Mark Hanna's daughter), and Eleanor Patterson. They had apportioned a division of labor between themselves and did not venture upon each other's territory. Consequently McCormick managed the *Tribune,* Joseph Patterson the *New York Daily News,* and Eleanor Patterson the *Washington Times-Herald.* Ruth Hanna McCormick ran the *Rockford Star* and *Register Republic* which were not part of the Tribune Company. In 1934 *Fortune Magazine* estimated the value of each share to be $26,800. The figure was conservative since the magazine roughly calculated earnings to be 12.5 percent of the stock's value.[27]

In the years from 1929 to 1941 the *Tribune* increased its circulation leadership over the other Chicago newspapers. Its readership had been gaining at the expense of the competition ever since 1910 (approximately when McCormick joined the paper), and it continued its advance until 1941. In 1911 the *Tribune* sold 220,000 copies daily. It competed in the tough morning field with the Hearst *Examiner,* the *Record-Herald,* and the *Inter-Ocean.* Ten years later the *Tribune*'s circulation had soared to 460,739, with competition from only the *Herald-Examiner.* In the six months ending March 31, 1929, the *Tribune* had attained, with its daily circulation of 837,146, approximately two-thirds of the morning readership. By 1941 it had a morning monopoly, the Hearst *Herald-Examiner* having expired of economic malnutrition in August, 1939. Its circulation reached 1,065,297, the second largest among American daily newspapers. The *Tribune*'s astounding advance had also been at the expense of the afternoon competition. In 1911 it had accounted for only 14.2 percent of Chicago daily English-language newspapers sold, in 1921, 26.3 percent, in 1929, 35.3 percent, and in 1941, 44.4 percent. It surpassed the *Daily News* to become Chicago's most popular paper in 1918.

On Sunday the advance was equally emphatic. In 1911 only 300,-000 copies of the *Tribune* were circulated on the Sabbath, but ten years later the figure was 787,952. In 1929 the Sunday circulation reached 1,143,014, and in 1941 it rose to 1,144,734. From 1929 to 1941, McCormick's newspaper advanced from second place in Sunday circulation (second to the Hearst competitor) to a leadership of 287,000 copies.[28]

The daily *Tribune* had about 60 percent of its circulation within the corporate limits of Chicago, about 20 percent in the suburbs, and 20 percent within what Frank Knox, publisher of the *Daily News,* liked to call "Scatterville." (The *Daily News,* unlike the *Tribune,* had only a small circulation outside the Chicago metropolitan area.) The *Tribune* was distributed throughout "Chicagoland," which according to McCormick's definition included most of Illinois, Wisconsin, and Indiana, with generous chunks of Michigan and Iowa. The Colonel forbade the syndication of any of the *Tribune*'s valuable features and comic strips within this huge area. Thus, if a reader in Peoria, for example, wished to catch up with the popular "Gasoline Alley" or "The Gumps" he had to buy the *Tribune*. The Sunday edition in particular had a sale throughout the Midwest and was carried by train to distant cities where it sold in all the main hotels and newsstands. Throughout the thirties only about half the *Tribune*'s Sunday circulation was sold within Chicago, and a sixth went to the suburbs. Approximately a third was distributed outside the Chicago metropolitan area. In 1931, it was estimated that 83 percent of all families in Champaign, Illinois, read the Sunday *Tribune,* 45 percent in Iowa City, Iowa, 38 percent in Madison, Wisconsin, and 33 percent in far-off Green Bay, Wisconsin. The *Tribune* therefore was more than simply a Chicago newspaper; its circulation and influence extended throughout the Midwest. McCormick must be given the major credit for the *Tribune*'s spectacular rise in circulation and power after 1910, as the greatest advances occurred while he controlled the newspaper.[29]

Although the *Tribune* circulated among all groups of people, it achieved its greatest penetration in the more affluent suburbs. In Chicago proper, the circulation of the newspaper in 1940 was 72 percent of the number of occupied dwelling units. In an industrial suburb such as Cicero the ratio fell to 53 percent; in Gary, it was 33 percent, in Hammond 40 percent, and in East Chicago 41 percent. In these working suburbs the *Tribune* circulation approximated that of the Hearst newspaper. But in several of the northern suburbs, the rate of *Tribune* circulation to occupied dwelling units was astonishingly high—101 percent in Evanston, 100 percent in Glencoe, 137 percent in Winnetka, and 163 percent in Kenilworth. Obviously the *Tribune* had a special appeal to the upper-income suburban reader.[30]

Within Chicago proper, *Tribune* circulation tended to be strongest in the areas of highest income and lowest in the more impoverished areas. Circulation per capita was highest on the North Shore, in some of the outlying areas, and in the Hyde Park–Woodlawn districts where the University of Chicago was situated. The *Tribune,* even within the city, went into Republican areas; the most staunchly

Democratic wards had a very low *Tribune* circulation. Where it was read, however, its roots ran very deep; in 1929, for example, it received 10,766 pieces of mail daily.[31]

Advertising followed circulation. Since the *Tribune* appealed to all economic classes and was distributed throughout the Midwest, it could demand more money from advertisers for each line of space than could the Hearst papers, for instance, with their comparatively small readership. During the thirties the *Tribune* achieved advertising leadership in the daily field. In 1929, on weekdays, it carried 560,000 fewer lines of advertising than the *Daily News*, which had been the traditional Chicago leader with its large allotment of grocery advertising and reputation as the "home" newspaper. Three years later the *Daily News*, nourished by a haughty *Tribune* refusal to lower its rates, led its morning rival by 2,570,000 lines. But in 1941 the *Tribune* surpassed the *Daily News* by 2,160,000 lines, a lead which had been growing steadily for some years. The Sunday *Tribune* throughout this period enjoyed a wide lead in advertising lineage over the competition. It must be remembered in assessing the *Tribune*'s financial position that although the *Daily News* surpassed the weekday editions of the *Tribune* in advertising lineage until 1936, the *Tribune* always received a greater advertising revenue, because its much larger circulation entitled it to charge more per line.[32]

For some inexplicable reason, newspaper profits are rarely made public. During the depression, the *Daily News* normally netted about a million dollars a year. Its circulation remained fairly constant: 432,796 in 1929, and 457,891 in 1941. *Fortune Magazine* estimated the *Tribune* net profits at over $10,000,000 in 1929, and $2,900,000 in 1933. Dividends were generous. Eleanor Patterson, who owned one-quarter of the Medill Trust, told Harold Ickes in January, 1939, that her income from the Tribune Company was $800,000 a year. Aside from the *Daily News* and the *Tribune*, no Chicago newspaper was a consistent money-maker. The *Herald-Examiner* regularly lost money, and its circulation sharply declined from 419,612 in 1929, to 362,123 in 1934, and to 324,270 in 1939. When Hearst encountered financial difficulties in the late thirties he was forced to amalgamate his morning newspaper with the evening *American.* The *American,* although generally regarded as profitable, did poorly from a circulation standpoint, dropping from 559,386 in 1929, to 459,938 in 1934, and 455,764 in 1941. In many respects the *Daily Times,* founded in 1929, was the most amazing phenomenon in Chicago journalism. Its circulation bounded from 142,347 in 1930, to 260,679 in 1936, and 422,446 in 1941. Frankly modeled after the *New York Daily News,* a tabloid, sensational, and filled with pictures, the *Daily Times* filled a void by being the only Chicago daily consistently to support the Roosevelt administration. It was never a great money-maker, but it survived.[33]

One reason the Tribune Company became such a profit-maker was its self-sufficiency. It owned its own lumber lands and pulp mills and even possessed a fleet of ships to carry newsprint to Chicago. This happy state of affairs was due to McCormick's farsightedness. Because of his experience as head of the Chicago Sanitary District, he knew electricity and canals and had picked up a general instinct for machinery. Accordingly, on December 4, 1915, the *Tribune* obtained control of three hundred square miles of Quebec territory. The newspaper built a company town, Shelter Bay, to house the workers—"scientifically planned and rigidly zoned," as an advertising brochure described it. These holdings were later augmented, and by 1940 the *Chicago Tribune* alone consumed 146,000 tons of newsprint a year, most of which was brought in on the *Tribune's* own shipping fleet. One of the major ingredients in the success of the *New York Daily News* was that after World War I the price of paper rose. The other New York newspapers were forced to pay higher prices while the *Daily News,* as part of the Tribune Company, bought its newsprint at a reduced rate. The other dailies increased their circulation price, which the *Daily News* refused to do. In McCormick's words "That clinched its success."[34]

The *Tribune* was a most distinctive newspaper. Politically it made a habit of swimming against the tide; whatever its faults it was never dull. Typographically it was expertly made up in a format which it had used steadfastly and successfully for years. The front page almost never varied in makeup—the bold banner headline and the cartoon appeared in issue after issue. Its format was "familiar as an old shoe to its readers" who always knew where to look for the various departments and features.[35]

The *Tribune* pioneered in the use of color, and this helped give the newspaper its bright, clean appearance. In a speech delivered to the American Newspaper Publisher's Association, McCormick insisted that "color must be as commonplace in the newspaper as elsewhere. Otherwise," he added, "we will give way to the colored sign, the neon tube, and those other advertising media where color is available to the advertiser." At the time of his death, *Editor and Publisher,* the trade weekly, declared that the immense growth of color printing was largely attributable to Colonel McCormick's foresight. By 1930 the *Tribune* was offering color to advertisers every day of the week as a regular service.[36]

After the commencement of World War II the newspaper was as lavish in its use of maps, many of which were full-page and in color. As the managing editor, J. Loy Maloney told an interviewer, "We try to present the news so that a kid can get it at a glance." Unfortunately this attitude often created distortion. It was difficult to compress the gist of the day's lead story into the rigid mold of a five-word banner headline. Many times the *Tribune* was accused of distorting the news when in fact the headlines were the chief villains; the newspaper's unvarying makeup afforded very little elasticity. Yet most of the distortions were in the direction of the newspaper's editorial viewpoint. One good sample of such a misleading headline appeared in December, 1929: LLOYD GEORGE CALLS LEAGUE 'FLAP—DOODLE.' If the reader bothered to read the story he would have discovered that Lloyd George had actually said something entirely different: "The League of Nations is in danger of failure from being run by flapdoodlers." The *Tribune's* explanation for any so-called distortion was that it refused to print "official pap." It never apologized for any of its stories, but simply claimed to be presenting the truth as it saw it. According to McCormick's definition, a newspaper's function was to "furnish that check upon government which no constitution has ever been able to provide."[37]

By 1929 the newspaper was a Chicago institution, and it sponsored such popular events as the All-Star football game, the Chicagoland Music Festival, and the Golden Gloves tournament. In analyzing the reasons for the success of the *Tribune* one must not forget the superb sports coverage, undoubtedly the finest in town, and the popular comic strips which could not be marketed elsewhere in Chicagoland (extending far outside the boundaries of Illinois). The editorial page was conservative and dignified in its makeup; the newspaper, although lively, seemed to hit a golden mean between the extreme sensationalism which made the Hearst newspapers repugnant to so many, and the dourly conservative appearance of the *New York Times.*

But there were deeper reasons for the *Tribune*'s popularity. It succeeded in establishing a framework of values for its readers, something which they could cling to and grasp. These were the individualistic values of small town, free enterprise America, the values of the poor inventor or businessman who could become a millionaire through hard work and perseverence, or of the orphan who might become president—in other words the values of Horatio Alger. This was the America of the McCutcheon cartoon, and of the "Gasoline Alley" and "Little Orphan Annie" comic strips. With the ostentatious and daily appearance of the United States flag on the front page, and the dictum of "My Country Right or Wrong," the *Tribune* seemed to typify the "American way of life" more than its competitors. The charge that McCormick was a fascist was of course absurd. What he wanted was a return to traditional American principles as he saw them.

Hence in an increasingly rootless age, the *Tribune* offered something readers could hold onto. Even during the depression when thousands were unemployed, the newspaper retained its high circulation by presenting this consistent set of values which could give unity and meaning for the individual. The Roosevelt administration was fated to clash with the *Tribune* because it presented a different and competitive framework of values. Consequently the newspaper denounced New Deal values as "un-American," since these values envisioned more regulation of free enterprise, greater social security, and greater cooperation for common improvement.

The *Tribune* used every journalistic device it knew to defeat Roosevelt and his measures, particularly during the presidential elections of 1936 and 1940, and the battle over lend-lease. Its efforts, however, were by no means confined to these periods. It regularly suppressed news sympathetic to the New Deal, played up the opposition to Roosevelt, and generally used every possible weapon to oust "that man in the White House."

John Gunther, in his *Inside U.S.A.*, devoted the greater part of a chapter to an analysis of the *Tribune*'s policies. He compared the paper to Texas: "aggressive, sensitive in the extreme, loaded with guts and braggadocio, expansionist, and medieval." Especially illuminating was his pointed comparison with a more formidable power than Texas:

> Another thing Colonel McCormick's *Tribune* reminds me of is Soviet Russia, which it has such a brilliant good time attacking. It is, like Russia, big, totalitarian, successful, dominated by one man as of the moment, suspicious of outsiders, cranky and with strong natural resources not fully developed; it has a strong nationalist streak, a disciplined body of workers, a fixed addiction to dogma, hatred of such assorted phenomena as the rich, the British, and crooked bourgeouis politics, and a compelling zest to fight for its own.[38]

In foreign affairs, the *Tribune* usually seized upon antagonistic and discouraging aspects of a given story, which of course served as a device to reinforce the idea of noninvolvement with the affairs of other nations. Two thirds of all front-page banner headlines dealing with foreign affairs in the 1926–1928 period and in 1935 contained one of the following words or a synonym: war, battle, revolution (rebellion or revolt), riot (massacre or "hundreds slain"), armed forces, crisis (peril, threat, menace), hands-off-warning (curb), break (in diplomatic relations), and save (guard or protect).[39]

Its editorial judgments were always brilliantly written in tones varying from caustic criticism to amused detachment. It was, reflecting the Colonel, a paper of many hates. H. L. Mencken once advised Leon Birkhead not to antagonize McCormick too much. "I warn you against the enmity of Colonel McCormick. When the blowoff comes at last, if you are on his list, he'll pen you upon a deserted island in Lake Michigan." These hates probably added to the newspaper's circulation, since people were often curious as to just what was on the Colonel's mind. In 1945 Louisville publisher Mark Ethridge declared, "I have always felt that those who said the [*Tribune's*] great hold came from comic strips and other features were wrong: it possesses an animal vigor." The *Tribune* itself agreed, "Comes the dawn. It ain't Orphan Annie. It's the hair on our chest."[40]

No other paper so willingly bragged about its accomplishments or was so determined to make the nation believe it was the "World's Greatest Newspaper."[41] No matter whether McCormick's views were popular or not, it is undeniable that Chicago was served good raw meat for breakfast. Judging from the alacrity with which both Democrats and Republicans bought the *Tribune,* they must have relished the diet.

NOTES

1.   Jack Alexander, "The Duke of Chicago," *Saturday Evening Post,* CCXIV (July 19, 1941), 74–75; Martin, *Harper's Magazine,* CLXXXIX, 409–410; George Seldes, *Lords of the Press* (New York: Julian Messner, Inc., 1938), p. 41; interview with Walter Trohan; interview with Frank Hughes, August 10, 1965.

2.   *Chicago Tribune,* April 2, 1955; interview with a *Tribune* executive; interview with Willard Edwards, July 24, 1967; interview with William Strand, July 25, 1967.

3.   Address at Yale University, quoted in *Editor and Publisher,* LXIII (November 22, 1930), 11. See also *Ibid.,* LXXXVIII (April 2, 1955), 16B, 64A; Trohan, *Journal of the Illinois State Historical Society,* LII, 482–83, 487–88; Gertz, *Public Opinion Quarterly,* VIII (Fall, 1944), 415–424.

4.   *Editor and Publisher,* LXVI (November 4, 1933), 36.

5.   Wayne Andrews, *Battle for Chicago* (New York: Harcourt, Brace & Company, Inc., 1946), p. 283; "The Enigma of One Robert Rutherford McCormick, the Internationalization of a Super-Nationalist or Watta Scholar!" (speech by Courtenay Barber, November 8, 1943), Barber Collection, University of Chicago Library; Michael Sayers and Albert E.

Kahn, *Sabotage! The Secret War Against America* (New York: Harper & Brothers, 1942), p. 165; John Roy Carlson, "Inside the America First Movement," *American Mercury,* LIV (January, 1942), 9–25; George Seldes, *One Thousand Americans* (New York: Boni & Gaer, 1947), p. 225; Stephen Becker, *Marshall Field III* (New York: Simon and Schuster, 1964), p. 271.

6.   *Fortune Magazine,* IX (May, 1934), 101; interview with Walter Trohan; interview with Herman Kogan, July 21, 1967; *The Trib,* XXI (January, 1940), 5; XXIII (December, 1941), 3; Chicago Tribune, *The W–G–N* (Chicago: The Tribune Company, 1922), p. 22; in an interview reprinted in *Editor and Publisher,* LXXIV (October 4, 1941), 4, Field stated that he was founding another morning newspaper because of the strongly isolationist viewpoint of the *Tribune.*

7.   Burton Rascoe, *Before I Forget* (New York: The Literary Guild of America, Inc., 1937), p. 235; *Editor and Publisher,* LXXVI (January 2, 1943), 27; Charles G. Dawes, *Notes as Vice-President, 1928–1929* (Boston: Little, Brown and Company, 1935), p. 209; interview with a *Tribune* executive.

8.   *Ibid.,* Robert R. McCormick, *What Is a Newspaper* (Chicago: The Tribune Company, 1924), p. 30; quoted in Volney E. Faw, "The Chicago Tribune and Its Control" (unpublished Master's thesis, The University of Chicago, 1940), pp. 15–16.

9.   William Cecil Rogers, "Isolationist Propaganda: September 1, 1939 to December 7, 1941" (unpublished Ph.D. dissertation, University of Chicago, 1943), pp. 52–53.

10.   *Editor and Publisher,* LXIX (July 25, 1936), 7.

11.   *Ibid.,* LXIV (July 16, 1932), 7.

12.   Dawes, pp. 148–49; Edward Beck to John T. McCutcheon, July 25, 1932, McCutcheon Papers, Newberry Library; S. E. Thomason to John T. McCutcheon, October 23, 1936, McCutcheon Papers; Dick Spencer III, *Pulitzer Prize Cartoons* (Ames: Iowa State College Press, 1951), p. 49.

13.   McCutcheon, *Drawn from Memory,* pp. 441–42.

14.   *Ibid,* p. 442; *Editor and Publisher,* LXVI (August 26, 1933), xix.

15.   Interview with Willard Edwards; interview with William Strand; interview with Charles Cleveland, August 1, 1967; interview with Everett M. Dirksen, July 27, 1967.

16.   John Hohenberg, *Foreign Correspondence: The Great Reporters and Their Times* (New York: Columbia University Press, 1964), pp. 274–77; Chicago Tribune, *Pictured Encyclopedia of the World's Greatest Newspaper* (Chicago: The Tribune Company, 1928), p. 334.

17. John Gunther, "Funneling the European News," *Harper's Monthly Magazine,* CLX (April, 1930), 636–7; Chicago Tribune, *Pictured Encyclopedia of the World's Greatest Newspaper,* p. 261; *Editor and Publisher,* LXIV (November 14, 1931), 5, and XXI (September 2, 1939), 33. The offices in 1928 were located in Tokyo, Manila, Sydney, Peking, Shanghai, Cape Town, Rome, Paris, Berlin, Warsaw, London, Riga, Madrid, Dublin, Buenos Aires, La Paz, Lima, Panama, San Juan, Havana, Mexico City and Honolulu.

18. Chicago Tribune, *Pictured Encyclopedia . . . ,* pp. 87, 632; Robert Desmond, *The Press and World Affairs* (New York: D. Appelton-Century Company, 1937), pp. 122, 127.

19. Gunther, *Harper's Monthly Magazine,* CLX, 638, 640.

20. *New York Times,* October 31, 1934, 7:4.

21. Interview with Walter Trohan.

22. Edmond Taylor, *The Strategy of Terror; Europe's Inner Front* (Boston: Houghton Mifflin Company, 1940), pp. 64, 81; John B. Powell, *My Twenty-Five Years in China* (New York: The Macmillan Company, 1945), pp. 320–21; Hohenberg, *Foreign Correspondence . . . ,* p. 275. Letter from Sigrid Schultz, March, 1968.

23. *Editor and Publisher,* LXII (April 12, 1930), 50; William Shirer, *End of a Berlin Diary* (New York: Alfred A. Knopf, 1947), p. 129.

24. Chicago Tribune, *The W–G–N,* pp. 89, 91; Walter Duranty, *I Write as I Please* (New York: Simon & Schuster, 1935), p. 122.

25. Robert S. Allen, *Washington Merry-Go-Round* (New York: Horace Liveright, Inc., 1931), p. 356; *Time Magazine,* LXV (April 11, 1955), 53; interview with Walter Trohan; interview with William Strand; interview with Herman Kogan; Robert R. McCormick, *An Address by Robert R. McCormick Delivered at the Dinner Following the Twenty-Fifth Semi-Annual Convention of the Advertising Department of the Chicago Tribune, December 29, 1932* (Chicago: The Tribune Company, 1932), pp. 6–7; McCormick, *Memoirs . . . ,* pp. 199–200.

26. Interview with a *Tribune* executive; interview with Walter Trohan; interview with Herman Kogan; Trohan, *Journal of the Illinois State Historical Society,* LII, 478; *The Trib,* XVIII (June, 1937), 14–15, and XIX (July, 1937), 4.

27. Volney E. Faw, "The Chicago Tribune and Its Control" (unpublished Master's dissertation, University of Chicago, 1940), p. 7; *Fortune Magazine,* IX (May, 1934), 108, 201.

28. Circulation figures are from American Bureau of Circulation (A.B.C.) figures, courtesy of *Chicago Tribune.* Newspaper circulations are also available in published form in *Editor and Publisher, International*

Year Book and in *N. W. Ayer & Son's Directory of Newspapers and Periodicals.*

29.   Edwin H. Ford and Edwin Emery, *Highlights in the History of the American Press* (Minneapolis: University of Minnesota Press, 1954), p. 378. The circulation breakdown by regions is available in *Editor and Publisher, International Year Book.* See also Chicago Tribune, *Book of Facts, 1931* (Chicago: The Tribune Company, 1931), pp. 19, 33–89; Selig Adler, *The Isolationist Impulse* (London and New York: Abelard-Schuman, 1957), p. 126; John Gunther, *Inside U.S.A.* (New York: Harper & Brothers, 1947), p. 363; Frank Presbrey, *The History and Development of Advertising* (Garden City, N.Y.: Doubleday, Doran & Company, 1929), p. 613. Letter from Burton K. Wheeler, March, 1968.

30.   Computed from the statistics presented in *Editor and Publisher,* LXXIV (August 23, 1941), 70.

31.   The *Trib,* X (April, 1929), 5.

32.   *Editor and Publisher,* LXII (March 8, 1930), 30, and LXV (March 18, 1933), 18, and LXXV (February 28, 1942), 11.

33.   In 1931 the net profit of the *Daily News* was $908,277, in 1932, $1,323,085, in 1933, $1,488,929, and in 1937, $1,046,697. *Editor and Publisher,* LXIV (February 20, 1932), 13, and LXVI (March 3, 1934), 58, and LXXI (March 5, 1938), 38. See also *Fortune Magazine,* IX (May, 1934), 188; Harold Ickes, *The Secret Diary of Harold Ickes,* II (New York: Simon and Schuster, 1953), 560, diary entry for January 22, 1939; *Editor and Publisher,* LXXII (September 2, 1939), 7. Even as late as 1967 the *Tribune* still refused to release any information concerning its earnings in this period.

34.   Chicago Tribune, *Trees to Tribunes* (Chicago: The Tribune Co., 1951), p. 13; Carl Wiegman, *Trees to News: A Chronicle of the Ontario Paper Company's Origin and Development* (Toronto: McClelland and Stewart Limited, 1953), p. 354; McCormick, *Memoirs . . . ,* pp. 195–96, 251.

35.   Robert R. McCormick, *An Address . . . at Yale University November 18, 1930 under the Auspices of the Paul Block Foundation of Journalism* (Chicago: The Tribune Company, 1931); Elmer Gertz and John Tebbel, "The Chicago Tribune," *American Mercury,* LVIII (March, 1944), 300.

36.   *Editor and Publisher,* LXII (November 16, 1929), 44, and LXIII (August 23, 1930), 10, and LXXXVIII (April 2, 1955), 64A.

37.   *Chicago Tribune,* December 5, 1929, 1:7; February 15, 1930, 10:1; *Editor and Publisher,* LXX (February 22, 1941), 5; Robert R. McCormick, *What is a Newspaper: A Talk before the Chicago Church*

Federation at the Hotel Morrison, October 27, 1924 (Chicago: The Tribune Company, 1927).

38.   Gunther, *Inside U.S.A.*, p. 359.

39.   Susan M. Kingsbury, Hornell Hart and Associates, *Newspapers and the News* (Bryn Mawr College Series in Social Economy, No. 1; New York: G. P. Putnam's Sons, 1937), pp. 31–33; Elizabeth Dewey Johns, "Chicago's Newspapers and the News: A Study of Public Communication in a Metropolis" (unpublished Ph.D. dissertation, The University of Chicago, 1942), p. 305.

40.   *New Yorker,* XXIII (August 2, 1947), 30; Ford and Emery, pp. 385–86.

41.   For example, the *Tribune* once wrote, "Homer would have liked to work on the *Tribune;* no blue pencil would have blurred the onamatapoeia of his lines. So would Horace, with his whimsicalities; Herodotus, with his wealth of incident. So would Balzac, Addison, Samuel Johnson, Dickens, Hardy, Kipling, and Mark Twain. Because in writing *Tribune* news each of these would have had opportunity to exercise his exceptional abilities." "Reporters," the statement went on, "like to work on the *Tribune* for the obvious reason that it is pre-eminently the best paper;" Chicago Tribune, *The W–G–N,* p. 127.

3

McCormick and the Hoover Administration, 1929–1933

At the basis of the *Tribune*'s foreign policy was a spirited chauvinism, a chauvinism that believed the world deteriorated the farther one traveled from Chicago. If Chicago was at the high end of the continuum, Europe was at its reverse. Colonel McCormick disliked the major European powers because he believed their leadership and social structure were entirely corrupt. Thus he argued against this country's putting trust in European "despots and monarchs or entering into any international alliances with them." Although the *Tribune* admitted that European culture was brilliant "at the apex," that did not in the newspaper's viewpoint "mean much to the base."[1]

> The whole structure of Europe is grossly materialistic. All society has to be occupied with material things, but European society has made this a gross preoccupation for centuries of acquisitive wars and struggle for peace, of peonage and villenage, of profligacy at the top and stolid plotting at the bottom with a culture, a scholarship and a civilization which has not had much meaning for the masses of the people in several hundred years.
>
> That's materialism packed down and solidified.[2]

Furthermore the *Tribune* suspected that Europe held sinister designs on the United States. European leaders, in the words of

Arthur Sears Henning, were anxious to "clip the wings of the American eagle and tap the fat wallet of Uncle Sam, or, as he is dubbed abroad, Uncle Shylock." In its vision of the existing world, the chief European powers literally wished to take over (by clever subterfuge or course) economic control of the United States. "The United States is in European eyes, less a nation with national interests to preserve and advance than a region to be exploited in the interests of the old world." What especially infuriated the *Tribune* was the condescending attitude of the Old World toward America. Thus the main reason, the newspaper asserted, that Sinclair Lewis was offered the Nobel prize for significant work in literature was that he described the "attributes of unpleasant people," and because it was "understood that Europeans admire the work which trims the damyank to their own satisfaction." The *Tribune* also maintained that European diplomacy was far too clever for naive American leadership. To McCormick's way of thinking, Old World leaders invariably duped United States leaders in the interest of their own selfish ends. Consequently America almost inevitably came off second best in its dealings with Europe because of the "Dazzling Brilliance of European Diplomacy." Perhaps the newspaper possessed a built-in sense of inferiority as well as an enormous chip on its shoulder when it bitterly castigated those Europeans who always criticized "our bad manners, lack of taste, slang, dollar chasing, nasal tones, and other errors."[3]

The natural question raised was this: why should European diplomacy always have been so incredibly superior? For one reason the United States government was "ephemeral, subject to popular hysteria and emotionalism. A crown is a continuity. . . . A republican executive thinks in terms of the next election. A king and his ministers think with regard to the next grandson." This did not mean the *Tribune* preferred the monarchical form of government, although it was ready to admit its superior diplomacy. On the contrary it believed that royal houses were still a "prevalent form of human debasement and futility," the chief prop of a social system of "caste, privilege and place without worth." For the *Tribune* the underlying center of power in Europe, outside of France, Germany, and Russia, still rested with royal houses, despite an ostensible veneer

October 15, 1929

of parliamentary control. There was a curiously anachronistic quality in the newspaper's image of European realities.[4]

The United States, even though no match for clever European diplomacy, offered incomparably better living conditions. McCormick really believed it was the only democracy, socially and politically, among all the nations of the world. In 1929 the faith was held particularly high; American society had brought within reach of even the poorest a life of "luxury and ease," the United States was now the world's financial center, and American methods of mass production offered hope for the economic liberation of even European labor (which was the main reason U.S. methods had not hitherto been more readily adopted in the Old World). Even in the depths of the depression, McCormick never lost his deep faith in the superiority of the "American way of life." He always believed that American youth was "entitled to the intelligent and vigorous exposition of American institutions and principles"; his belief in the basic soundness of the old American values was never to waiver.[5]

Not only was the United States the finest nation in the world, the Midwest was undoubtedly its most desirable section:

> The central states are not an appendage. They are the productive center of the nation. Within a few hours' ride of Chicago is the center of the nation's population, the center of its manufacturing industry, and the center of agricultural production. . . . The other sections of the country, and particularly the eastern seaboard, can prosper only as we prosper. We and we alone, are central to the life of the nation.[6]

This statement, although on the surface mere chamber of commerce posturing, was indicative of a deeply held conviction that the Midwest somehow possessed more of the peculiar qualities of "Americanism" than did the other regions of the United States. The chief reason for this, McCormick argued, was that the central states, unlike the original thirteen, had never been colonies. The United States was their mother country. "Their first settlers, veterans of the Continental Army, brought with them the fierce patriotism of the soldier of which veterans of all succeeding wars have continually renewed the flames." It constantly rankled the *Tribune,* however, that the Midwest was not first in everything, that Chicago, after all, was only the "second city." Thus, New York City, which it naturally considered completely unrepresentative of America's best, was the butt of its choicest diatribes. "New York society and New York letters," the *Tribune* thundered, "are colonial in their attitude to the old world." Eastern seaports were somehow un-American in their geographical location; they faced the outer world and were "the port of entry of foreign capital and foreign citizens, foreign philosophy, and foreign political doctrines." Eastern capital was supposedly inextricably linked with European financial interests. Few words were too strong to describe New York's "flimsy American aristocracy." Eventually, the Newspaper optimistically hoped and expected, the second city would become first, and Chicago could overtake the Eastern behemoth.[7]

The *Chicago Tribune* was the chief example of the optimistic, "I will" spirit so characteristic of the Midwest metropolis in the 1920s. As late as 1932, a magazine writer took note of Chicago's viewpoint:

> They are determined to make of Chicago the world's largest city, the world's most beautiful city, the world's most cultured city. There is not much chance that it will fail to have its fifty millions of population. There is not much doubt that it will dominate the stream of American Civilization.[8]

This was the message preached day after day by the *Tribune*.

McCormick would have agreed with the thesis associated with Frederick Jackson Turner that the true point of view in the history of the United States was not the Atlantic Coast, but rather the Great West. Driven to its logical conclusion, the Turner thesis asserted that the traits of the frontier—"that buoyancy and exuberance which comes from freedom"—were of a superior order to the European originals. According to Turner, "What the Mediterranean Sea was to the Greeks, breaking the bond of custom, offering new experiences, calling out new institutions and activities, that the ever retreating Great West has been to the eastern United States directly, and to the nations of Europe more remotely." McCormick's belief in midwestern superiority (it was superior because it had never been colonial), and resulting provincialism was not too far removed from the views of the noted historian, although there is no evidence that he was *directly* influenced by Turner. Certainly Turnerism is capable of serving as an intellectual justification of "isolationism."[9]

The *Tribune* evidently desired that the United States be as untainted by foreign contamination as possible. It grudgingly observed that the national origins plan, passed in 1927, was a just rule of admission for immigrants, but admitted that it preferred "as complete a shutting off of immigration as . . . humanly possible." Claiming that the proportion of criminals among aliens was especially high, it supported measures requiring the registration of aliens with "the authorities until granted full citizenship." According to the *Tribune,* an especially troublesome problem was the influx of Mexicans, which should have been severely restricted. The unlimited immigration of Mexicans, the newspaper warned, would eventually "lower the American standard of living and introduce into the social composition of the American population a large element unready historically and racially to be assimilated."[10]

The depression reinforced these nationalistic arguments since unemployment would be increased by the influx of additional foreigners. A cartoon by John T. McCutcheon in November, 1930, illustrated this viewpoint. It portrayed the "American unemployed" beseeching Uncle Sam to "Shut the Gates for Two Years." In the background was a huge group of foreigners—the "Flood of European Immigration" all ready to swarm in and compete for the few available jobs.[11]

It was a heavy burden on McCormick's shoulders that American leadership (and this included the leadership of the Republican party) was blind to these truths. The diplomatic corps in particular was infested with unsound, foreign notions:

> High grade men, strongly American, strongly democratic in their instincts, have not emerged in the diplomatic service in numbers enough to make the selection easy. The snobbery and laziness of minor jobs in the field break down the better qualities of young men entering the work. . . . The days of imitation and of toadying to foreign castes and titles are over. They should have been over since the time of Ben Franklin, but the diplomatic service has still to find it out.[12]

The reference to America's "toadying to foreign castes and titles" pointed especially to those of the British. McCormick believed, or professed to believe, that the State Department was headed by diplomats who wanted nothing more out of life than to gain the social prestige of being presented at the British court. Consequently the only reason State Department employees attended and supported international conferences was because of the social distinction the conferences gave, the opportunity to partake of the "social ritual of Europe . . . the glamour of ancient forms and the sophistication of old world manner and method." American diplomacy, the Colonel argued gloomily, displayed "none of the stalwart pride that our diplomatists of early days exhibited." It had become cringing and obsequious. Whenever any other nation would threaten to withdraw from a conference, American diplomats automatically fell "to their knees through fear of the failure of a conference and the abrupt ending of their enjoyable prominence and prestige." The *Tribune* was more responsible than any other voice in disseminating the idea that State Department employees were effete cooky-pushers. The only way to rectify this distasteful situation, to the Colonel's way of thinking, was return to good, old-fashioned "shirt-sleeve" diplomacy. Those, such as President John Grier Hibben of Princeton, who criticized United States foreign policy, tariff restrictions, and isolationism were denounced for "seeking the good opinions of Europeans whose culture they regard as superior." To disagree with McCormick usually resulted in a reply that one was more interested in social prestige or gaining the good opinion of foreigners than of being pro-American. In fact it was impossible to disagree with the *Chicago Tribune* and still be considered patriotic.[13]

Although deeply suspicious of the Old World, the *Tribune* was by no means "isolationist" when it came to the New World. A fair description of McCormick, one which has been more generally applied to the historian Charles Beard, is that he was a continentalist. To him the Eastern and Western hemispheres were two completely detached entities. The one was old, the other new; one was corrupt, the other full of promise and opportunity. "We are all men of a new world, having certain common characteristics of the pioneer, a certain viewpoint and response to life which differentiates

January 15, 1935

us from the world of our European ancestors." In the same editorial the *Tribune* actually argued for a "continental patriotism." It asserted that the construction of a Pan-American highway would bind Latin America more closely with the United States and extend the bonds of cooperation. However, the newspaper contended that if a Latin American nation, such as Haiti, were incapable of ruling itself, the United States had every right to intervene and take charge of its affairs. Eventually the Colonel hoped to see the removal of European influence from the areas south of the border and development of the Latin American standard of living under the tutelage of the United States. Even Canada, although a member of the British Commonwealth of Nations, could not escape this destiny. "They are people of the new world and of the new times" and as such would be tied closely economically and culturally to the United States. In short, an active foreign policy from the Arctic Ocean to Tierra Del Fuego was in the legitimate interests of American diplomacy.[14]

The *Tribune*'s attitude toward Great Britain exemplified its antiforeign outlook. Although this was the country the Colonel knew best, it appeared the summation of all that was wrong with Europe. Although McCormick did not deny that England was a political democracy, he argued that the nation was socially an oligarchy. The newspaper asserted that the monarch still provided the keystone to the whole parliamentary system, a system which retained "caste, aristocracy and position, dignity and privilege fixed by birth or by royal grant," and it criticized the special rights enjoyed by the Church of England. According to the *Tribune*'s analysis, eventually the system would work to the nation's detriment as it blocked the advancement of able men in industry and trade and perpetuated rot.[15] In fact when it came down to the essentials, England was a rather miserable place in which to live:

> London, metropolis of an aristocratic caste system and a populace which is content with the thin gruel of a political democracy, not a social one, becomes year by year a worse place for the average man. Its faults and its vices have been built into it by centuries of aristocratic indifference to the common lot.[16]

At the top, however, England was enormously rich, sated with the spoils from the World War. Whatever the fighting had cost

Britain, according to the newspaper, the advantages had more than compensated for the expenditures. For one thing the United Kingdom had picked up additional colonies from the fighting. "The white man's burden is rubber, oil, opium (for the heathen Chinese), tea, hardwood, copra, cotton, silk, and ships to carry them." If British policy appeared pacific in nature, it was only because it had already looted the entire world.[17]

Despite all this vast wealth, Great Britain owed the United States a considerable war debt, a fact which probably created more isolationists in America than any other single consideration. Recognizing a popular issue, the *Tribune* constantly reminded its readers of these debts, and declared that the British people were moral crybabies for falling behind in their payments—that they had been encouraged by their government to "nurse a sense of injury," and that the "average Englishman is suffering because of his moral superiority and because of the unscrupulousness of other people, particularly of Americans." It scoffed at the suggestion that the debt could not be paid: "They [the major powers of Europe] now rule the world. . . . The sick man is well. He hates all the expenses of his illness." A McCutcheon cartoon in 1929 purported to show how the "annual exodus to Europe of 700,000 American tourists" gave Europe plenty of dollars with which to pay the debt. The *Tribune* thought that the easiest way for the British to pay this debt would be for them to hand over to the United States all their possessions in the Caribbean, or if that proved impossible, transfering certain units of their navy to the American; this could "at least take care of the interest payments." In November, 1932, when Great Britain was supposed to pay approximately one hundred million dollars to the United States, the *Tribune* suggested that the transfer of two battleships would do very nicely as a payment.[18]

Perhaps the main reason McCormick was so critical of Great Britain was that he considered it a natural rival, even an enemy, to the United States. In 1931 the *Tribune* darkly warned of the possibility of a war between the two great naval powers. The Colonel claimed to have had some personal experience in this regard. In a speech delivered in 1943 at the Detroit Athletic Club, he asserted that the two nations had in the recent past been perilously close to war:

> You may have forgotten the tremendous tension that arose between Great Britain and this country over our naval building plans before the treaty limiting our navy was adopted. Both countries regret the treaty now, but Great Britain's insistence forced it.
>
> At that time the tension was so great that our general staff feared an army of 300,000 regulars, then in England, would be landed in Canada and marched against this country, which had completely demobilized.
>
> The idea appears fantastic, but it did not appear fantastic to our general staff at that time. I know, because I worked with the general staff on plans on defense—for the defense of Detroit.[19]

Consequently one of the chief requirements of American security was to have a navy superior to that of the British. Arthur Sears Henning contended that with an American navy equal to Great Britain's the latter nation "would be unable to trample on the neutral trading rights of the United States in another war as she did in the world war between 1914 and 1917, and would be compelled to accept the freedom of the seas." McCormick could not envision an Atlantic community of nations with the great seapowers leagued together against the land masses. To his way of thinking, the chief rivals to the United States were precisely the members of this Atlantic community; the natural allies of America were to be found only in the New World.[20]

Although the two nations should be rivals, McCormick always believed that in reality the British government obscured this natural relationship by secretly manipulating American foreign, and even domestic policy. A matter-of-factly written news story of August, 1929, stated how an increase in the re-discount rate of the New York Federal Bank on August 12, 1929, followed closely a visit to the United States of Sir Montagu Norman, Governor of the Bank of England. Collusion was taken for granted. The *Tribune* insisted the American political leaders of both parties possessed an instinctive English viewpoint, whereas in Great Britain there was no corresponding American viewpoint. Especially singled out were Henry

March 31, 1931

Stimson and Dwight Morrow—Republican politicians who found in "upper circles of British society an idealization of social conditions. If they could be quite certain that there was an American ruling class they would think themselves of it." McCormick suspected that it was the one great dream of these leaders to cement a closer political connection between the United States and Great Britain. For example, the *Tribune* asserted that 1930 was going to go down in history as the year the United States joined the British Commonwealth (because of the London Naval Treaty).[21]

The *Tribune* tried to have it two ways: contending that Great Britain was unbelievably wealthy and also in steady decline. Both points of view served the newspaper's purpose: the first because it could be argued that Britain was rich enough to pay back her debts; the second demonstrated the inferiority of her system. According to the second viewpoint the British Commonwealth was disintegrating because the ordinary man in the dominions fought against the class stratification so dear to the English. The *Tribune* pointed out that the British Empire did not consist of contiguous territory. "Time and space are against it and not for it." Prophetically it predicted that the Union of South Africa would eventually break all ties with the United Kingdom.[22] In a news article, Henry Wales stated:

> England is slipping. London is losing the power and prestige which it formerly held as the center of the earth's finance and as the hub of the world's commerce. England does not yet admit its decadence. London does not yet acknowledge that it has passed the zenith of its heyday, and is now headed along the downward curve.[23]

England's decline furnished a lesson for America. In fact England provided so many lessons that one is driven to the conclusion that its "lessons" had little to do with actual conditions. In later years when McCormick was busy sticking pins into the Roosevelt administration England was to become an example of prosperity! But in 1931, at the time of the run on the British pound, the English were in the *Tribune*'s bad graces. At that time they were in prosperous circumstances only when it served McCormick's argument; that is, when the subject of war debts was being discussed. The lesson that

Britain more normally furnished, by 1931, was that a nation living beyond its income inevitably would decay. Socialism and the dole had thus nearly wrecked what had been "the richest nation on earth." This demonstrated, for the *Tribune* at least, that soaking the rich and "provident" to provide for the needs of the "less fortunate" only proved disastrous.[24] McCormick, in a speech delivered in Rockford, Illinois, on December 1, 1932, argued:

> No other country has ever put the slogan of 'soaking the rich' into such systematic and continuous operation. It has cost Britain the destruction of her basic industries and her world-wide trade, reflected in an army of workless permanent for the last ten years. Fallacies are always fallacies. There has been no more magnificent example of killing and eating the geese that should supply the golden eggs.[25]

Strangely enough, several people who were close to the Colonel (and who shared his views) deny vociferously that he was anti-British; rather that the opposite was true. McCormick said much the same thing after returning from a trip to Africa in the early fifties. He interviewed Kwame Nkrumah, later the president of Ghana. Nkrumah told McCormick that he had heard the publisher was extremely anti-British. He then turned to the Colonel and said confidentially, "So am I." McCormick seemed puzzled why Nkrumah should have heard he was anti-British when it was so obviously a "fiction"! Yet the English were always the subject of constant sniping by the *Tribune*. The newspaper, if not anti-British, certainly relished twisting the lion's tail.[26]

Ironically, McCormick, a bitter antagonist to Mayor William Hale Thompson's Republican machine, held very similar foreign policy views. Thompson, it may be recalled, ran for mayor regularly on an anti-King George ticket and in 1931 thundered, "The *Tribune*, greatest curse Chicago ever had, sold out to King George to get 1,200 square miles of Canadian land." The difference of course was that Thompson was vulgar; the *Tribune* had a more sophisticated facade.[27]

But McCormick's attitude toward Britain was mild compared with his views on Russia. Of all nations, the *Tribune* believed that the Soviet Union possessed the worst dictatorship and posed the greatest threat to American security. In its estimation the "dictatorship of the proletariat" was all dictatorship and no proletariat, and the USSR was little more than an inchoate mass of people submerged in bureaucracy, red tape, rules, and lack of innovations. Thus to the *Tribune* communism represented a backward movement in the march of civilization. The newspaper admitted, however, that there was only a slight chance of the overthrow of the Stalin regime, which remained in power because of "the Russian capacity for suffering and inaction in the face of suffering." Nevertheless, the *Tribune* optimistically foresaw some "danger of peasant revolts."[28]

In reality communism was a new religion retaining much of the outward symbolism of the old. "It has its ikons, its sacred relics, its rites, and its pageantry. It demands that its devotees blind themselves to the realities of misery, oppression and cruelty and adhere to a doctrine as an act of faith." The embalmed body of Lenin had become for the Soviet leadership a religious symbol, and the victims of Russian courts were often "plainly impressed by the general religious sense of their guilt." The *Tribune* compared judicial procedure in the Soviet Union with that of the Salem witch trials.[29] In its best style, the newspaper in 1930 ran an editorial concerning a Stalin speech:

> Stalin recently made a seven hour speech, the length of it being sufficient proof that the irreligious reds are in reality very primitive religious people. A praying Cromwellian colonel of a regiment of Roundhead saints from the Eastern Association of Independents would not have preached more than five hours before the battle of Marston Moor or after it, and not even the Fifth Monarchy men would have gone seven at any time. It is not even done in the Tennessee hills.[30]

As the preceding quote indicates, the *Tribune* could not take the Russians entirely seriously. McCormick and his editors refused to believe that any nation which so denied the values of free enterprise could be a going concern. How could a nation which went against such preconceived ideas successfully exist? The *Tribune* of course believed the Russians were rapidly declining in power; Stalin had economically wrecked the nation—a task abetted "by the incompetence of the Russian masses." Those aspects of Russian communism which seemed to work were the parts influenced by American capitalism. Carey Orr in particular was fond of portraying the typical Bolshevik leader as a wild-eyed, incompetent revolutionary, with dirty face and shaggy, unkempt beard, carrying the communist manifesto in one hand and a bomb in the other. Russia was, after all, "a land of simple people who pass from one despotism to another, altering . . . not at all in degree and little in kind," a people, in short, "incompetent except for plain husbandry, crafts and arts." Since communism contradicted everything in which McCormick believed, it had to be unsuccessful.[31]

Although the *Tribune* ostensibly underrated Russian economic growth and power, this disguised a real fear, strengthened by the advancing shadows of the depression, that the United States was ripe for communist subversion. The belittling of Russia only masked an almost obsessive concern that a communist takeover of the United States was imminent. Difficult as it now is to believe, even the Hoover administration seemed vulnerable to red subversion. The *Tribune* cranked out many stories on this theme. At the time of the 1932 Republican convention, Carey Orr drew a front page cartoon showing Lenin sitting on Lincoln's seat in the Lincoln memorial, put there by the "radical congress." In a front page editorial, allegedly written by the Colonel himself, the *Tribune* claimed that the United States government was reaching out for dominance over manufacturing and commerce. A month later McCormick delivered a speech pointing with grave concern to the growing power of the federal government under Hoover. John T. McCutcheon had a forceful remedy for the whole communist problem in the United States; he urged in a cartoon that people who believed conditions were better in the USSR "should be forcibly put on a boat and sent over to that country to enjoy its blessings." The *Tribune* often went to absurd lengths to find the red menace omnipresent. In 1929 it reported that communism held sway over many Waukegan school children and blamed this state of affairs on such "pinks" as Clarence Darrow and Jane Addams.[32]

The Moscow bureau posed a problem. The *Tribune* refused to station a correspondent in the Soviet capital because of censorship. Consequently, its Russian correspondent, Donald Day, located himself in Riga, Latvia. After removing George Seldes from Moscow in 1923, McCormick left no representative there, and thus the *Tribune* was compelled to rely for its Soviet news upon sources outside that nation or occasional visitors. Arguing that although "this procedure may reduce our volume of news from Russia," the newspaper asserted that the quality of the news would be improved since any reporter stationed in Moscow would be merely the prisoner of government handouts. Unfortunately the *Tribune* forgot that covering the Soviet Union from Riga was roughly comparable to covering the United States from Havana, or China from Hong Kong. Day was violently anticommunist and tended to see reds around every corner. Riga was filled with all sorts of refugees and was a hotbed of rumors. Although enjoying McCormick's support, Day failed to gain the full confidence of the Chicago office, which distrusted some of his more anti-Soviet statements. (Day defected to the Nazis in World War II and issued propaganda broadcasts from Berlin against the Allies.)

A typical report from Day to Chicago proclaimed that drinking was on the rise in the Soviet Union (because the workers were unhappy, of course), or that the people lived in unbelievable squalor. He was forced to depend too heavily upon refugees for his information, and much of his reporting was suspect. Nevertheless, he succeeded in giving pertinent information concerning the 1931 Russian famine. Some of his more critical stories, derided by his fellow correspondents, in fact turned out to be true. With breathtaking exactness, Day wrote in 1932 that the Soviet regime had cost the lives of 3,883,891 people, and he put the number of exiles at 7,000,000. But he often received his news from untrustworthy sources; for example one of his sources of information for these statistics was Alfred Rosenberg, the prominent German Nazi.[33]

In March, 1929, Mark Rasumny visited Russia and wrote up his impressions for the *Tribune*. His picture of conditions was unrelievedly grim. The people looked "strangely serious, unnaturally stiff and reserved." When he saw the way people in Moscow actually lived, he "better understood" the faces he met on the sidewalks. Rasumny made much of the fact that crime rates in Russia were high; in Rostov-on-Don he estimated there were ten to twelve robberies a night. The *Tribune* headline writer changed this to twenty robberies a night. (There was no estimate of the number of robberies occurring in Chicago on an average evening.) While visiting Jewish communities, Rasumny discovered that the people were "thin and emaciated," their eyes "deep sunken and hungry." He found a general discontent with the Stalin regime and smugly concluded that civil war was imminent.[34]

Henry Wales, the *Chicago Tribune* Paris correspondent, went on a fact-finding tour for the newspaper in March, 1931, and made a different assessment. Surprisingly, and probably to the *Tribune*'s embarrassment, his reports praised the accomplishments of communism. In what must have been a dig at the newspaper for which he worked, he found it difficult to account for the "daily harvest of jingo news in American dailies"; and as far as he could observe, there was "no foundation for any of the alarming reports." Admittedly the Soviet Union was undergoing a food shortage, but Wales claimed that conditions were no worse than they had been in Germany, Austria, or Hungary after the war. He wrote that his copy was not censored and asserted that there was a labor shortage in Russia in contrast to the widespread unemployment elsewhere. Russian prisons were "not below those of western European nations in hygiene, and the regime under which they operated is considerably less severe." Everywhere he found churches; the only ones that were closed were those whose congregations failed to support them with voluntary offerings.[35] Wales was positively whimsical when he described the dreaded G.P.U.

> Everything in Russia is blamed on the G.P.U. Those poor boys in the secret police haven't got a single friend, anywhere, but every one must be some lonesome mother's darling. Day after day, week after week, month after month, year after year, certain circles of the capital buzz with reports of wholesale arrests and car lot executions and innumerable offenders sent into exile. . . . One wonders how the housing shortage can exist in a city, which is also depleted nightly by the raids of the sinister secret police.
>
> There have been enough stories published of starving, freezing populations to have exterminated all the inhabitants by this time—if they were true.[36]

It was very much to the *Tribune*'s credit and an acknowledgment of the freedom extended to its correspondents that it ran the series, although its editorial page made the dispatches appear more anti-Soviet than they actually were. After Wales returned to Paris, the *Tribune* claimed that his reports had been heavily censored by Soviet authorities.[37] Despite his differences, Henry Wales remained with the newspaper for a number of years.

Two Atlanta girls, Alva Christensen and Mary L. De Gire, visited the Soviet Union in January, 1933, and wrote dispatches far closer to the *Tribune*'s editorial position. Headlines helped give the gist of their stories for those readers too tired to read the entire text:[38]

U.S. GIRLS FIND	U.S. GIRLS FIND
RICH DON BASIN	RUSSIANS WORK
A HIDEOUS PLACE	AT POINT OF GUN

When William Shirer interviewed Russian refugees, the *Tribune* featured the story prominently. Shirer once cross-examined a group of people for six hours because their stories seemed to him so incredible. Finally convinced, he found "a tale of human suffering so terrible that it seemed like the account of another and strange world—an animal kingdom where all is butchery and starvation and the human touch is unknown."[39]

The *Tribune* believed those correspondents who found Soviet living conditions most intolerable. Perhaps one reason the newspaper so prominently displayed their stories was that during the depression it did not want any unemployed reader to gain the impression that life in Russia was preferable to unemployment in the United States. Thus it argued comfortably that a "survey of actual conditions will show that except for a small percentage the American unemployed are better fed, better clothed, and better off in all essentials of physical condition than the mass of Russian employed." It belittled the American "intelligentsia in their present mood of enthusiasm for the bolshevik system."[40]

McCormick sturdily fought any suggestion that the United States should offer recognition to the Soviet leaders. Soviet diplomatic immunity would, in the opinion of the editorial page, produce "mischief making under the direction of the Red Internationale," and give the Soviets undeserved prestige. Anyway, what did the USSR have to give the United States in return for recognition? The *Tribune* could not resist casting aspersions at those politicians who disagreed with its position on this matter. Characteristically it claimed that Senator Borah's pleading for recognition only emphasized "his lack of qualification for the position he has as chairman of the committee on foreign relations." But until 1933 it could be thankful that four American administrations had refused recognition to the Soviet Union, an act which, in the *Tribune*'s opinion would have been "humiliating, futile, and injurious to international responsibility."[41]

The European country which the *Tribune* most admired was Germany. The reason for this was that of all nations in the Old World, it seemed to be the one which most resembled the United States. The newspaper pinned great expectations upon the German republic, before Hitler took over the national leadership, and constantly criticized the British and French for thwarting its ambitions. Although acknowledging that Germany was partly responsible for World War I, the *Tribune* asserted that its guilt was by no means exclusive. By 1929 the material damage wrought by the German army had been all but obliterated, and the *Tribune* even argued that reparations had already more than compensated the Allies for war damages. To its way of thinking, spoils was a more apt term than reparations for the booty that was being exacted from Germany. During the World War, the United States had asserted that it was fighting to make the world "safe for democracy," to destroy monarchical government. Why, the *Tribune* logically argued, should the Weimar Republic be saddled with the onus of the previous monarchy?[42] In one editorial, written in 1929, it gave the German people its highest praise:

> The German people are fitted to fulfill and make good use of free institutions. They are law abiding and order loving. They labor and they think and they are not easily swept off their feet by emotion. Their social and political character is substantial and they have developed science and industry to a height unsurpassed by any other people. . . . Germany is easily the most modern nation in Europe and fitted best to deal with and

exploit for her own and the world's benefit the expanding possibilities of our time.[43]

Unfortunately for this dream, the National Socialists in 1930 increased their representation in the Reichstag from twelve seats to one hundred and seven. The *Tribune* never had any delusions about the nature of Hitler, declaring that this increase in Nazi strength could "hardly comfort anyone who believes that what Europe and Western Civilization most need at the moment is peace and stability." It continued, however, to be hopeful about Germany's future, although its optimism was more tempered than it had been formerly:

> But for Germany we continue to have faith in republicanism. The Germans are the most stable and orderly people of the continent, with a very high level of character and intelligence. If any people in the world are fit for self government and popular institutions they are.[44]

The newspaper especially praised the aging Paul von Hindenburg who supposedly represented the finest traits of the German character. To help the Hindenburg regime survive, it urged the Allies to permit the union of Germany and Austria, return the Saar, and perhaps even return some of the colonies; this would, in its opinion, give the German Republic needed popular support. When the German economy began to deteriorate in the thirties, the *Tribune* blamed the decline on the Treaty of Versailles and the intransigence of the Allies. As the newspaper bitterly noted, the economic condition of Germany was not "an unforseen consequence of the peace. It was provided for in the design." It strongly attacked the French for not allowing Austria and Germany to form a customs union, and predicted correctly that they would later regret that refusal.[45]

Through the able reporting of Sigrid Schultz, midwestern audiences received a vivid and informed picture about German internal politics. From 1919 to 1941 Miss Schultz represented the *Tribune* in Berlin. She was also, in the thirties and early forties, the Berlin commentator for the Mutual Broadcasting System. Her father was a portrait painter of the wealthy. "In later years," she once wrote, "when I became a reporter, my father's acquaintances provided me with valuable contacts usually barred to foreigners." Schultz had lived in Germany during World War I. She intensely hated the Nazis and indeed distrusted the entire German nation. Her anti-German outlook was evident when she wrote during World War II, "Our alleged unkindness at Versailles had nothing to do with Germany's dedication to another war and, should that war fail, to still another." William Shirer, her good friend, praised her as "buoyant, cheerful, and always well informed." Harry Flannery described her as "one of the most capable newspaperwomen" he had ever met. Although her views often differed from the *Tribune*'s, she had the highest respect for the Colonel and this respect was reciprocated.

Miss Schultz constantly sounded the warning about what would happen if Hitler came to power: Germany would be governed by a "reactionary dictatorship, snarling at neighbor countries, with all powerful leaders cracking the whip over the bulk of the electorate." In her first interview with Hitler, he staggered her by shouting at the top of his voice, "My will shall be done," as if he were the diety. Neither was the *Tribune*'s editorial page blind to the danger. Hitlerism, it said, was "reactionary and destructive of the freedom upon which, we profoundly believe, human progress depends." Perhaps, the newspaper was to assert, if the Allies had only been less exacting of Germany in the twenties there would have been no Hitler government. The *Tribune,* during the heated days of World War II, was often criticized for being pro-Nazi: the contention was absurd as the evidence amply demonstrates. Colonel McCormick was against Hitlerism from the very beginning. In fact the *Tribune* fares very well in any comparison with the most prestigious American daily, the *New York Times,* which in 1932 averred, "Hitler is not as extreme as his proclamations and will follow a policy of moderation."[46]

The *Tribune* was no more favorable to Italian fascism, which maintained power by "the most ruthless force." Mussolini suffered from an "inordinate ambition and the cultivation of a provocative belligerence certain to bring Italy dangerous enmity if not isolation." McCormick argued that fascism was almost as bad a form of government as communism; neither allowed inquiry and dissent. But Italian matters during these years received only a minor share of the newspaper's attention; certainly the Colonel was far more obsessed with the communist form of totalitarianism.[47]

During the Hoover administration the great issues in foreign policy were war debts, naval disarmament, and the Manchurian question. The war debts problem has already been discussed to some extent in relation to Great Britain. In 1931, when the Hoover moratorium went into effect, the *Tribune* did not criticize what were, after all, the economic facts of life, but it did urge the president to stress openly his opposition to a general debt cancellation. With solicitous concern for the American unemployed, an Orr cartoon portrayed two unemployed men talking to each other, "I tell you, Bill, I'm worried about those European nations an' all the debts they owe us—Poor England with scarcely money enough to maintain the largest navy in the world—poor France with only 3½ billion dollars in gold—an' Italy in such bad shape, so that Mussolini can only challenge the world to fight once a month instead of every two weeks—tsk-tsk. An' us rolling in the lap of luxury with scarcely 10 million idle, My! My!"[48]

After the conclusion of the 1932 presidential campaign, the *Tribune* filled the entire second page of one issue with a map of the territory acquired by the Allied powers in the war. Not entirely coincidental was the appearance of a chart showing the debt payments then due the United States from these same powers. The implication was that some of this plunder could be turned over to the United States if cash were not immediately forthcoming.[49] The *Tribune* could be very forceful in its handling of this issue, an example of which is its treatment of the Hoover moratorium in its news columns.

JOHNSON RIPS INTO MORATORIUM

President Hoover's foreign debt policies and his proposal for a one year moratorium were ripped to pieces today and the pieces held up for the world to see by Senator Hiram Johnson. . . .[50]

On the issue of naval disarmament, the *Tribune* argued that the United States should have the largest possible navy. It distrusted the aims of American diplomacy, which appeared to be operating under the assumption that the real force for peace in the world was moral, not military. That the United States was second in naval power proved a continuing frustration. The views of the *Tribune* on this matter were so vigorously expressed that they earned the antagonism of several other newspapers, although McCormick's paper could be counted on to answer such criticism with stern bluntness. When, for example, the New York *World* condemned *Tribune* naval "jingoism," the Chicago newspaper retorted that it wished the *World* had "the same hospitality for American public opinion that it has for the European point of view."[51]

The *Tribune* continually asked why American naval power should be restricted just to insure the success of some international conference. The United States had world responsibilities, and a growing commercial and financial involvement in almost every country. Its investments and interests needed protection. "There has never been a time in the known history of mankind," the *Tribune* stated, "when naval power has not been one of the chief agencies of international order and of the expansion of civilization." Sea power, it argued, was thus as essential to the welfare of the United States as it was to the British empire.[52]

The newspaper then cast aspersions on the motives of those groups and people who did not see the naval problem in precisely the same light. For example the *Tribune* strongly lashed out at the Federal Council of Churches for favoring naval disarmament. (One of the most refreshing aspects of the *Tribune* is that it went after pressure groups other newspapers would have been afraid to touch. On the other hand, its criticisms often knew no bounds.) Noting that the head of the Council of Churches had been an English citizen until he was 31, the *Tribune* denounced the organization in no uncertain terms:

> The influence of the federal council is active and widespread and is persistently opposed to the development of our naval strength and to all defense measures. The general membership doubtless is merely pacifistic, but we may well give some serious thought to an organized pressure which was directed, or at least largely influenced, by a man of alien birth, and that birth in the country with which alone we have serious naval competition.[53]

In September, 1929, after the Senate began investigating the activities of the shipbuilder's lobby in favor of a large navy, the *Tribune* thought it would be worthwhile if the investigation would include lobbies of "fanatic" pacifist groups, "foreign inspired" groups, and those church organizations arguing against a large navy. "It has been a wise and not a weak standard of conduct," the *Tribune* thundered, "which in times past has kept the organized clergy out of political action."[54]

The *Chicago Tribune* was the most important American newspaper to criticize the London Naval Conference of 1930. Some of the headlines seem almost unbelievable by present day standards:[55]

BRITISH FIGURES BARE DRIVE TO 'SINK' U.S. NAVY

NAVAL CUTS FAVOR BRITISH

BRITISH AMAZED	BRITISH GIGGLE
AT GENEROSITY OF	AS UNCLE SAM
BIG HEARTED U.S.	GIVES UP SHIRT

Much the same point of view was expressed by John Steele, the newspaper's correspondent in London, and particularly by Arthur Sears Henning. Their articles were marked by a strongly anti-British bias. Henning tried his best. One dispatch began on this high level: "Like his ancestors at Bunker Hill, Secretary Adams is holding his fire until he sees the whites of their eyes." Even if the United States achieved the magic "parity" in tonnage, Henning warned, the British preponderance in naval bases would insure her military superiority on the high seas. Britain also could be counted on to retain a certain superiority in the fact that her merchant ships could be more easily converted to naval purposes than could United States merchant vessels. Privately McCormick and Henning believed that Charles Dawes, the ambassador to the Court of Saint James had sold out to the British, just as former ambassador Walter Hines Page had done during the World War.[56]

The final success of the London Conference in 1930 and the conclusion of a treaty received no applause from the *Tribune* which dourly noted "that the American navy is to be considered as an auxiliary of the British, intended to be used in alliance and joint operation, for the protection of trade and possessions. . . . In such a scheme," it added, "it would be composed of the ships required by the British. . . . It is the program which would be recommended by the admiralty to the British dominions if they were building." The newspaper unfairly contended that there undoubtedly were secret provisions in the London Treaty which would explicitly commit the United States to future "entanglements." The only way the United States would have combat parity under the treaty's stipulations would be if "the battle could be arranged at a convenient time and place not too far from New York City." In the Pacific Ocean the newspaper grimly warned that the fleet would not be able to operate much beyond the Hawaiian Islands, leaving the Philippines open to enemy attack. In its published form the treaty was an extremely disappointing document, the *Tribune* argued, although perhaps all that could have been expected from an internationalist and pacifistic administration.[57]

In retrospect it can be seen that the *Tribune* was correct in its distrust of naval disarmament. The United States entered World War II with a thin margin of safety. But the newspaper was often dishonest in its reporting. Unwary readers must have been astonished when the treaty was finally ratified in the Senate by a margin of fifty-eight to nine, for had the *Tribune* not assured them all along that it was very unpopular? The newspaper dourly concluded that Hoover's victory was "a triumph of hope over experience." The *Tribune* was almost alone, except for the Hearst press, in opposing the treaty. Most American dailies lauded the results of the London Naval Conference, and some, such as the New York *World,* wished that the U.S. fleet had been cut even more.[58]

After the passage of the treaty and with the aggressions of Japan in Manchuria, the *Tribune* became more concerned about the naval threat of Japan than of the British. The London Treaty now foredoomed the United States to an inevitable choice between a war that "self-respecting strength could have avoided," or national humiliation. With everything west of Hawaii "cast adrift" all the United States had left in the Pacific were "hostages in Japanese hands." (The *Tribune* had desired the fortification of Guam and the Philippines.) Increasingly the logical enemy appeared to be Japan.[59]

Another problem which plagued the Hoover administration was that of the relationship between a weak, disunited China and a fast-developing Japan. The dream of a strong, prosperous China had for years fascinated many Americans. The *Tribune* was not alone in believing there was a lucrative future to be had in the China trade, a trade which many believed held far more possibility for development than did the trade with Japan. Especially during the depression the fancy of a flourishing, unified China seemed to hold promise for American recovery. Why this belief should have been so prevalent is obscure, for American trade with China in 1929 was only 40 percent as great as with Japan, and in 1933, only 33 percent as much. But the *Tribune* was as hopeful as everybody else. "Stabilization in China means the creation of a market for American manufacturers and investment and would not only hasten in the restoration of our own prosperity, but if brought about as it might be by the establishment of a strong and enlightened government would soon make China a potent and welcome factor in world civilization."[60]

Easier said than accomplished! Not that the *Tribune* lacked suggestions about how the Chinese government could rectify the existing situation. It was hopeful that the Chinese leadership would create a "comparatively small army thoroughly disciplined and well equipped," and renovate its transportation system. It praised the Chiang government and contended that the United States should provide substantial financial assistance to bring about stability, although the newspaper was vague as to whether the bulk of this aid should be public or private. The *Tribune* criticized American business leaders for being "too little conscious of the momentous character of the Chinese situation." Since nothing could be expected "from our political leadership," private enterprise should, to its way of thinking, provide the initiative for Chinese economic growth. Chinese development was obviously to be modeled after the American example.[61]

Sympathetic as it was to Chinese aspirations, the *Tribune* was not entirely sure that China was worth admitting to the family of nations on terms of complete equality. It argued strongly that the United

States should retain its extraterritorial privileges. "Chinese laws and legal agencies have not reached a stage of modern development which justifies confidence," it explained. "Chinese govermental conditions are not yet sufficiently stable and responsible to justify the surrender of foreign concessions to their administration and protection." Until the Chinese established a government able to keep internal peace the United States should retain those privileges.[62]

China was burdened with two overly powerful neighbors: the Soviet Union and Japan, and it was embroiled in conflict with both of them during the Hoover administration. Like many Americans the *Tribune* found it difficult to say where the right and wrong lay in the dispute between China and Russia. Although naturally sympathetic with the Chinese, it believed the United States government would be wise to stick to the traditional policy of minding its own business.[63]

The danger from Japan proved more threatening, at least in the early thirties. The *Tribune* put much of the blame for this upon the United States, which had made so many concessions to the Japanese in the Washington treaty that Japan was left militarily supreme in the western Pacific. It blamed the "pacifists" for allowing American naval strength to deteriorate to the point that if war developed between Japan and the United States, it would be because of the inability of America to defend its own interests. The *Tribune* held no brief for the Japanese government, which displayed little disposition to quell the "rather general belief that a mad dog is loose." In December, 1932, Philip Kinsley visited Japan and reported that the average Japanese citizen, although full of admiration for America, expected eventual war between the two nations. Despite the heavy drain upon Japanese finances caused by the Manchurian adventure, he found the militarists in full control.[64]

Certainly the *Tribune* was not aggressive in its attitude toward Japan. It urged the United States to pour more money into its navy, so the Japanese would respect American strength, but it was appalled by the thought of an embargo directed against Japan, a policy mainly advocated by those "pacifists and Ph.D.'s" who were hell-bent on war only after scuttling the U.S. Navy. To the *Tribune*, a boycott or embargo was "the exact equivalent of presenting a bayonet at the

throat of an opponent and demanding his surrender, with the difference that the threatened opponent is not deterred from reaching for
his gun." Manchuria simply was not worth a war, especially since
Japan, in expanding its empire, was only emulating the example
of the European powers and the United States. "Japan, looking
about for parallels, along which its conduct travels, might observe
Texas, or for more recent although lesser examples Haiti and
Nicaragua, even if nothing at all were to be made of Guam and the
Philippines."[65]

The *Tribune* was deeply suspicious of and antagonistic toward the
Asian policies of Secretary of State Henry Stimson, whom it once
called a "mad-dog," and usually portrayed him as a naive innocent,
ever ready to sally forth on foolish adventures to police the world
and by underhanded means trick the United States into the League
of Nations. There was, in its opinion, no reason for his constantly
sticking pins into Japan.[66]

> Americans are learning to be on guard against their secretary
> of state. He steps into things, and some day will lead with his
> chin, if, indeed, that it not what he constantly does. There is
> scarcely a section of the globe in which he has not been found
> in a dilemma which immediately raised the question why he got
> in it. And when he hunts trouble, it is always alone.[67]

It was with relief that Philip Kinsley could report after the Presidential election of 1932 that the Japanese "were profoundly thankful for the passing of Mr. Stimson." He summed up his dispatch
optimistically: "With a little enlightenment on both sides of the
ocean war between Japan and America may be forgotten."[68]

The *Tribune* recognized that the Philippines were vulnerable to
Japanese attack, blaming this situation on the concessions of the
Washington Treaty. Although independence for the Philippines was
adjudged premature, one *Tribune* reporter touring the islands
acknowledged that if the Filipinos had any say on the subject, they
would have voted for immediate freedom. But McCormick had
little respect for the Filipino people, and called them "bright young
midgets" and the "little brown brothers."[69]

The *Chicago Tribune* was fortunate in having a capable far-
eastern specialist stationed in Shanghai, John Powell, who was also

the editor of the *China Weekly Review*. Powell was the first foreign correspondent to visit the Chinese-Russian front in September, 1929, where he saw evidence of the fighting which had occurred the previous month. He visited Mukden immediately after the Japanese seized Manchuria in 1931, and Shanghai when they captured that city the following year. His dispatches were to prove so infuriating to the Japanese that they denied him access to the official military communiques in March, 1932.[70]

In summary the *Tribune* desired close ties with China in order to foster further trade, and argued for the sending of financial assistance to promote its economic stability. Yet in the final analysis it would rather have seen China go down the drain than go to war with Japan, even while arguing for a stronger military establishment in the Pacific and the retention of the Philippines.

In the final analysis, McCormick, during the Hoover administration, cannot be fairly classified as an "isolationist." His beliefs were more complicated than that, and "isolationist" is, at best, a difficult word to define. His insistent patriotism, support for armaments—especially where they concerned the navy, advocacy of universal military training, and desire for an independent (not necessarily isolated) course for the United States on the world scene, stamp him more as a nationalist. Europe was corrupt and to be abjured, but the same was not true for Latin America nor for the Far East. There was nothing unique in this viewpoint. The Far East, especially, had for a century represented a region of glittering promise for American policy makers, and the United States public had nursed long memories of European rapacity and injustice.[71]

Although the *Tribune* had energetically supported Herbert Hoover for the presidency in 1928, it was not long before the embers of enthusiasm grew cold. The Hoover administration lasted approximately twenty minutes in McCormick's favor. After the inaugural address, wherein the new president outlined his ideas for reform and development, Arthur Sears Henning received a telegram reading, THIS MAN WON'T DO. That was that. Doubtless this was because Hoover had promised greater enforcement of the Volstead Act, limitations on armaments, and had praised the world court. The

Tribune regularly criticized Hoover even before the depression tarnished his reputation. By October 2, 1929, Henning was worriedly asking whether Hoover were not scrapping "cardinal principles of our traditional policies of national defense" and setting forth on the "greatest adventure of idealism in the history of the world."[72]

Three months later, Carey Orr pointed out in a cartoon that the 1928 Republican platform committed the party to avoiding foreign "entanglements" but that "irresponsible leadership" was leading towards that end. Those "irresponsible" leaders could hardly have been anybody other than Stimson and Hoover. In February, 1930, Henning declared that Hoover was pro-British. The *Tribune* did not restrict its criticisms to foreign policy and asserted that the president lacked political acumen. In analysing the reasons for Hoover's poor relationship with congress, it argued, "The processes of government are hardly the processes of engineering, and an administration does not get a law in the same way that a constructor would build a dam."[73]

Under Hoover the Republican party was chained to the evils of internationalism, prohibition, and pacifism. Badly needed in McCormick's opinion was a thorough cleansing of the party, with some major hints that Hoover constituted the element to be cleaned out. The *Tribune* fervently supported the Colonel's sister-in-law, Mrs. Ruth Hanna McCormick, in her battle against Senator Charles Deneen for the 1930 Republican Illinois Senatorial nomination. She defeated Deneen. To the *Tribune* the primary demonstrated that the American people wanted nothing of the Versailles Treaty, the League of Nations, or the World Court. (The November results, wherein Mrs. McCormick was overwhelmingly defeated by Democratic candidate James Hamilton Lewis, apparently signified nothing as there was no editorial comment on the election.) The decline in the Republican fortunes in the general election of 1930 was blamed on none other than Herbert Hoover, who failed in McCormick's estimation to follow traditional Republican policies. Hoover "was showing Bryanism in foreign policy, Bryanism in prohibition, Bryanism in economic regulations." As the paper shrewdly noted:[74]

Mr. Hoover was not responsible for the disillusionment of American business men as to the new era and its permanence, but when the illusion cracked he had nothing in his medicine chest for it. Another man might not have had, but another man would not have had the handicap of a reputation for miracles. And another man might not have had his party so far away from home.[75]

When Representative Fiorello La Guardia of New York City declared that it was "the duty of the federal government to take such action as to eliminate suffering, hunger and want in the future," the *Tribune* retorted that such a statement could "be heartily applauded in Moscow." In truth the newspaper was not very concerned with the sufferings of the unemployed, even during the worst years of national suffering. Rent strikes, for example, were nothing more than communist plots. It constantly criticized Hoover for being too much a socialist, too much the prisoner of the "communistic urges predominant in Washington," and too much the candidate of Bishop James Cannon, Jr., and of the "Methodist Board of Temperance, Prohibition, and Public Morals." The *Tribune* was not alone in showing this curious myopia—was it not H. L. Mencken, for example, who once wrote that the chief issue of the 1932 campaign was prohibition![76]

McCormick did have one remedy for the depression—cut taxes, reduce spending, balance the budget, pare every government department to the bone (except the navy), and stop all federal subsidies. Government costs had to be slashed to "avoid the fate which has overtaken Britain." Hoover's great fault was that he wished to reduce only the navy expenditures. To illustrate where high taxes were leading the nation, the *Tribune* on Christmas Day, 1931, presented the following as a news story on its front page:

TAX BURDENED JUDEA SAVED BY JOHN BAPTIST

Until now, for several years, Palestinians had been forming the habit of looking for poverty to spread farther and farther; for political abuses to become worse and worse. The taxation situation, due to lavish public expenditures on arenas, temples and extravagant public works has recently become intolerable. In fact, it has been learned that the present rate takes nearly 40 per cent of the country's production.[77]

McCormick embarked on an unusually active speaking program to denounce the high rate of government spending. He was utterly convinced that he knew the causes of the economic decline. "Over a month ago," the Colonel told the Hamilton Club, "the economists in the *Tribune* traced the cause of our depression and found it to be the unprecedented extravagance of government."[78] In March, 1932, he stated to the Better Business Bureau, "Last January I was able to announce accurately that the world-wide depression was due to government extravagance which had impaired the accumulations of the world to the point where they could not longer finance necessary trade and industry." He was proud "that the movement for national economy starts in Chicago." If the Hoover policies were followed, McCormick claimed, the United States would come to "complete and inescapable ruin." "The time has come," he summed up, "to get rid of foreign doctrines," in short what the United States needed was a "Patriot Movement."[79]

No wonder Carey Orr declared that the Republican "report card" would give them Fs in "foreign affairs, prosperity, prohibition, naval affairs, and general deportment." About the most feasible alternative left for the Republicans would be to dump Hoover and draft Calvin Coolidge as the standard-bearer in 1932. The *Tribune* disillusionment with Hoover was so great that at the time of the 1932 Republican convention the newspaper carried the banner headline: HALF BOLSHEVIK: HALF FREE.[80]

Even early in 1932 it was evident to astute observers that Hoover probably would be defeated in his bid for reelection. Attention thus focused on the Democrats. The *Tribune,* early in the year, believed that Governor Roosevelt did "not impress the nonpartisan as a strong man or a national winner." It preferred him, however, to Newton Baker who was "thoroughly disqualified" by his pro-League of Nations viewpoint. In the newspaper's estimation, Senator James Reed was a very able candidate who probably could not obtain the nomination. The *Tribune* then gave its considered opinion that the best candidate from the Democratic standpoint would be Governor Thomas Ritchie of Maryland who had "won a great deal of admiration for most of his proposals and doctrines of government."[81]

Since the *Tribune* thought Roosevelt weak and ineffectual (and

WILL IT COME TO THIS?

June 15, 1932

more to the point suspected he was a big spender), and preferred Coolidge to Hoover, it sat on its hands during most of the 1932 campaign, doing an impartial job of reporting the news. Clifford Raymond, an editorial writer, later recollected that toward the end of the campaign, McCormick called him into his office. "Now Cliff, I want you to treat Roosevelt nicely in your editorials," the Colonel said. "I want that boy that I went to school with at Groton to know I wish him well on his career." Not until November 4, 1932, did the newspaper decide to support Hoover, albeit tepidly (most of the editorial condemned Stimson's foreign policy). Arthur Sears Henning correctly predicted the Roosevelt victory although he underestimated the Democratic margin. The *Tribune* faced Roosevelt's election with remarkable equanimity. "Even if we prefer," it stated, "as conditions now are and as prospects are to be viewed that President Hoover and the Republican party should continue in administration we are not, because of that, justified in anticipating the election of Gov. Roosevelt as a calamity." Perhaps the *Tribune* was so favorably disposed to Roosevelt because of local politics since it had strongly supported Anton Cermak over William Hale Thompson in the 1931 mayoralty race and was campaigning with all the resources of its editorial page for Henry Horner against Len Small in the gubernatorial battle. National issues balanced off rather well between the two parties for the *Tribune*: the Republicans were superior on the issue of federal involvement in the economy, the Democrats were stronger against prohibition.[82]

On March 2, 1933, the *Tribune* had an interesting valedictory for Herbert Hoover. It argued that he "had not acquired public confidence as a strong and consistent leader." Although giving expression to the highest "principles of American individualism," Hoover paradoxically had become, in reality, "the greatest state socialist in our annals. . . . He could praise individualism with eloquence, but he could also build Boulder Dam." The editorial ended by condemning his views on prohibition and foreign policy which "subordinated American interests to European."[83] It was not long, however, until the *Tribune* would judge Hoover in a much kinder light.

NOTES

1. *Chicago Tribune,* June 27, 1929, 14:1.

2. *Ibid.,* August 18, 1929, 14:1.

3. *Ibid.,* March 20, 1929, 14:1; September 23, 1929, 14:2; October 15, 1929, p. 12, Orr cartoon; September 19, 1930, 14:2; December 13, 1930, 14:2; October 24, 1931, 12:2.

4. *Ibid.,* October 6, 1929, 12:2; June 10, 1930, 14:2.

5. *Ibid.,* May 27, 1929, 14:2; June 10, 1929, 14:2; June 13, 1929, 12:1; June 26, 1929, 14:2; April 12, 1932, 12:2.

6. *Ibid.,* April 14, 1929, 12:1.

7. Robert R. McCormick, *How We Acquired Our National Territory* (Chicago: The Tribune Company, 1942), p. 48; *Chicago Tribune,* October 19, 1929, 12:2; November 30, 1930, 14:1; Chicago Tribune, *The Destiny of Chicago; Reprinted from the Chicago Tribune* (Chicago: The Tribune Company, 1929).

8. Morris Markey, "Land of the Pilgrim's Pride, the Urgent City," *McCalls,* LIX (March, 1932), 67.

9. See Frederick Jackson Turner, *The Frontier in American History* (New York: Henry Holt and Company, 1921), pp. 3, 37, 38.

10. *Chicago Tribune,* June 5, 1929, 14:2; September 2, 1929, 12:1; March 21, 1930, 14:2.

11. *Ibid.,* November 25, 1930, p. 1.

12. *Ibid.,* March 26, 1929, 12:2.

13. *Ibid.,* July 6, 1929, 6:2; May 15, 1930, 14:1; December 22, 1932, 10:2; February 7, 1933, 12:2.

14. *Ibid.,* March 4, 1929, 12:2; December 16, 1929, 12:1–2; January 3, 1930, 14:2; February 5, 1930, 14:2; May 9, 1930, 14:1; July 17, 1930, 12:2; September 10, 1930, 14:1–2; September 16, 1930, 14:2; March 6, 1932, 14:2; August 6, 1932, 7:1.

15. *Ibid.,* June 26, 1929, 14:2; July 13, 1929, 8:1; September 15, 1929, 12:2; October 22, 1929, 14:1.

16. *Ibid.,* January 28, 1930, 14:2.

17. *Ibid.,* May 14, 1929, 14:1.

18. *Ibid.,* May 30, 1929, 12:2; June 4, 1929, 14:1; June 23, 1929, p. 1; October 14, 1931, 10:1–2; November 17, 1932, 12:1. President Hoover proposed to Prime Minister MacDonald that the British consider selling Bermuda, British Honduras, and Trinidad to the United States as credits upon the war debt. In Hoover's words, "He did not rise to the

idea at all." Herbert Hoover, *The Memoirs of Herbert Hoover,* II (New York: The Macmillan Company, 1952), 345–46.

19.   *Chicago Tribune,* February 13, 1931, 14:2; Robert R. McCormick, *An American's Creed, Delivered before the Detroit Athletic Club, December 15, 1943* (Chicago: The Tribune Company, 1943), p. 10. McCormick's statement that "Great Britain's insistence" forced the Washington Treaty is an example of how he could twist historical fact to "demonstrate" an anti-British statement.

20.   *Chicago Tribune,* October 6, 1929, Sec. 3, p. A.

21.   *Ibid.,* August 12, 1929, 1:8; This story was written by Arthur Crawford. October 8, 1929, 12:2; February 26, 1930, 12:1; September 30, 1930, 14:1–2.

22.   *Ibid.,* September 10, 1930, 14:1–2; September 29, 1930, 14:2.

23.   *Ibid.,* August 22, 1931, 5:5.

24.   *Ibid.,* September 18, 1931, 12:2; October 29, 1931, 12:1; November 5, 1931, 12:2; December 3, 1932, 14:1.

25.   Quoted in *Ibid.,* December 2, 1932, p. 6. The speech was published in Robert R. McCormick, *Mussolini, Moscow or America; An Address by Colonel Robert R. McCormick* (Chicago: The Tribune Company, 1932).

26.   Robert R. McCormick, *Another Voyage to Three Continents, Based on a Series of Addresses Broadcast over WGN, WGNB and the Mutual Broadcasting System, February 16–March 29, 1952* (Chicago: The Tribune Company, 1952), pp. 19–20; interview with Chesly Manly; interview with Mrs. McCormick.

27.   See Alex Gottfried, *Boss Cermak of Chicago, A Study of Political Leadership* (Seattle: University of Washington Press, 1962), p. 206.

28.   *Chicago Tribune,* September 3, 1929, 12:2; February 23, 1930, 14:1.

29.   *Ibid.,* July 2, 1930, 14:2; November 8, 1930, 14:1–2; December 7, 1930, 12:2.

30.   *Ibid.,* July 2, 1930, 14:2.

31.   *Ibid.,* August 7, 1931, 2:2; September 27, 1931, 12:1–2.

32.   *Ibid.,* May 19, 1929. The headline to this news story read BARE RED'S SWAY OVER WAUKEGAN SCHOOL CHILDREN. *Ibid.,* August 5, 1931, p. 1; June 15, 1932, p. 1; July 8, 1932, p. 6; *Editor and Publisher,* LXV (June 18, 1932), 6.

33.   *Chicago Tribune,* April 14, 1929, 12:1–2; March 31, 1929, 10:3–4; October 23, 1932, 8:1; interview with Walter Trohan; interview with a *Tribune* executive; Seldes, *Lords of the Press,* p. 53; George Seldes, "The Men Who Fake the News," *New Masses,* XXXIV (January

30, 1940), 14–17; Oswald Garrison Villard, "Red Menace and Yellow Journalism," *The Nation,* CXXXII (June 3, 1931), 602–603.

34.   *Chicago Tribune,* April 5, 1929, 16:1–4; April 12, 1929, 21:1–6; April 15, 1929, 16:1–4; April 18, 1929, 15:1–5.

35.   *Ibid.,* March 8, 1931, 1:3; March 9, 1931, 3:3; March 12, 1931, 11:2; March 25, 1931, 16:2; April 2, 1931, 20:1; April 5, 1931.

36.   *Ibid.,* April 4, 1931, 9:2; March 25, 1931, 16:2.

37.   *Editor and Publisher,* LXIII (April 4, 1931), 32.

38.   *Chicago Tribune,* January 19, 1933, 6:1; January 20, 1933, 4:1.

39.   *Ibid.,* June 19, 1932, p. 15.

40.   *Ibid.,* September 2, 1931, 12:2; August 1, 1932, 12:2.

41.   *Ibid.,* June 7, 1929, 14:2; March 26, 1930, 12:2; March 9, 1931, 10:1.

42.   *Ibid.,* August 22, 1929, 12:1.

43.   *Ibid.,* August 13, 1929, 14:2.

44.   *Ibid.,* September 16, 1930, 14:1.

45.   *Ibid.,* October 14, 1930, 14:1; March 24, 1931, 14:2; June 9, 1931, 14:1.

46.   *Ibid.,* March 13, 1932, 1:1; September 6, 1932, 10:2; September 14, 1932, 12:2; Sigrid Schultz, *Germany Will Try it Again* (New York: Reynal & Hitchcock, 1944), pp. viii, ix, 9; *New York Times,* January 9, 1932, p. 16; interview with Walter Trohan; William Shirer, *Berlin Diary* (New York: Alfred A. Knopf, 1941), pp. 41–42; Harry W. Flannery, *Assignment to Berlin* (New York: Alfred A. Knopf, 1942), p. 22.

47.   *Chicago Tribune,* June 2, 1929, 14:1–2; April 12, 1932, 12:2.

48.   *Ibid.,* June 22, 1931, 12:1; November 27, 1932, p. 1. The *Tribune* usually ran a spate of articles and cartoons on war debts each November and December since those were the months when the interest payments were due.

49.   *Ibid.,* July 10, 1932, p. 21; November 13, 1932, p. 2.

50.   *Ibid.,* December 22, 1931, 1:8.

51.   *Ibid.,* October 19, 1929, 12:2.

52.   *Ibid.,* June 9, 1921, 12:1; August 30, 1929, 12:1; November 10, 1929, 14:1.

53.   *Ibid.,* June 15, 1929, 10:1.

54.   *Ibid.,* September 12, 1929, 14:1; June 5, 1931, 12:2.

55.   *Ibid.,* December 20, 1929, 1:1; February 7, 1930, p. 1; February 9, 1930, 2:2; February 10, 1930, 1:1; The second of these headings served as the eight column banner headline for the day.

56. Robert Allen, pp. 356–57; Drew Pearson and Constantine Brown, *The American Diplomatic Game* (Garden City, N.Y.: Doubleday, Doran & Company, Inc., 1935), p. 126; *Chicago Tribune,* January 19, 1930, Pt. 2, p. 5; January 30, 1930, 12:1; Tiffany Blake to John T. McCutcheon, February 26, 1930, McCutcheon Papers.

57. *Chicago Tribune,* February 11, 1930, 14:2; May 30, 1930, 8:1; June 8, 1930, 14:2; June 13, 1930, 14:1; September 1, 1930, 8:1.

58. *Ibid.,* August 3, 1930, 14:1; *Literary Digest,* CVI (August 2, 1930), 5–6.

59. *Chicago Tribune,* February 18, 1931, 14:2; October 28, 1931, 12:1.

60. *Ibid.,* September 1, 1930, 8:1; March 27, 1931, 14:2; U.S. Dept. of Commerce, *Statistical Abstract of the United States, 1934* (Washington, D.C.: Government Printing Office, 1934), pp. 428–29.

61. *Chicago Tribune,* August 2, 1930, 6:2; March 30, 1931, 14:1–2; September 1, 1932, 10:1.

62. *Ibid.,* January 2, 1930, 14:1; July 31, 1930, 10:2.

63. *Ibid.,* December 4, 1929, 14:1; December 5, 1929, 14:1–2.

64. *Ibid.,* September 1, 1930, 8:1; September 23, 1931, 12:2; March 8, 1932, 10:2; December 5, 1932, 8:1; December 6, 1932, 12:1; December 12, 1932, 6:3.

65. *Ibid.,* February 25, 1932, 10:2; March 1, 1932, 12:1; September 29, 1932, 10:2.

66. *Ibid.,* October 13, 1931, 12:2; January 11, 1932, 10:1–2; Eleanor Tupper and George E. McReynolds, *Japan in American Public Opinion* (New York: The Macmillan Company, 1937), p. 347.

67. *Chicago Tribune,* August 21, 1932, 12:1.

68. *Ibid.,* December 13, 1932, 8:7.

69. *Ibid.,* May 21, 1929, 14:1; October 28, 1931, 12:1; February 17, 1932, 8:2. Hoover believed that the Philippine Islands should be given their independence provided that the separation was absolute. This meant that the United States would have no responsibility for their defense. William Starr Myers, *The Foreign Policies of Herbert Hoover, 1929–1933* (New York: Charles Scribner's Sons, 1940), p. 169. He vetoed a bill granting independence in December, 1932, on the grounds that the Philippines were not economically ready to follow an independent course. *Ibid.,* p. 171.

70. *Chicago Tribune,* April 2, 1932, p. 16.

71. See e.g. Robert Endicott Osgood, *Ideals and Self-Interest in America's Foreign Relations; The Great Transformation of the Twentieth Century* (Chicago: The University of Chicago Press, 1953), 58–70; William

E. Livesey, *Mahan on Sea Power* (Norman: University of Oklahoma Press, 1947); and Theodore Roosevelt, *Fear God and Take Your Own Part* (New York: George H. Doran Company, 1916), 18, 39, 87–88, 107, 136, 228–29.

72.   *Chicago Tribune,* October 21, 1929, 5:1; Trohan, *Journal of the Illinois Historical Society,* LII, 477–78.

73.   *Chicago Tribune,* January 5, 1930, p. 14; January 14, 1930, 14:1; February 17, 1930, 1:1.

74.   *Ibid.,* April 2, 1930, 14:1; April 6, 1930, p. 1, Orr cartoon; April 10, 1930, 14:1, also p. 1, McCutcheon cartoon; November 9, 1930, 14:1.

75.   *Ibid.,* November 6, 1930, 14:1.

76.   *Ibid.,* January 6, 1931, 14:1; January 11, 1931, 14:1; May 3, 1931, 14:3; August 6, 1931, p. 13. The eight column banner headline over the August, 1931 story read: REDS HERE FOMENT RENT PLOT, and the item began, "A communist plot to foment a rent strike among Chicago's colored residents came to light yesterday afternoon. . . ." No attempt was made by the newspaper to investigate how conditions were among the Negro population. See also Henry L. Mencken, *Making a President: A Footnote to the Saga of Democracy* (New York: A. A. Knopf, 1932).

77.   *Chicago Tribune,* September 23, 1931, 12:1–2; October 1, 1931, 12:1; December 25, 1931, 1:6.

78.   Robert R. McCormick, *The Cost of Government: An Address Delivered before the Chicago Assembly of the Hamilton Club, Chicago, February 18, 1932* (Chicago: The Tribune Company, 1932), p. 5. On the same theme see also McCormick, *The Rise and Fall of the Third Estate: An Address by Colonel Robert R. McCormick before the Chicago Bar Association, April 16, 1932* (Chicago: The Tribune Company, 1932), p. 14; Robert R. McCormick, *The National Peril: An Address by Colonel Robert R. McCormick, April 16, 1932* (Chicago: The Tribune Company, 1932), pp. 14–15; and Robert R. McCormick, *Help Save Your Country: An Address by Colonel McCormick under the Auspices of the National Organization to Reduce Public Expenditures, July 19, 1932* (Chicago: The Tribune Company, 1932), p. 4.

79.   Robert R. McCormick, *An Address by Colonel Robert R. McCormick at the Annual Dinner of the Chicago Better Business Bureau, March 16, 1932* (Chicago: The Tribune Company, 1932), p. 5; Robert R. McCormick, *An Address by Robert R. McCormick before the Chicago Association of Commerce, April 6, 1932* (Chicago: The Tribune Company 1932), p. 18; Robert R. McCormick, *The National Peril . . . ,* pp. 14–15; Robert R. McCormick, *The Sack of Rome and the Sacking of America: An Address by Colonel Robert R. McCormick before the*

Kansas City Branch of the Federation of American Business, Kansas City, Missouri, July 7, 1932 (Chicago: The Tribune Company, 1932), p. 6; Robert R. McCormick, *Mussolini, Moscow or America.*

80.   *Chicago Tribune,* November 21, 1931, p. 1; June 15, 1932, p. 1; *Editor and Publisher,* LXV (June 18, 1932), 6.

81.   *Chicago Tribune,* January 16, 1932, 12:1.

82.   Chicago Tribune, *A Century of Tribune Editorials* (Chicago: The Tribune Company, 1947), p. 106, editorial of April 22, 1932; *Chicago Tribune,* November 4, 1932, 14:1; November 6, 1932, 1:8, 10:2; April 2, 1955, 3:3.

83.   *Ibid.,* March 2, 1933, 12:1. How different was the assessment of William Starr Myers, who wrote in an authorized treatment of the Hoover administration, "Never in our history was peace more assured to the American people nor did the United States stand higher in the esteem of the world than on March 4, 1933. Hoover's record stands as an open book to be read by the American people." Myers, p. 255.

4

The Break With FDR, 1933-1937

Colonel McCormick supported the Roosevelt administration for several months after its accession to power. Twenty-one years later, he could almost truthfully assert that no president had been more warmly applauded by the *Chicago Tribune* than Franklin Roosevelt had upon taking office. The calamities of the depression had produced an almost unanimous consensus for the leader who appeared so confident and brave in his assertion that the only thing to fear was fear itself. Roosevelt's handling of the bank crisis aroused universal acclaim and his attempts to slash the national budget soothed conservatives. The *Tribune* was not alone during those troubled days in praising Roosevelt's "superb leadership." McCormick went so far as to offer the president the use of his home whenever he should visit Chicago.[1]

But the honeymoon was of short duration. McCormick had neither the temperament nor the desire to support consistently any administration. He broke with Roosevelt, although not violently at first, long before most Republican leaders did so publicly. Tiffany Blake, the newspaper's chief editorial writer, had private doubts from the beginning: he considered the inaugural address to be so much "hot air." In a letter to John T. McCutcheon, addressed March 4, 1933, he related that the Colonel was spending all his time on his military biography of Grant, "Leaving us to face the Red Army with such skill in military tactics as we may possess." It was not expedient, however, to criticize the president too early in 1933. In May, Blake was again lamenting to McCutcheon that "criticism seems futile at this time. . . . We can only hope for the best and wait for a more favorable situation to begin fighting for the restoration of American ideas."[2]

On May 1, 1933, the *Tribune* began publishing some of this criticism. Arthur Sears Henning wrote apprehensively of rumors in Washington (they may well have been started by him) that the administration was drifting into a dictatorship similar to those of Hitler and Mussolini. He reported that there was considerable worry that Congress had become a mere rubber stamp similar to its Italian and German counterparts. The *Tribune* believed that if Congress had adjourned after slashing federal expenditures and passing the beer bill, the United States would have been in far better condition.[3]

One of the most important reasons McCormick had for turning against the New Deal was his concern about the National Recovery Administration. From the inception of this agency, the newspaper argued that the NRA was fascistic—to state that it was revolutionary was "merely to state the obvious." In time its criticisms of the NRA were to grow more vehement. According to its stated criticism, United States business was comprised of orphans, widows trying to eke out a small living, and crippled barbers, all being victimized by this ruthless and overbearing governmental agency. Although the *Tribune* displayed the familiar NRA eagle on its front page, in time the eagle began getting smaller and smaller while the American flag kept getting bigger and bigger.[4]

McCormick criticized the NRA in part because he believed it was a threat to the freedom of the press. Especially obnoxious to his viewpoint was the effort of the Roosevelt administration to treat newspapers like any other industry and subject the press to licensing under a code which publishers would be asked to sign. The Colonel was chairman of the Freedom of the Press Committee of the American Newspaper Publisher's Association. On June 9, 1933, a meeting was held in New York, attended by many of the leading publishers of the nation. In McCormick's words, "It was the overwhelming view of those present that, if the recovery act were applied to newspapers, it would constitute an abridgement of the provisions of the

Constitution, guaranteeing freedom of the press." Thus, it was clear to McCormick and the conferees "that newspapers were exempt from the provisions of the act." Most of the publishers decided, however, that it would be poor tactics to "insist upon constitutional rights" and they decided to sign the agreement, although incorporating into it a declaration maintaining the freedom of the press.[5]

Through the summer of 1933, the *Tribune* criticized the New Deal more on this point than on any other. Roosevelt replied to McCormick's criticism at a press conference by declaring that the Colonel was "seeing things under the bed." The rift between the two men, although not as wide as it later would be, was complete.[6]

The other primary reason for the *Tribune*'s break with the president was the New Deal's reliance upon public spending to pull the nation out of the depression. Since McCormick believed the depression "had been brought on us by our taxing bodies which have spent the accumulation of thrifty citizens to exhaustion," he obviously was not going to be patient with the administration's attitude. As a candidate Roosevelt had promised a 25 percent cut in expenditures; in fact he had sent a personal telegram to McCormick in June, 1932, assuring the Colonel he would slash government expenditures wherever possible. Then, according to McCormick, "he reversed himself completely and launched a spending program that was . . . without precedent."[7]

The Colonel, however, was only human and not averse to a little federal largesse as far as the Midwest was concerned. Unashamedly the *Tribune* urged Washington to buy the Chicago Sanitary and Ship Canal for a mere hundred million dollars, although under more ordinary circumstances it would foment at great length against reckless spending and pork barrel extravagance, especially if the extravagances were for New York or Florida. Perhaps the Midwest, since the *Tribune* considered it more American than any other section, was the most deserving of federal aid. It certainly remained the newspaper's firm opinion that the Midwest possessed more desirable characteristics than any other section. For this reason the *Tribune* continued to advocate the moving of the national capital west of the Appalachians, specifically to the "vicinity of Grand Rapids" which was "in a setting of great natural beauty and in as fine and healthful a climate as can be found anywhere in the country." The question of how much the move would cost and add to "government extravagance" was conveniently ignored.[8]

Although generally critical, the *Tribune* was not as bitterly opposed to the Roosevelt administration at the end of 1933 as it was to become later. At times the newspaper seemed to possess a relatively understanding position on the problems facing the administration. Once, for example, it stated:

> The immediate effect of paying billions for public works and other billions to the city folks for little work, and to farmers for refraining from work is to make trade active. Whether recovery will then come of its own momentum is a question over which some people may differ from the President. But while the money is being spent retail trade is bound to be active.[9]

Such generally conciliatory editorials gradually disappeared. By 1934 relations between McCormick and the administration were obviously deteriorating. John Boettiger (soon to be Roosevelt's son-in-law) wrote a story in April indicating that President Roosevelt was just another Kerensky, weakly attempting to keep things together before a serious revolution occurred.[10] In a later article, Boettiger compared Henry A. Wallace to Lenin, Mussolini, and Hitler. The *Tribune* editorial page heaped scorn on the "Frankfurter Red Hots" who it believed were bringing democracy to an end. By 1936 McCormick went so far as to state, "A band of conspirators including one Felix Frankfurter, like Adolph Hitler, born an Austrian, impregnated with the historic doctrines of Austrian absolutism, plans to inflict this Oriental atrocity upon our Republican people." Thus the New Deal became regarded as a gigantic foreign conspiracy to subvert the "American way of life." The bitterness ran deep.[11]

At the time of the 1934 elections the *Tribune* campaigned with its usual enthusiasm for an increased Republican representation in congress. Without this increase, the newspaper declared, there would be no real meaning left in the phrase—"life, liberty, and the pursuit of happiness." Like Naziism, fascism, and communism, the New Deal required a subservient congress. And unlike the Republican party, the Democratic party was not even an "American party" at all, because it included men like Upton Sinclair, Norman Thomas, and Rexford Tugwell. The *Tribune,* however, in 1934 professed to be confident that the American people were ready to turn against the New Deal. Arthur Sears Henning predicted, for example, that the GOP would gain at least thirty to forty representatives in the House. When, much to the newspaper's consternation, the Republicans actually lost seats, all it could do was retort that the victory had been gained for the New Deal because all the people on relief voted Democratic. "Tax Payers voted Republican," it added petulantly.[12]

In 1935 the resentment against Roosevelt continued to grow more extreme, and McCormick grew ever more doleful. "Cheered as I am by this spurt of business during this early winter," he announced pessimistically to his advertising staff in January, "I cannot foresee any general boom. A tyranny has never brought prosperity to the people it ruled and it will not now." Patriotism flourished on the pages of the *Tribune,* as if the newspaper were intent, singlehandedly if necessary, on saving the American Way of Life. It urged investigations of communism in the schools and praised C. R. Walgreen for worrying about the subversive doctrines allegedly taught at the University of Chicago. Since "Mr. Roosevelt and his revolutionaries are through with American government as it has existed," by necessity these investigations had to be conducted for the time being on the local level. But the *Tribune* hoped, even after the 1934 debacle, that the American people were at last awakening to the terror in their midst. The newspaper believed that it saw signs in 1935 that Roosevelt's popularity was dipping, and Arthur Sears Henning, ever optimistic, believed that "every indication" demonstrated that the Democratic party would split, with Huey Long on the left and the conservatives on the right leaving it. This would make, he averred, the election of a Republican president in 1936 a "probability."[13]

The most important foreign news story of 1933 was Hitler's accession to the German chancellorship. From the beginning the *Tribune* had realized the detrimental effects a Nazi regime would have on Germany, and it consistently portrayed Hitler as a ruthless dictator.

The most unfortunate aspect of Naziism, according to the *Tribune,* was its anti-Semitism. That was why in March, 1933, the newspaper denounced the newly formed Hitler government as a "survival of the dark ages" although initially it had mistakenly thought that Hitler would attempt to control some of the more repulsive anti-Jewish activities of the storm troopers. The German republic in which the *Tribune* had placed such confidence was at last dead—"probably for generations" the victim, the newspaper claimed, of an overly harsh policy on the part of the French.[14]

During the grim days of March, 1933, the *Tribune* emphasized with front-page banner headlines, Hitler's anti-Semitic measures. JEWS FACE DRASTIC BOYCOTT and HITLER NAZIS DECLARE WAR ON WORLD JEWRY the front page screamed. Sigrid Schultz, writing from Berlin that year, added her crisply anti-Nazi comments and her cables were supplemented by those of Edmond Taylor, equally repelled by the regime. In March and April, 1933, Taylor traveled through the Reich to seek information on Hitlerism. He soon ran into trouble. Fiercely anti-Nazi, he reported that German Jews had built up the schools, universities, libraries, and culture of Germany and how they were being systematically persecuted. In retaliation for these stories the Nazi authorities arrested Taylor, although they soon released him. He was forced to conclude with regret that despite the almost total loss of German freedom, the Hitler government was becoming increasingly popular with the people. Sigrid Schultz documented in detail the Nazi book-burning campaign, whereby even such innocuous items as Helen Keller's autobiography were destroyed.[15]

Even Colonel McCormick left on a mission to investigate conditions in Hitler's Germany. He wanted to see how Hitler had attained power and why the Nazis had "revived the Middle Age persecution of the Jews." On his return, the Colonel explained for the benefit of the Chicago audience that he had found the answer. "I have found the explanation and will give it in as few words as possible." The few words took the greater part of a week to relate.[16]

It is often underemphasized just how good a reporter McCormick actually was. He had a fine eye for detail and when he was not pontificating, vividly portrayed the life of the common people.

Although McCormick did not ignore the Nazi persecution of the Jews, he tended to apologize for it, to cast the blame not so much on the German people or even the Nazis but upon the Allies. The German troubles, he argued, were essentially the legacy of the Treaty of Versailles. "Admission of war guilt, economic slavery, and loss of national self-respect had rankled in the German mind for fifteen years." Thus persecution of the Jews was merely a reaction against the economic poverty caused by the treaty. He ended his dispatches with what he considered an apt comparison:

> Poor Jews, poor Germans.
> A bitter road lies ahead for both.
> A final word. What do Germany and Hitler most remind me of?
> Mexico and Madero.[17]

With all this pessimistic news, the *Tribune* recommended that American tourists not visit Germany, since their safety could not be assured. Why visit a country, it asked, when it had been delivered over to the "control of Apache boy scouts."? Much better it was to remain home and visit the Chicago Century of Progress Exposition![18]

As Sigrid Schultz's correspondence from Berlin was not censored (in this regard the German leaders were more lenient than their Italian counterparts), she was able to send remarkably honest dispatches to her home newspaper. In March, 1934, she described how Hitler had taken over absolute control of the largest Protestant church in Germany, and how the Nazis were ordering ministers to include Hitler in their Sunday prayers. She outlined for *Tribune* readers the tensions between the Nazis and the Catholics and stressed, as did the newspaper's editorial page, the "paganism" of the Hitler regime. Later she wrote about the convents raided by the Nazis and of the priests taken to prison camps. Both the *Tribune* and Miss Schultz played up the Nazi persecution of the Christian churches. Neither did Miss Schultz pull any punches with President Paul von Hindenburg despite the newspaper's previous veneration of the former marshal, and usually pictured him as an aging dotard who knew "only what Chancellor Adolf Hitler wants him to know is happening in Germany. . . . Like all dutiful German citizens," she continued, "he reads the German papers and accepts what they tell him." But by 1936 she was astutely predicting that Germany was looking eastward for future living space and that Hitler's plans included war with the Soviet Union.[19]

Other reporters gave much the same anti-Nazi viewpoint in their columns. Edmond Taylor reported from Munich in 1934 that politically minded Germans were beginning secretly to call Hitler's regime a failure. Economically, he declared, Germany was headed for a crash. But the most pointedly anti-Nazi comments were reserved for *Tribune* reporters stationed outside Germany. Charles Farmer, in Luxembourg, for example, contended:

> Hitler is beginning to realize that putting over his "new deal" is vastly more difficult than he thought. He suffered a nervous breakdown when early in April he was told Germany's financial situation is far more precarious than he believed. He wept for hours and his friends rushed him to the seashore, smuggled him on the Deutchland, Germany's pocket battleship and took him cruising until he had pulled himself together, which took much longer than was expected.

The *Chicago Tribune* Press Service predicted from Copenhagen in 1936 that Germany was headed for inevitable war because of its ambition to dominate central and southeastern Europe from the North to the Black Seas.[20]

After 1934 there was a tendency on the *Tribune* editorial page to let up in criticisms of Hitler. Chances for war were visibly rising and the newspaper wished to appear neutral in the developing power struggle between Germany and the Allies. In May, 1934, it pointed out that Germany was a strange land "of excitements, repressions, and totem pole enthusiasms, a land of Teutonic Ku Klux, all the more formidable for being thoroughly efficient." But the *Tribune* played down, as it had not done previously, stories on the plight of the Jews. It appealed for a policy of appeasement on the part of the western Allies, no matter how terrifying the new Germany appeared. The Fuhrer should be "cajoled . . . into respecting the rights and the peace of other nations." Thus the best policy for Great Britain in its viewpoint, was to have a "benign" rather than a "savage" policy toward Germany.[21]

Even though the *Tribune* criticized many of the worst domestic features of Hitler's regime, it tended to excuse the Nazis in their foreign policy. Hitler was, as McCormick had pointed out in 1933, the product of the Treaty of Versailles. Two years later he had not changed his mind. As the *Tribune* held in 1935, Hitler's cradle was not in Berlin but in Paris. One year later the newspaper gave the same argument:

> The whole peace was an act of folly and stripping Germany of its colonies was a part of it. It is conceded that the victors had been terrified and they had despaired of the success which came to their side. They had not expected mercy if defeated and they intended to give none. In such a state of mind they sought their future security as well as their revenge by binding the German people to perpetually humiliating conditions. In doing so, they destroyed the German republic and produced Hitler, now their chief menace.[22]

Thus despite its hatred of Naziism there was no stronger proponent of appeasement than the *Chicago Tribune*. The more imminent war became, the more anti-British the tenor of its editorial page. Increasingly the Germans were pictured as merely products and prisoners of a dishonest peace.

The *Tribune* continued to hold a low opinion of Mussolini, and declared—accurately as it turned out—that fascism would not outlast his regime. Part of the trouble, in the newspaper's viewpoint, was Mussolini's overspending and Italy's mounting debt which in the long run presaged ruin and "probable war." The more the Italian economy became centralized the more it tended to bog down. In short Mussolini's sins approximated those of the New Deal. Furthermore the Italian dictator was criticized for his ridiculous posturing:

> Mussolini intends to be the revival of imperial Rome and the part must be dressed. It must be constantly dressed, impressively, menacingly, pompously. Dictators must be allowed to know their business, the nature of which is at times dreadfully juvenile, as most affairs of the emotions are even when they are savage."[23]

David Darrah, who reported Italian news from Rome for the *Tribune* after 1926, was fiercely anti-fascist. He had to be more circumspect, however, in his reporting than did Sigrid Schultz from Berlin, because the Italian regime attempted to impose a censorship on the dispatches leaving Rome for other countries. Darrah was later to write that "there was always this shadow of the man with the blue pencil behind everything we did and the spectre of that black room on the third floor in the Piazza S. Silvestro." He did his best to brave the censorship difficulties. On February 23, 1935, he noted the lack of popular enthusiasm for any fascist military adventures and three months later reported that the government faced the disapproval of the people and the "severest financial difficulties." He added that the King of Italy was everywhere rumored to be against the Ethiopian adventure and discovered general "popular dislike" for the project. Furthermore Darrah mentioned that there had been "difficulties" in connection with the mobilization of a division in Sardinia.[24]

For this unfriendly reporting, Darrah was summarily thrown out of Italy in 1935. The Italian police held him for twenty-four hours during which time he was not even allowed to go home to pack his clothes, nor communicate with American authorities. The *Tribune* fully backed its correspondent and transferred him to Paris, where he could write as many anti-Mussolini pieces as he desired, without any censorship. The newspaper never attempted to replace him in Rome. Mussolini's dictatorial action, the *Tribune* argued, held an ominous lesson for Americans:

> Mussolini must have felt that the American public had no right to the facts regarding Italy. If so, he overlooked the circumstances that much American money has been lent to Italy and the even more important circumstance that Americans have every reason to be interested in the progress of dictatorships, for our government has displayed strong leanings in that direction. . . . It is instructive to the American people to observe to what lengths a dictator will go in his attempts to destroy the freedom of the press.[25]

When Italy invaded Ethiopia in 1935 it seemed a portent of greater aggressions in the future. The *Tribune* immediately dispatched a correspondent, Will Barber, to the troubled scene. Barber reported from the French Somaliland in June, 1935, that it was his

THE UNDER DOG

November 5, 1935

impression after observing Mussolini's army that the dictator had plunged into the war without proper preparation. He witnessed the lack of supplies among the Italian troops, and wrote that the soldiers were short of water and a half dozen men were dying each day from sunstroke alone. Barber graphically depicted the Italian soldiers sleeping naked in the streets in their desperate effort to escape the searing heat, of working in the blazing sun without helmets because none had been given them, and of even having to beg money for food. After viewing conditions from the Italian side of the lines Barber traveled into Ethiopia where he held an unprecedented interview with Emperor Haile Selassie, who told of his determination to fight for his nation's integrity. Barber was the first American correspondent to reach Addis Ababa and he filled *Tribune* pages with informative articles dealing with Ethiopia's geography and economic situation. Especially interesting was his critical article on the slavery still practiced in the nation. He was the first American correspondent permitted to visit the Ethiopian fighting front and he traveled into the Ogaden desert to get a first hand view of the armies.[26]

In only a few days, Will Barber was dead: the victim of malaria. He was but thirty-two years old. His dispatches, which had brought fresh laurels to the *Chicago Tribune* foreign service, earned him a posthumous Pulitzer Prize. In an obituary, Robinson Maclean of the *Toronto Telegram* testified that Barber had scooped the world by interviewing the Emperor and by "going into the yellow hell of the Ogaden desert." The *Tribune* did not replace Barber, depending upon other news services for its information, including the pro-Italian Herbert L. Matthews of the *New York Times*.[27]

After the commencement of the war, the *Tribune* argued that Great Britain was meeting the Italian aggression in its usual masterful, if hypocritical fashion. The newspaper could never rid itself of the notion that British diplomacy could be anything but devilishly clever. Perhaps irresponsibly, the *Tribune* argued both an anti-Italian and an anti-British point of view, contending that Great Britain would be feigning false virtue in opposing the Italian aggression because it had conquered its own colonies in similar fashion. On the other hand it believed that the hesitancy of Great Britain to stop Italy only demonstrated the weakness and futility of the League of Nations.

> The day the first Italian bomb drops on Addis Ababa the ancient city of Geneva should be rocked to its foundations. The respectability of the League of Nations will be in shreds and tatters. The record will be a monument to the little band of "willful men" known as the irreconcileables in the United States Senate, who retained their mental poise when an emotional wave of illusionary humanitarianism was about to sweep the United States into this fickle, futile, and false brotherhood of men. That first Italian bomb should bring the pretenses of the League down like a flimsy tower of bricks. Its marble front was only paint.[28]

In September, 1935, the *Tribune* found it difficult to believe the English would not risk their fleet and shut the Suez Canal to Italian vessels. When, much to the newspaper's surprise, the English refused to act, it argued that this failure of nerve marked a major event "in the dissolution of the most widely spread empire, long the greatest of world powers." Derisively it pointed out that the English and French failed to act because "the doctrine that a colonizing nation can't take what it can get" was a strange one to them, and alluded to the French suppression of Syrian nationalistic sentiment and the English squelching of home rule sentiment in Egypt. France and Britain would have been condemned by the *Tribune* if they had acted in the Ethiopian crisis, and condemned if they had not. Either way, the Colonel made sure that the avenues of criticism were not closed.[29]

Although several of his defenders argue that McCormick was basically pro-British in his attitudes, the evidence for this startling assertion is practically non-existent for the period from 1933 to 1937. It is true that the *Tribune* praised British economic policies which aided that nation in recovering from the depression faster than did the United States. An article by John Boettiger in 1934, for instance, noted that England had no NRA, AAA, or CWA, and was experiencing an amazing return to prosperity.[30]

But this praise for Britain was not so much a means of lauding the British government as a club to hold over the Roosevelt policies.

Much more commonly the *Tribune* presented dark forebodings of British decline, although whether this caused McCormick any sleepless nights remains a moot point. The declaration of the Oxford Union that it would not fight for king and country was "ominous evidence of the deterioration of British morale." The British refusal to fight Mussolini over Ethiopia only signified retreat to the Colonel (not that standing up to Mussolini would have gained the *Tribune* imprimatur—most likely the newspaper would then have accused the British of hypocritically trying to appropriate most of the world's colonies). "If the old power is not gone it has at least become so uncertain of itself that it retreats rather than advances."[31]

Although in later years it was to deride in the harshest manner the failure of British leadership during this period, the *Tribune* from 1933 to 1937 argued that a policy of appeasement toward Nazi Germany was a proper course of policy. Anything but pro-Nazi, the newspaper contended that communism constituted a far worse threat to world stability than Hitler's Germany. A cartoon drawn by Carey Orr in March, 1936, showed, for example, the French Republic fleeing a harmless daschund (Nazi Germany) and running blindly into the open arms of a huge, grinning bear (Soviet Russia). Furthermore the *Tribune* argued that whatever one thought of the Hitler regime, Germany possessed an impeccable case for Allied concessions. Surely the "fat boy of Europe" (Britain) could give in to some of the German demands for the sake of world peace.[32]

McCormick was especially critical of the British press, which he contended was not free. According to British court procedure, for example, a newspaperman could land in jail if he were not careful how he reported a trial. The Colonel was most greatly appalled at how the British press handled the abdication crisis, when it imposed a voluntary censorship upon itself. To his way of thinking this was nothing more than subservience to the state, and certainly there would have been little precedence in American journalism for such a questionable practice. He lambasted British newspapers for "sedulously noting every event that can give an unfavorable impression of American character," although McCormick with his ever-sensitive patriotism retaliated in like manner to the British. He strongly condemned those segments of American society most favorable to England. As an example, the *Tribune* severely scorned those movie producers who depicted British imperialism in a friendly light.[33]

For a newspaper which claimed that monarchies were decadent, the *Tribune* allotted a generous amount of space to the abdication crisis, probably the biggest news story of 1936. It was often caustic in its criticisms of the British royal family, but this did not entirely disguise a strong curiosity about the latest royal doings. Although occasionally praising King George V, the *Tribune* was critical of the royal institution when Edward became monarch. "A royal family with a middle aged bachelor king and a strong willed mother, probably undisposed to accept the dowager estate, falls short of the ideal."[34]

On September 28, 1936, the *Tribune* prominently displayed its first picture of Mrs. Wallis Simpson "often seen in company with King Edward of England." A six column headline on October 15, 1936, announced that Mrs. Simpson was seeking a divorce, and two weeks later, the *Tribune* went to the unusual length of giving the complete testimony of the divorce hearing. Its readers certainly could not have complained that they were not given full details.[35]

When the king abdicated, the *Tribune* threw off all restraints; the story was given as much coverage as physically possible. By this time its reporting of the event had become sympathetic to Edward, probably to cast the British ministry in as unflattering a light as possible. Thus the *Tribune* argued that Baldwin acted as he did merely to preserve the social caste system, and that the common people supported the king. "Once again, as time after time in the History of England," it declared, "the people of London are cheering for the king," as if a revolution were imminent. The *Tribune* contended that the upper class despised Edward's sympathy for the workingman. Presumably as a public service, the *Tribune* polled the Simpsons of Chicago on what they thought of the matter, and breathlessly announced they supported the king three to one.

> The ministry, the church, and the majority of commons opposed the marriage because it offended sentiment and not because the king proposed to do a thing outside his constitutional prerogative. Many well informed persons are convinced

that there were other objections to Edward. The marriage question offered an opportunity to get rid of a monarch whose interest in social conditions proved to be an embarrassment to upper class government and might become a danger. Edward was sympathetic, headstrong, and outspoken when he viewed slums and neglected areas, and he went about in them a great deal.[36]

The Spanish Civil War provided the first arena of military conflict between the fascist and western powers. *Tribune* correspondents covered the war thoroughly and well. Jay Allen in particular turned in some superb reporting. He was on the scene almost immediately after the landing of General Franco's African troops in July, 1936, only one day before his car was perforated with twenty-three bullet holes. A week later, Edmond Taylor, who had been one of the first American correspondents to reach the front on the rebel side, stationed himself with the rebel army in northern Spain, Henry Buckley was sending dispatches from Madrid, and Jay Allen was reporting from Gibraltar.[37]

Edmond Taylor's later recollection of the war showed what the first glimpse of battle meant to a young reporter:

> Even apart from the bodies, I didn't think the battlefields were pretty. It was a shock to me to see real battlefields: not a picturesque inferno landscape, but an incredible kind of tinny litter, waste, and destruction done by the soldiers themselves, like a filthy house, except that people other than soldiers don't smear human excrement all over their floors. I could see that there might be moments of great dignity in war so long as a man was on his feet, but not once he was hit and down.[38]

The most enterprising of the reporters was Allen, in part because he was most familiar with the Spanish scene. He obtained an interview with General Franco in July, 1936, and was told of Franco's determination to establish initially a military dictatorship in Spain. Later on, the Generalissimo promised, there would be a plebiscite to determine the will of the nation, but first Spain had to be saved "from the communists" and pacified. Three days later, Allen prematurely wrote that Franco's game was up, that the loyalists were certain to win the war. What he failed to foresee was the quick dispatch of Italian aid, although when Italian flyers finally joined the rebels, it was Allen who broke the story.[39]

Jay Allen was bitterly anti-fascist and he claimed, almost from the beginning, that Franco was a mere tool of the Germans and Italians. He also documented how the Portuguese were giving important aid to the rebels, and wrote a story, which became world-famous, about four thousand men and women slaughtered in Badajoz (just across the border from Portugal) simply "for the crime of defending their republic against the onslaught of the generals and the land owners." Allen wrote this story at four o'clock in the morning "sick at heart and in body, in the stinking patio of the Pension Central." Unfortunately his views were too leftist to suit the *Tribune,* especially when the newspaper was fighting the 1936 presidential campaign on the theme that Roosevelt had bartered his soul to the communists. He reported for McCormick for a few months and then was discharged.[40]

Despite this, the *Tribune* made a sincere effort to present unbiased news from Spain. Although Allen was fired for his strongly pro-loyalist views (which at times affected the quality of his reporting), neither Edmond Taylor nor Henry Buckley, both capable reporters, favored the rebel cause. The *Tribune,* never one to hide its successes, touted itself over the expense it had gone to insure reliable news. "The *Tribune's* account of the Spanish revolt," an advertisement boasted, "has been far and away the most vivid and comprehensive one provided by any newspaper."[41]

Perhaps the *Tribune* was relatively unbiased in its presentation of the Spanish news because it tended to view the conflict as one simply between the communists and the fascists. In August, 1936, the newspaper cynically observed that if the rebels won, a military dictatorship was probable and if the loyalists won, a communist dictatorship. "Spain's Left Republican government wants neither but, win or lose, it may be wiped out." Some editorials appeared to favor Franco, while others favored the loyalists. But perhaps the most typical *Tribune* observation was that "Whoever wins the civil war, the Spanish people, rich and poor alike, have lost." Surprisingly, however, the newspaper did not favor the United States for cutting off the shipment of war materials to loyalist Spain since the Spanish government, despite what one thought of it, was legitimate and had been voted validly into power. In one of its more pro-loyalist editorials, the *Tribune* asserted:

> The conflict in Spain can be reduced to a simplified form. It is a war in which a duly constituted government is defending itself against the attack of insurgents who would overthrow it. That government may be disliked by many people. Its arms and purposes may be regarded as bad. Still other people may hold the government and its policy for the Spanish people in great esteem.[42]

The Spanish situation was made more complicated and more sinister in its possible implications by the intervention of foreign powers. It is surprising that the *Tribune* did not favor an embargo of war materials from the United States to that beleaguered nation; most isolationists by contrast favored such an embargo. After the intervention of Germany and Italy (and to a lesser extent the Soviet Union) into the Civil War, the newspaper began to recognize how important the defeat of Franco was for the security of France and Great Britain. As early as August, 1936, Jay Allen had conclusively proved that the German ship *Kamerun* carried munitions to Portugal for prompt reshipment to the Spanish fascists. Even more important to the Franco cause was Italian aid, and the *Tribune* commenced viewing the war in terms of a strategic struggle by Great Britain and Italy for control of the Mediterranean. Thus the conflict took on the nature of a battle for empire, as much as a battle between ideologies. The newspaper took it for granted Britain would win, not fully realizing the extent to which British leadership was paralyzed.[43]

Although the *Tribune* was constant in its criticism of Naziism and fascism, communism remained by far the more reprehensible system of government. In fact the newspaper would probably have editorially supported the loyalist government in Spain, except for its fear of a red takeover. In comparing fascism to communism, the newspaper displayed some of its values by stating that the former was generally the better system because it promised "on the whole a more orderly government" and most importantly "less damage to the economic organization." Donald Day's dispatches from Riga only served to reinforce McCormick's views. His stories of misery in the Soviet Union continued to confirm what the *Tribune* had said for years. Thus the newspaper stressed stories of Stalin's ruthlessness during the Roosevelt administration just as it had during the Hoover years.[44]

The *Tribune* never forgave Franklin Roosevelt for his recognition of the communist regime in November, 1933. At the time of recognition, the newspaper asserted in shocked tones that Russian radicalism had swallowed up the Democratic donkey. The editors claimed to be especially aghast over the appointment of William Bullitt as the first American ambassador to the Soviet Union, snidely observing that it was not wise "to send to a foreign country a representative who prefers the institutions of that country to his own."[45]

The *Tribune* was ever ready to claim a cause and effect relationship between Roosevelt's recognition of the Soviet government and any internal turmoil (especially labor trouble) in the United States. In an amazing series of *non sequiturs,* McCormick made note of the progress of the communist conspiracy in a speech delivered July 30, 1934:

> Maxim M. Litvinov, foreign minister of the Soviet, landed in America on Nov. 7, 1933.
>
> On Nov. 11 rioters at the packing plant of George A. Hormel & Co. at Austin, Minn. drove out company officials and seized possession of the plant.
>
> Ambassador Bullitt from America took up his residence in Moscow on March 7. On March 21 street fighting in New York began as rioters fought with police in the city theatrical district.[46]

To the *Tribune* the San Francisco general strike of 1934 clearly demonstrated the same communist penetration into the American labor unions and political parties. The paper's headline writers recurringly emphasized the supposed similarities between experience. Articles on Russia became a means of flailing the New Deal. Examples are these two, by no means unrepresentative, headlines:[47]

SPORT IN RUSSIA	SOVIET BRAIN TRUST PLANS
IS REGIMENTED	'TVA' TO MODERNIZE SIBERIA
BY BRAIN TRUST	

McCormick sincerely believed that almost everybody who was not a conservative Republican was tinged with communism. As a result he enthusiastically endorsed Elizabeth Dilling's book *The Red Network,* which by innuendo and implication denounced such people as Robert Hutchins, William Borah, Graham Taylor, Jane Addams, John Dewey, Paul Douglas, Albert Einstein, J. Ramsey MacDonald, Reinhold Niebuhr, Mrs. Franklin Roosevelt, and Lilian Wald as dangerous radicals.[48]

One of the most surprising aspects of the *Tribune's* attitude toward the Soviet Union was that McCormick honestly believed for a few glowing months in 1936 that the newly written Soviet constitution was the "most momentous event in Europe, and indeed it probably may be asserted in the world since the world war." To the *Tribune* the constitution seemed to anticipate a momentous swing to the right, with its provisions for universal suffrage, the setting up of a parliament, secret elections, freedom of speech and the press, religious worship, and protection for certain forms of property. Perhaps communism, thought the *Tribune,* would even evolve into something better.

> If the constitution is realized, as it may be hoped it will be, Joseph Stalin, it is hardly too much to say, will rank as the great statesman of his time, if not one of the greatest of all time.
> The fruits of liberty may be slow in ripening. Russian tradition and habit of mind are not favorable to immediate efficiency in the use of free institutions. But the aspiration to liberty is in the hearts of all men, though at times it may be discouraged by misfortunes or overwhelmed by conditions. Give a people a parliament and free utterance in press and forum, in the end they will learn how to enjoy and defend their rights and perfect their institutions.[49]

The *Tribune* believed that at the rate the USSR and the United States were evolving, the Soviet Union could, in the not too distant future, become the more democratic society. But this was a passing chimera and by the fall of 1936 the newspaper was again accusing the Soviet communists of nefariously involving themselves in the American election. Never again would McCormick have faith in the possibility of communism evolving into anything different.[50]

August 4, 1935

During Roosevelt's first administration the *Tribune* continued to excuse Japanese expansion just as it had done during the Hoover years. It accurately pointed out that the United States was no respector of Chinese sovereignty either since China was the "permanent station of an American regiment." The American case was by no means simon pure:

> The new Manchurian territory of Japan is about two-thirds of the territory the United States acquired by invading Mexico. It is much less than the area of British India where the British, in spite of Indian revolutions, still are. The German colonies, which the allies took as spoils of war, somewhat challenge European criticism of the Japanese on the Asiatic mainland. Is it more reprehensible to take from China than from Germany?[51]

The newspaper compared Japan's "special interest" in Manchuria and the Asiatic mainland with the United States's interest in the Caribbean. Thus, it argued, the war between the two nations over Japan's alleged aggression in Manchuria would be "inexcusable folly" as the interests of the two were not contradictory to each other. The *Tribune* was even willing to contemplate the division of China into "more manageable units"—a major shift from its editorial position of previous years when it had envisoned a strong, unified China. Obviously if America had to choose between Japanese and Chinese friendship, the *Tribune* was pulling for Japan. In 1929 its policy had been pro-Chinese; that attitude was to be one of the casualties of the Japanese aggressions.[52]

McCormick praised the Roosevelt-Hull foreign policies in the Orient as less belligerent and more friendly to Japan than the Hoover-Stimson policies. Hull especially was applauded for doing "nothing to aggravate the situation Mr. Stimson created." At no time during Roosevelt's first administration did the *Tribune* criticize the president for his Japanese policy, although it blamed him for almost everything else. The newspaper hoped, however, that the United States would tone down some of its high moral pronouncements, declaring also that the Japanese could reciprocate by curbing some of their own emotionalism at the same time. It argued, as it had in the past, that the United States should repeal those provisions of its 1924 immigration act which specifically forbade Japanese immigration into the United States—since under the quota system only a hundred and eighty-five Japanese could have been admitted anyway.[53]

The *Tribune* possessed a shrewd awareness that what the Japanese respected above all was power. Although certainly not unsympathetic to Japan's goals in the Far East, it would not hurt, in the *Tribune*'s viewpoint, for the United States to build up its Pacific defenses, and not enter into any more disarmament treaties such as the Washington Treaty (1923) which had so seriously undercut American power in the western Pacific. To criticisms that an American military buildup in the Pacific would only antagonize the Tokyo government, the *Tribune* declared that if America continued to be weak and indifferent, war would be inevitable anyway. McCormick had a keen interest in the development of air transport in the Pacific, and urged the development of a strong military base in the Aleutians, to supplement Hawaiian defense facilities. One reason the *Tribune* favored an increase in the military buildup in the Pacific was that even it did not entirely trust the Japanese government. It admitted that Japanese policy was occasionally "extraordinarily arrogant" and worried that the military appeared to be running the government. John Powell, the newspaper's Shanghai correspondent, was implacably anti-Japanese and privately warned McCormick that Japanese publicity was "designed for the purpose of keeping the war spirit alive."[54]

Although favoring a strong defense, the *Tribune* urged the United States to sever its commitments with the Philippines as soon as possible since the islands appeared to be the most serious defense problem the American military faced. When the decision was made in 1934 to grant the islands their independence, the newspaper pleaded for immediate withdrawal by the United States. It wished the "little brown brothers" well but believed the American government had to consult its own best interests on the matter. The United States had "no more obligation to defend them than we have to defend any other nation independent of our control." In December, 1935, Chesly Manly reported from Manila that the Philippine people were uncivilized and not really worth saving anyway. Indeed it would probably be a blessing to everyone concerned if the Japanese were forced to accept the responsibility of the Philippines!

> The Malay mind is not susceptible to western civilization. The natives can memorize what the book says but they can't put this knowledge into practice or arrive at any ideas of their own. A clerk in a store may speak good English and purport to understand you perfectly when you order a certain brand of cigarets, but he will bring you some other brand.[55]

In the final analysis it is surprising how uncritical the *Tribune* actually was of Roosevelt's foreign policy during his first administration. Indeed, it openly stated that Cordell Hull made a finer secretary of state than had Henry Stimson, and aside from the New Deal's recognition of the Soviet regime, was not notably opposed to the administration's diplomatic policies. Actually there was little to criticize. Roosevelt was probably less an internationalist before 1937 than had been Herbert Hoover; the *Tribune* was content. Anyway, the newspaper spent so much time denouncing the domestic aspects of the New Deal that it had little energy for the foreign aspects.

Although the paper regularly found fault with Naziism and fascism, the edge of its criticism was blunted by its support of an appeasement policy, and also by its attitude toward Roosevelt. For example, Carey Orr, in a 1935 cartoon, portrayed Roosevelt, Stalin, Mussolini, and Hitler as the "Four Horsemen of the Apocalypse."[56] This, obviously an attempt to make the Roosevelt administration seem as destructive and evil as possible, had the obverse effect of making Hitler, for example, appear less evil than he really was, because he was being reduced to FDR's level. Although Hitler was often criticized by the *Tribune* in the strongest terms, the reader could take comfort from the supposition occasionally expressed by McCormick's paper, that after all he was really no worse than Roosevelt, or at least the two were comparable. He was obviously a person with whom the United States could easily coexist. Certainly there was nothing in its attitude toward Hitler to justify a belligerent foreign policy on the part of the United States toward Germany.

Despite the 1934 election setback, the *Tribune* confidently believed that 1936 would witness the final defeat of the New Deal.

THE FOUR HORSEMEN OF THE APOCALYPSE

July 8, 1935

Almost from the beginning of the campaign, it backed Governor Alf Landon of Kansas for the Republican presidential nomination, hopefully characterizing him in November, 1935, as "a westerner who has shown that he can win elections against landslide majorities" and a candidate who could gain the enthusiastic support of all segments of the party.[57]

McCormick evidently believed the Republicans could win the election. In February, 1936, he was confident that if the party made wise nominations, Illinois would be in the Republican column in November. The Democrats, he asserted, had on their side only "the lazy . . . the worthless . . . the larcenously inclined." "In the aggregate," he added, "these classes number in the thousands but they do not constitute a majority in Illinois, or anything like a majority." By June, 1936, McCormick personally assured Landon that he would carry not only Illinois but also Chicago.[58]

The campaign officially began for the *Tribune* on New Year's, 1936 with the insertion of a new plank on the editorial page— "Turn the Rascals Out." On March 11, the newspaper's masthead carried the new motto: "Only 236 days left to save the country." This refrain was repeated each day until the election and *Tribune* telephone operators would take up the chant whenever they answered a call. (On election day the *Chicago Times* had a little fun with the *Tribune* by carrying the banner headline—52 DAYS TO XMAS!)[59]

Meanwhile the newspaper encouraged the Landon candidacy by giving the Kansas governor constant publicity. On May 9, 1936, an editorial found that Landon was "a man possessed of common sense, . . . thoughtful, prudent, with a mind ripened by experience in business and public life." If no hard news story presented itself, the *Tribune* found space anyway to emphasize Landon's attributes. For example, on May 19 a front page headline blared: LANDON TIPS OFF YOUTH TO SOME SIMPLE TRUTHS. The story told of an address by Landon to a graduating class of twenty-nine high school seniors. The speech was given in full on page two, taking four columns of presumably valuable space.[60]

What the *Tribune* opposed was the nomination of rival Chicago publisher Frank Knox, whom McCormick detested. When Knox sought the endorsement of the Republican state convention after losing the downstate vote to Senator William Borah in the Illinois presidential primary, the *Tribune* coldly remarked, "Personal ambitions should be satisfied by the verdict of the primaries. It was the best that could be expected and any one who tries to queer it is a traitor to the party here and throughout the country." To prove that Illinois public sentiment in fact supported Landon, the *Tribune* conducted a special poll which demonstrated that the Kansas governor had 56 percent of Illinois Republicans back of him. In its enthusiasm for Landon's strong showing, the newspaper somehow neglected to make anything of the fact that Roosevelt garnered 20 percent more votes in the poll than all the Republicans combined. Instead, the *Tribune* interpreted the survey as demonstrating that "with Landon the party can win." Even if the Kansas Republican were to lose the election, under his leadership the party could "still live as an instrument for the future salvation of the United States."

> Landon should be nominated because Landon can be elected. He can beat Roosevelt. Some people think that the playboy of the White House cannot be defeated, that four years more of the darling of the Gods are ineviable, no matter how you read the cards. Landon says it is not so. With Landon the Republican party can say it is not so. . . .
> Roosevelt can be beaten by a man in whom the majority of Americans recognize the characteristics they like to think they at their best possess themselves. Roosevelt can be beaten by an American. If he isn't there will not be many left.[61]

Much to the Colonel's satisfaction, the Republicans did nominate Landon. He was not so happy over the convention's choice of Frank Knox for the vice presidential nomination but grudgingly admitted that Knox at least was a better man than John Nance Garner. His original choice for vice president was Senator Arthur Vandenburg, and Edward Beck and Chesly Manly spent an entire afternoon trying to persuade Vandenburg to make the race. Finally the Michigan senator relented but by then it was too late as the party bosses were already nominating Knox.[62]

All the means of publicity available to the *Tribune* were used to insure the election of the Landon-Knox ticket. This does not mean the newspaper felt it was losing its objectivity. In a letter to Edward Beck in June, 1936, the Colonel made it quite clear he wanted "strict impartiality" during the campaign, urging that the Roosevelt stories be adequate and written without bias. "As far as interpretive stories or paragraphs are used," McCormick declared, "they must be real interpretations and not hostile arguments." But the *Tribune* strongly believed that a newspaper could not be "objective" in the traditional sense of reporting. So many means of communication were open to Roosevelt, the Colonel argued, that it would be necessary to see that Landon received "a fair share" of the news space available. The "fair share" attained almost 100 percent. McCormick believed that since Roosevelt, by his personal magnetism and presence, dominated the radio and the speaking platform, it was only fair for Landon to dominate the press.[63]

Thus the *Tribune,* although ostensibly "objective," actually chose to ignore and misrepresent the Democrats, often by crude and vulgar journalistic tricks. In the week before the Democratic national convention, for example, almost nothing could be found in the newspaper concerning the impending event. Space was available only for the Landon campaign. When the Democrats convened in Philadelphia, even the *Tribune* could not totally ignore the event, but it chose to carry such eight column banner headlines as "DROP ROOSEVELT." AL SMITH. (Arthur Sears Henning commented in his column that this was a "verbal bombshell.") When the Democrats chose to ignore such advice and renominated Roosevelt by a unanimous vote, the *Tribune* countered with the banner: NEW DEAL ASKS MORE POWER. On the front page, Carey Orr portrayed Roosevelt in a Hitler mustache and hairdo saying, "I like this role best." Not surprisingly the newspaper failed to run the usual front page picture of Roosevelt after his nomination although it had done so with Landon.[64]

Some of the *Tribune* devices to depict the Democrats in an unpleasant light demonstrated the most tawdry aspects of sensational journalism. The newspaper persisted in calling James Farley "Fat Jim" even in so-called "straight" news stories. On the other hand Republicans were depicted as tough and lean, eminently suited to the arduous task before them. Apparently, to its way of thinking, the rugged prairies of Kansas bred superior stock to the effete East.

If the reader were willing to read into a story that Roosevelt was physically crippled, the *Tribune* did not especially care. In a particularly nasty editorial the paper asserted:

> All the reports from Topeka tell the same story. Gov. Landon is fit and so are the men around him. Physically he and they are hard, and mentally keen. They are in condition to dish it out and take it. . . .
>
> The contrast is presented in Philadelphia. Fat men are running that show. When they chuckle—and they are doing a great deal of chuckling this week—their bellies quiver. It makes their jeweled watch chains jingle. Boss Farley is the first fat man among many fat men. . . .
>
> The Republican leaders are vigorous men, trained in Kansas heat and Kansas blizzards. They start with a physical and moral advantage whose value will increase as the campaign progresses.[65]

After the adjournment of the Democratic convention, the campaign began in full swing for the *Tribune*. On June 29, 1936, the paper's eight column headline blared: OPEN CAMPAIGN TO SAVE U.S. Throughout July, Landon made the front page with monotonous regularity while Roosevelt's name disappeared for weeks at a time.

Perhaps the most prevalent *Tribune* theme during the campaign was its attempt to link Roosevelt with international communism. A typical Orr cartoon in August portrayed a grim and dejected Russian revolutionary (bearded and carrying a time bomb) whining over the latest news headline: LANDON GAINING IN AMERICA. More specifically, Donald Day sent a dispatch from Riga which purported to demonstrate that Stalin had given orders for all American communists to support Roosevelt. In retailiation, the *Chicago Times* offered $5,000 if the *Tribune* or any other newspaper could prove this story true. McCormick ignored the challenge.[66]

The first cartoon Joseph Parrish ever drew for the *Tribune* depicted "Communist Tugwell" leading Roosevelt down the path to Stalinism. Consequently the newspaper played up alleged similarities between the "two dictators" and their programs. Not to be outdone by Parrish, Orr portrayed the campaign as one between "patriots throughout America" and the "Roosevelt squadron of foreign forces—Fascism, Naziism, and Communism." A front page

THE DEMOCRATIC KEYNOTER MAKES SOME COMPARISONS

"WASHINGTON"

SEN. BARKLEY

ROOSEVELT COMPARED TO THE FATHER OF OUR COUNTRY –

"LINCOLN."

COMPARED TO THE GREAT EMANCIPATOR –

"NO! NO! NO!"
TAKE IT OFF! SOME-
BODY MIGHT
SEE YOU!

I LIKE THIS ROLE BEST!

– BUT NOT COMPARED TO THE GREAT DICTATOR

June 26, 1936

story in October carried the headline: RECORDS SHOW ROOSEVELT AIM: A REVOLUTION. The insinuations and innuendos mounted as the day of election grew more imminent. Donald Day reported that Moscow was renewing a "vicious attack" against Landon because of its worry over the GOP's "growing strength." Somehow the newspaper always managed to leave the impression that the Roosevelt campaign was run from the Russian capital.[67]

The Colonel did not believe Roosevelt was merely the arch communist in the United States; McCormick also held the somewhat contradictory position that the President was the arch Nazi as well, as the following editorial insinuated:

IN FASCIST BERLIN

Protestants may not worship God as they see fit.

Catholics are persecuted for daring to instruct their children in their faith.

Jews are outcasts without citizenship rights. . . .

As long as the Constitution of the United States stands as the supreme law of the land, and the Supreme Court retains the power to invalidate laws and decrees which violate it, there can be no fascism in our country, no inequality on account of religion or race.

Mr. Roosevelt thinks our constitution is out of date.[68]

Outwardly at least, the *Tribune* did not hold that it was fighting a lost cause. As in 1934, it was confident that the American people would reject Roosevelt. When the *Literary Digest* poll substantiated Republican claims, the *Tribune* predicted that Landon's margin of victory would be even greater than that forecast by the *Digest*. Arthur Sears Henning was not as convinced. He acknowledged that the "majority of intelligent persons doubtless marked and returned their ballots" to the *Literary Digest,* but worried that "the unintelligent, particularly illiterates, undoubtedly threw the ballots away."[69]

If one could doubt the *Tribune*'s confidence, none could deny its enthusiasm. A typical *Tribune* lead read: "Governor Alfred M. Landon tonight brought his great crusade for the preservation of the American form of government into Los Angeles." A typical *Tribune* headline blared: ROOSEVELT AREA IN WISCONSIN IS HOTBED OF VICE.[70] As an example of how the newspaper blanketed its readers with news favorable only to Landon, the following are the headlines of all the stories pertaining to the campaign in the issue of October 11, 1936. The news treatment was in no ways unrepresentative.

LANDON PLEA: 'END MUDDLE'
ALF M. LANDON; THE CRAFTSMAN IN GOVERNMENT
ROOSEVELT BIDS FOR FARM VOTE IN G.O.P. ATTACK
LANDON CAN TAKE CARE OF HIMSELF, TEACHER REVEALS
ATHLETE OWENS TO BACK LANDON IN SPEECH TODAY
NEW DEAL'S RED TINGE 'PROVEN' SAYS COUGHLIN
CHILDISH! SAYS LEMKE MANAGER OF ICKES TIRADE
ROOSEVELT BIDS FOR MINNESOTA'S COMMUNIST AID
J. A. REED RAPS ROOSEVELT FOR ASSUMED POWER
KNOX WARNS OF "FALSE SACRIFICE" FOR SECURITY
FIGHTING SPIRIT OF VOLUNTEERS SPURS LANDON
LANDON'S MESSAGE TO COLORED PEOPLE MADE PUBLIC IN N.Y.

When Roosevelt visited Chicago in 1936, he received an enthusiastic welcome, but news of this was not allowed to appear in the *Tribune*. The newspaper asserted instead that "fat Bosses" were ordering union labor members much against their will to march in the presidential parade. In fact it compared these alleged methods to whip up large and enthusiastic crowds with those of Hitler and Mussolini and declared this coercion provided "a new experience for many American citizens." The *Chicago Times* printed an exposé criticizing these *Tribune* journalistic practices. According to a *Tribune* photograph, Roosevelt buttons were lying all over the presidential route, discarded by irate citizens. The *Times* asserted, with photographic evidence, that the emblems actually had been scattered on the street by the *Tribune* photographer.[71]

The *Tribune* also failed to report the extent of the public antipathy manifested toward the newspaper during the Roosevelt visit. The sight of the press buses caused a fury in the crowd and jeering voices challenged the *Tribune* and Hearst reporters to show their faces. As Marquis Childs reported it, the crowd shouted, "Where's the *Tribune?* Down with the *Tribune*. To hell with the *Tribune!*" These shouts were heard along the entire march and the police, fearing an attack on the press cage, had to brandish their night sticks. An editor for the *Herald-Examiner* later reported, "We were concerned for the safety of our people." The situation at the *Tribune* was doubtless as tense.[72]

Despite its unwillingness to mention Roosevelt's name, the *Tribune* was far more anti-Roosevelt than it ever was pro-Landon. Surprisingly little attention was devoted to Landon's policy views; the newspaper spent most of its editorial space railing at New Deal, hoping to tear down every aspect of the Roosevelt administration. Like Herbert Hoover, but unlike Alf Landon himself, McCormick favored, in Arthur Schlesinger's words, "a root-and-branch assault on every idea as a menace to the republic." Its tactics proved destructive rather than constructive. The Colonel gave generously of his time and money to the cause, although he was never to make Landon's inner circle of advisers. Near election day he even took the beloved John T. McCutcheon off the front page because he wished "to battle this out to the drop of a hat."[73]

To the end the *Tribune* remained ostensibly optimistic. On November 1, an editorial warned readers that the election would be "the most fateful . . . in the history of the American people," but hopefully claimed that Roosevelt's windup speech in Madison Square Garden "was the speech of a man who was beaten and knew he was beaten." Solemnly it concluded that the president "was going through the motions of winding up a campaign, but it is difficult to believe that he fooled even his own pay rollers who packed the hall." McCormick was confident enough that he arranged a "victory dinner" on election night to which he invited many notables. His partisanship had blinded his judgment.[74]

The trumpets of victory were soon stilled as the sad returns poured in. The verdict of the American people was one of the most conclusive in history. How could one explain Landon's defeat; here was a candidate whom the *Tribune* expected to be the strongest in the Republican party. Pessimistically (and uncharacteristically) the newspaper concluded that there was something basically wrong with the American people. Arthur Sears Henning argued that the president owed his reelection "largely to the support of workingmen and the socialists and communists and other radically minded groups."

If that observation were true, then such groups obviously made up an American majority! The *Tribune* sourly concluded that during Roosevelt's second term the communist party, under Earl Browder, would come more and more to dominate the administration.[75]

The election was an indictment of the American press, as approximately 75 percent of United States newspapers supported Alf Landon. Within the Chicago city limits, the pro-Roosevelt circulation was 258,078, the pro-Landon circulation a whopping 1,373,559. Yet Roosevelt was to carry the city by the stunning vote of 1,099,141 to 543,755, sweeping forty-eight of the fifty wards. Harold Ickes rarely spoke more accurately than when he wrote in his diary: "Never have the newspapers, in my recollection, conducted a more mendacious and venomous campaign against a candidate for President, and never have they been of so little influence." Luckily for the president, he had found alternate means of reaching the American people.[76] The Colonel argued that government and the press were natural enemies, the duty of newspapers was "to furnish that check upon government which no constitution has ever been able to provide." Thus he believed the *Tribune* had the right, nay the duty, to "compensate" for FDR's primacy on the radio, his magnetic presence, and his control of the government by offering only pro-Landon material. In his instructions to Edward Beck in mid-1936, which directed "strict impartiality," the Colonel also argued that since so many means of communication were open to Roosevelt, it was necessary that Landon receive "a fair share" of the total news space available. Beck did not misunderstand the Colonel's intent. The *Tribune* felt it had to rig its case against the president because it believed the case was being rigged in favor of FDR in all other mass media.

But the rigging proved self-defeating, perhaps bolstering the party faithful but certainly, as the election figures made evident, not converting any of the wayward. Although Landon himself generously declared that the *Tribune* provided positive help during the campaign, the evidence is that it was too blatant, too childishly obvious, to make much of an impression, except negatively. The pity was that such a capable editorial staff was forced to write on such an intellectually dishonest level.

Notes

1. Robert R. McCormick, "Why I Broke with F.D.R.," a speech given over WGN, August 7, 1954 (in the library of the *Chicago Tribune*), p. 1; *Chicago Tribune,* March 11, 1933, 10:1–2; Franklin Roosevelt to Robert R. McCormick, May 16, 1933, Edward S. Beck Collection, Chicago Historical Society.

2. Tiffany Blake to John T. McCutcheon, March 4, 1933, May 2, 1933, McCutcheon papers.

3. *Chicago Tribune,* May 1, 1933, 1:8; June 17, 1933, 14:1.

4. *Ibid.,* June 13, 1933, 12:1; interview with Walter Trohan.

5. McCormick, "Why I Broke with F.D.R.," p. 5; Robert R. McCormick, *The Freedom of the Press: A History and an Argument Compiled from Speeches on this Subject Delivered over a Period of Fifteen Years* (New York: D. Appleton-Century Company, 1936), pp. 53–54; Philip Kinsley, *Liberty and the Press: A History of the Chicago Tribune's Fight to Preserve a Free Press for the American People* (Chicago: The Tribune Company, 1944), pp. 4–5, 45.

6. McCormick, "Why I Broke with F.D.R.," p. 6.

7. *Editor and Publisher,* LXV (March 11, 1933), 21; McCormick, "Why I Broke with F.D.R.," p. 3; Waldrop, p. 216.

8. *Chicago Tribune,* October 24, 1933, 14:2; October 12, 1935, 14:1.

9. *Ibid.,* January 21, 1934, 10:2.

10. Boettiger once apologized to Harold Ickes for the critical way in which he was ordered to write his stories. Nevertheless, after marrying the president's daughter, he became editor of the Hearst *Seattle Post-Intelligencer,* also a strongly anti-New Deal daily. See Ickes, I, 204.

11. *Chicago Tribune,* April 11, 1934; April 24, 1934, 1:1; Robert R. McCormick, *An Address by Col. Robert R. McCormick, Civic Opera House, Chicago, February 12, 1936* (Chicago: The Tribune Company, 1936), p. 4.; interview with Willard Edwards.

12. *Chicago Tribune,* November 2, 1934, 14:1; November 6, 1934, 12:1; November 4, 1934, 1:8; November 10, 1934, 14:1.

13. *Editor and Publisher,* LXVII (January 5, 1935), 12; *Chicago Tribune,* April 24, 1935, 10:1–2; June 2, 1935, 17:2; July 19, 1935, 12:1; August 5, 1935, 1:1.

14. *Ibid.,* March 13, 1933, 10:1–2; March 24, 1933, 12:2.

15. *Ibid.,* March 27, 1933, 1:1; March 29, 1933, p. 1; March 31, 1933,

p. 7; April 1, 1933, 2:3–4; April 19, 1933, p. 7; *Editor and Publisher,* LXV (April 8, 1933), 8.

16. *Chicago Tribune,* August 9, 1933, 2:4.

17. *Ibid.,* August 11, 1933, 3:2; August 12, 1933, 6:1.

18. *Ibid.,* August 27, 1933, 14:1; July 1, 1933, 12:2.

19. *Ibid.,* March 4, 1934, 1:4; April 4, 1934, 14:1; July 17, 1934, 5:1; March 20, 1935, 14:1; April 5, 1936, 2:2.

20. *Ibid.,* May 17, 1934, 9:1; July 9, 1934, 3:1; July 12, 1936, 12:1.

21. *Ibid.,* May 14, 1934, 12:2; July 31, 1934, 10:2.

22. *Ibid.,* February 9, 1936, 14:2; December 29, 1936, 8:2.

23. *Ibid.,* May 29, 1934, 10:1; December 14, 1934, 16:2; January 8, 1935, 10:2.

24. *Ibid.,* February 23, 1935, 5:1; May 31, 1935, 1:4; June 10, 1935, 12:2–5; Darrah, p. 303.

25. Darrah, pp. 303–333; *Editor and Publisher,* LXVIII (June 15, 1935), 9; *Chicago Tribune,* June 15, 1935, 12:1.

26. *Chicago Tribune,* June 22, 1935, 8:1; June 28, 1935, 1:3; September 23, 1935, 2:3–4.

27. *Ibid.,* October 8, 1935, 12:2; October 7, 1935, 3:2–2; John Hohenburg, *The Pulitzer Prize Story* (New York: Columbia University Press, 1959), pp. 138–42. For Matthews' viewpoint, see Herbert L. Matthews, *The Education of a Correspondent* (New York: Harcourt, Brace and Company, 1946), pp. 25–63; Herbert L. Matthews, *Two Wars and More to Come* (New York: Carrick & Evans, Inc., 1938), pp. 13–173.

28. *Chicago Tribune,* September 4, 1935, 10:2.

29. *Ibid.,* September 23, 1935, 12:2; April 22, 1936, 12:2; May 5, 1936, 10:1.

30. *Ibid.,* March 19, 1934, 3:1–3.

31. *Ibid.,* March 10, 1933, 10:2; June 25, 1936, 12:2.

32. *Ibid.,* October 11, 1934; March 14, 1936, p. 1.

33. *Ibid.,* April 30, 1934, 10:1; August 31, 1934, 12:2; May 3, 1935, 16:2; December 9, 1936, p. 1, Orr cartoon.

34. *Ibid.,* January 25, 1936, 10:2.

35. *Ibid.,* September 28, 1936, p. 2; October 15, 1936, p. 1.

36. *Ibid.,* December 6, 1936, 16:1; December 7, 1936, 14:1; December 9, 1936, 4:1; January 1, 1937, 14:2.

37. *Ibid.,* July 21, 1936, 12:1; July 22, 1936, pp. 1–2; *Editor and Publisher,* LXIX (July 25, 1936), 6.

38. Frank C. Hanighen (ed.), *Nothing but Danger: Thrilling Adventures*

of Ten Newspaper Correspondents in the Spanish War (London: George G. Harrap & Co. Ltd., 1939), p. 70.

39. *Chicago Tribune,* July 27, 1936, 2:2–4; July 30, 1936, 1:8; August 4, 1936, 1:8.

40. *Ibid.,* August 21, 1936, 9:6; August 30, 1936, 2:2–6; Jay Allen, Elliot Paul, Luis Quintanilla, *All the Brave* (New York: Modern Age Books, 1939), pp. 24–26; Ickes, II, 388.

41. *Chicago Tribune,* July 25, 1936, p. 11.

42. *Ibid.,* August 9, 1936, 22:1; August 21, 1936, 10:1–2; September 8, 1936, 14:1; December 31, 1936, 8:1.

43. *Ibid.,* August 26, 1936, 12:2; November 9, 1936, 12:1.

44. *Ibid.,* August 30, 1933, 14:2.

45. *Ibid.,* November 23, 1933, p. 14; November 29, 1933, 12:2.

46. *Ibid.,* July 31, 1934, 5:2.

47. *Ibid.,* June 9, 1934, 11:1; December 2, 1934, 15:2–3.

48. See Elizabeth Dilling, *The Red Network: A "Who's Who" and Handbook of Radicalism for Patriots* (published by the author, Chicago, 1934), pp. 259–336.

49. *Chicago Tribune,* June 13, 1936, 12:1–2.

50. *Ibid.,* June 16, 1936, p. 4.

51. *Ibid.,* April 29, 1933, 10:2; May 14, 1933, 14:1; See also *Ibid.,* January 12, 1935, 8:2.

52. *Ibid.,* May 22, 1933, 8:1; June 2, 1933, 16:2; March 18, 1935.

53. *Ibid.,* January 25, 1934, 10:2; October 27, 1933, 12:1.

54. *Ibid.,* December 7, 1933, 14:1; February 3, 1934, 12:2; October 30, 1934, 12:2; December 13, 1935, 14:2; January 12, 1936, Pt. 7, p. 10; November 18, 1936, 14:2; December 22, 1936, 8:2; January 15, 1937, 12:2.

55. *Ibid.,* January 28, 1934, 16:2; November 21, 1935, 12:2; December 23, 1935, 9:1–5.

56. *Ibid.,* July 8, 1935, p. 1.

57. *Ibid.,* November 18, 1935, 14:1.

58. *Ibid.,* June 23, 1936, 7:1; *Review of Reviews,* XCIII (February, 1936), 42.

59. *Chicago Times,* November 3, 1936, p. 1.

60. *Chicago Tribune,* May 9, 1936, 14:1; May 19, 1936, 1:8, p. 2.

61. *Ibid.,* May 22, 1936, 14:1; June 7, 1936, 14:2; June 8, 1936, 4:1; June 10, 1936, p. 1, editorial.

62. *Ibid.,* June 13, 1936, p. 1, editorial; interview with Chesly Manly;

Arthur Vandenburg to Edward S. Beck, July 6, 1936, Edward S. Beck Collection, Chicago Historical Society.

63.   *Editor and Publisher,* LXIX (June 27, 1936), 30.

64.   *Chicago Tribune,* June 22, 1936, p. 1; June 24, 1936, p. 1; June 26, 1936, p. 1.

65.   *Ibid.,* June 24, 1936, 14:1; June 28, 1936, 6:2–4.

66.   *Ibid.,* August 7, 1936, p. 1; August 9, 1936, 3:1; Seldes, *Lords of the Press,* pp. 55–56; Seldes, *Facts and Fascism,* p. 82.

67.   *Chicago Tribune,* September 14, 1936, 10:2; September 27, 1936, 15:1; October 3, 1936, p. 1; Orr cartoon, October 5, 1936, 1:1; October 14, 1936, 17:1.

68.   *Ibid.,* September 23, 1936, p. 1; quoted in *The New Republic,* XC (March 17, 1937), 181.

69.   *Chicago Tribune,* November 1, 1936, 8:1.

70.   Quoted in *New Republic,* XC (March 17, 1937), 181; and Faw, p. 111; *Chicago Tribune,* October 16, 1936.

71.   *Editor and Publisher,* LXIX (October 24, 1936), 16; *Chicago Tribune,* October 16, 1936, p. 1; *Chicago Times,* October 14, 1936, p. 6.

72.   Marquis Childs, *I Write from Washington* (New York: Harper & Brothers, 1942), p. 114; John J. McPhaul, *Deadlines and Monkeyshines: The Fabled World of Chicago Journalism* (New York: Prentice-Hall, Inc., 1962), p. 287; *Chicago Times,* October 15, 1936, p. 3; Thomas L. Stokes, *Chip Off My Shoulder* (Princeton: Princeton University Press, 1940), pp. 449–50; interview with Willard Edwards.

73.   Arthur M. Schlesinger, Jr., *The Politics of Upheaval* (Boston: Houghton Mifflin Company, 1960), pp. 603–41; John Gunther, *Taken at the Flood: The Story of Albert D. Lasker* (New York: Harper & Brothers, 1960), pp. 187–88; Robert R. McCormick to John T. McCutcheon, October 23, 1936, McCutcheon Papers, Newberry Library. Letter from Alf Landon, December, 1967.

74.   Ickes, II, 63, 76. Ickes received his information from Paul Leach of the *Chicago Daily News* and Mayor Kelly of Chicago; interview with Charles Cleveland.

75.   *Chicago Tribune,* November 4, 1936, 1:8, 16:1.

76.   *New Republic,* XC (March 17, 1937), 178; Ickes, I, 702; *Chicago Daily News Almanac and Year Book for 1937* (Chicago: Chicago Daily News, Inc., 1937), pp. 795–97.

5

Prelude to War, 1937–1939

The *Tribune* refused to soften its criticisms of the New Deal during the first two and a half years of Roosevelt's second term. There was much to censure, as these years were by most criteria the most unsuccessful of the Roosevelt administrations. *Tribune* animosity displayed itself from the beginning; there was no second-term honeymoon.

The newspaper's treatment of Roosevelt's second inaugural address demonstrated its continued intransigence. This speech ranks among FDR's most famous, for this marked the occasion he announced that he saw one-third of a great nation ill-housed, ill-clad, and ill-nourished. Although the news value of the speech was obvious, the *Tribune,* continuing its policy of underplaying everything the president said, chose to hide it on an inside page. Its eight column banner headline screamed instead: TROOPER SLAIN: NAB PAROLEE.[1]

The most important domestic developments of the second Roosevelt term were the court fight and the emergence of the Congress of Industrial Organizations. The *Tribune* stand on each was predictable. The rise of the CIO particularly held sinister implications. As before, McCormick attempted to connect the more active labor leaders with world communism. Thus, when rioting broke out at the Republic Steel plant in Chicago in May, 1937, with a resultant loss of life, the newspaper ran the front page banner: RIOTS BLAMED

ON RED CHIEFS. An ensuing editorial found no difficulty in affixing the responsibility, and blamed the riots on the "communist inspired" and "murderous" mob. McCormick never doubted that the CIO was riddled with communism. One representative *Tribune* headline announced that the CIO was the RED STEPPING STONE TO A SOVIET U.S.[2]

> John Lewis and the C.I.O. are the best organized, largest moneyed, and hardest driving force in Mr. Roosevelt's liberal Democratic party. Lewis more than any other man determines what the political program of the party shall be. There can be no concealment of the dominant position of the communists in the C.I.O. nor of the dominance of the C.I.O. in the Democratic front line.[3]

With its despairing view of the American future, the newspaper continued in its attempts to saddle the Democratic party with a communist appellation. The word "communist" took on a broad meaning. In fact anyone who differed from the *Tribune* took the risk of being called a red, or a fool, or perhaps both. According to the paper's stated viewpoint, the reason 85 percent of the press opposed the president was his communism. Of the remaining 15 percent "perhaps 5 percent is openly communistic, another 5 percent is secretly communistic . . . and the rest are still deceived." The *Tribune* gloried in its anticommunism, proud that it could not be corrupted. "Every blandishment known to intrigue and politics," was showered upon its Washington press corps. Luckily (especially if they wished to retain their jobs) they remained "unaffected by polls undertaken with preconceived prejudices among the C.I.O. reporters in Washington." Here the *Tribune* was undoubtedly demonstrating its sensitivity over the fact that a poll of Washington reporters by Leo C. Rosten had called it the single worst newspaper in the nation. In rebutting the common criticism that it falsified the news, the *Tribune* claimed that actually it was giving its readers a good news balance by failing to listen to these CIO-communist blandishments.[4]

> A certain determination, indeed a strong sense of editorial responsibility is required to keep the news columns evenly balanced in spite of this pressure of propaganda. It is notable that

newspapers shrinking from the duty to give a fairly balanced news presentation attempt to alibi themselves with claims of fairness, but this is an evasion of duty and only adds to the wrong to the public in putting its readers off their guard.[5]

Not only did the newspaper continue to call Roosevelt a communist, but it repeated the canard that he was also a fascist. When the story broke that Supreme Court nominee Senator Hugo Black had once been a member of the Ku Klux Klan, the *Tribune* asserted that the senator had belonged "to an organization which for its bigotry and devotion to the violent suppression of minorities would recommend itself to Goering and Goebbels." But the newspaper felt that it was not Black so much as Roosevelt himself who stood exposed as a bigot before the American people. When the president made his famous Quarantine speech at the dedication of the bridge on Chicago's outer drive in October, 1937, the *Tribune* at first sneered that it was nothing but a clumsy attempt to foster a "war scare" to head off public antagonism toward Black.[6]

Yet, all things considered, Roosevelt was more often labeled communistic than otherwise, the fascist gambit being used only when political opportunism might dictate. An Orr cartoon of October, 1938, showed the New Deal going after Nazi spy rings while ignoring the "far greater danger" of Soviet sabotage, Bolshevik wrecking, communist spies, red activities, Moscow agents, and the CIO. The newspaper insinuated that Mayor LaGuardia of New York City might be a member of the communist conspiracy. And a month later the *Tribune* revealed that Harold Ickes, the irascible secretary of the Interior, had "admitted" membership in the American Civil Liberties Union, "a communist front organization." On July 4, 1939, Colonel McCormick in a speech solemnly warned the American people that the administration was conspiring to involve the United States in another war because it wished to scrap the constitution and supplant it with Soviet communism. Consequently, the newspaper cast the name "dictatorship bills" at all New Deal measures and argued that the sooner they were repealed the better. This irresponsible name-calling, although sincere, was a forerunner of the McCarthy era of the 1950s. Throughout these years, the newspaper continued to compare and put on the same level Roosevelt New

Dealism with Russian communism, Italian fascism, and German Naziism.[7]

To McCormick, the last hope for American freedom continued to lie in the Republican party. In May, 1938, the *Tribune* noted despairingly that if the Republicans failed to win in 1940 it would mean the end of the "American system of government." The newspaper remained quieter during the 1938 campaign than it had in 1936, but after the election in which the Republicans doubled their membership in the House of Representatives, trumpeted the result in an eight column banner: NEW DEAL WRECKED BY G.O.P. With a new generation of Republican leadership coming to public attention, the *Tribune* believed (temporarily) a bit more optimistically in the future, a future represented by the "Deweys, the Tafts, the Lodges, the Saltonstalls, the Stassens, and many others."[8]

As early as 1938 the *Tribune* predicted that Roosevelt wanted American involvement in a European war so he could finally achieve his great dream in life—complete dictatorship. Thus McCormick feared war because he lacked confidence in the administration which would fight it. A war would only "mean the destruction of the democratic way of life." Roosevelt, the newspaper alleged, wanted war since it was the only way he could have prosperity, a third term, and absolute power. During the Hoover administration the *Tribune* had been notably militaristic. This viewpoint rapidly changed because the newspaper distrusted the man who would be wielding the weapons of militarism. Because of its hatred for Roosevelt, it was changing some of its most basic convictions.[9]

Tribune carping at Great Britain continued unabated as that nation moved closer to war. Its published viewpoint was that the United Kingdom was a fascist power, antagonistic to Nazi Germany only because of imperialistic rivalry. Colonel McCormick visited England in the summer of 1937 to see for himself the condition of the nation. The trip did nothing to alter his viewpoint. On August 22, a headline announced:

> WHY DID EDWARD
> FALL? FASCISTS
> DEPOSED HIM

A PICTURE OF BRITAIN
UNDER NAZI YOKE

In the article under the headline, McCormick declared that "England has gone Fascist and Fascism permits no independence whatever of subject or sovereign." His main evidence pointed to the self-imposed censorship which British newspapers had clamped upon themselves just before the abdication crisis. McCormick then realized, as he said in his article, that the English press was "not really free." The "Nazi government," according to the Colonel, "got rid of Edward because it wanted no social nonsense from the monarch, no asking of embarrassing questions about the poverty of the masses."[10]

David Darrah, who was as anti-British as he had previously been anti-Mussolini, claimed to see many of the same phenomena in British society that he had witnessed in Italy. A dispatch in late 1937 argued thusly:

> In other words, there is a distinct tendency to Fascism every-where. Britain is professedly a democracy with parliamentary rule. Actually it is a Venetian oligarchy. Groups of interests and a few powerful and determined men—former Prime Minister, Stanley Baldwin, Montagu Norman, Lord Derby, and the Archbishop of Canterbury, to mention a few—are more power-ful than parliament.[11]

The newspaper also emphasized the similarities between Germany and Great Britain in order to play down the seriousness of their conflict. Following this reasoning, the *Tribune* saw no compelling reason "Nazi" England (a term it often used in its headlines) should be inimical toward the aspirations of Nazi Germany. "The British government," it declared, "would rather deal with a reasonable Fascist government than with an unpredictable democracy. . . . We go on the idea that the British government is not what it is, an undemonstrative Fascist government perfectly able to get along with other Fascisms if they are friendly." This sounded surprisingly similar to the rhetoric Earl Browder was delivering at the same time. Britain was licked at the outset in the *Tribune*. If the Conservatives had been out of power and Labor in, the paper would have claimed undoubtedly that it was "socialistic," if not communist.[12]

Royalty was always held up to scorn for the *Tribune* reader, although the newspaper never attacked George VI personally. The *Tribune* still half believed that kings had autocratic powers, and ex-kings could return to power and depose governments with mighty armies behind them. An obsession about the British royal family, however, did not entirely conceal a strong curiosity, although the peculiar trappings of British officialdom, the pageantry of royalty, were constantly derided. The *Tribune* raised a storm of protest over whether the American ambassador would wear knee pants at the coronation of George VI. All three of the newspaper's cartoonists (Orr, Parrish, and McCutcheon) devoted much ink to this momentous issue. The editorial page denounced the Roosevelt administration for going "colonial" and an extremely improbable headline noted:

BRITISH GUFFAW AT U.S. SHANKS IN KNEE PANTS
RIDICULE ENVOYS FOR PLAYING "FLUNKEY"

This headline was buttressed with a story by David Darrah which claimed the English were worried that the American representative at the coronation would not look well in knee pants.[13] James W. Gerard, the head of the delegation, was held up for *Tribune* ridicule:

Mr. Gerard apparently has a fine pair of legs, two well rounded calves which will keep him from looking like a bottle on a pair of toothpicks when he displays himself from the knees down to such public gaze as may be interested in him.

Mr. Gerard's wearing knee pants only pointed up how American leaders were determined "to conduct themselves as amateur Englishmen, like all other colonials." In short, the Declaration of Independence was just a myth.[14]

King George was finally given his "shaky crown." The *Tribune* treated the poor gentleman rudely at the time of the coronation, in much the same spirit as a boy paints mustaches on advertising posters. The issue of May 15, 1937, carried a series of pictures of the king illustrating how he would look with various types of beards.

This studied rudeness toward the royal family continued in many stories. On October 26, 1938, a prominently displayed news item related that the duke of Kent and his "pretty" wife Marina were "banished" to Australia (he was appointed governor general) because of the queen's jealousy. "Marina, sleek and leggy fashion plate, has stolen newspaper and magazine photographic laurels from the not so slender Elizabeth for months." Finally "to the vast amusement of Mayfair," Elizabeth grew jealous and tried to outglamour Marina, but to no avail. "Banishment" to Australia was the eventual remedy.[15]

When the king and queen visited America in the summer of 1939, the *Tribune* advised the American people to greet the royal family with the "utmost cordiality and respect" but with no "fawning." It hoped that the hospitality would be a greater success than the diplomacy, hinting darkly that an alliance was in the making. The *Tribune* was sensitive to the slightest indication of such an alliance. An example of this sensitivity occurred when the paper carried an eight-column front page banner headline: F.D.R. DRINKS TOAST TO KING. A worried Carey Orr drew a cartoon underneath this headline advising Uncle Sam to "hang on to your pocketbook, uncle." It was much to the *Tribune*'s relief when the royal couple finally departed.[16]

More significant than these pot shots at the British royal family, but not unrelated, was the newspaper's barrage of criticism at the whole Allied position vis-à-vis Germany. The Allies, according to this viewpoint, were responsible for their own predicament since they were responsible for the Treaty of Versailles. "The treaties and boundaries in question were conceived in greed and duplicity." The *Tribune* also blamed the Allies for bringing about the conditions which killed the German Republic. "They killed democracy," the newspaper thundered. "They killed liberalism, culture, intelligence, good will, and liberty. In the place of a friendly society they raised up dictatorship, brutality, ignorance, serfdom, and military power."[17]

To prevent war the newspaper recommended that the Allies do all they could to appease and conciliate Germany—in effect to buy off Hitler. The *Tribune* refused to sympathize with France and England's "determination to hang on to their loot," and believed that the restoration of the German colonies "would put Hitler and his Nazis in good humor." It derided British hypocrisy and was indignant because that nation had acquired territory by force of arms. The newspaper failed to see any moral forces working in the European situation; if war developed between the Allies on one side and Germany on the other, the war would be entirely imperialistic in nature. The Colonel, rather surprisingly, took a viewpoint similar to that of the communists, but the exigencies of antiwar politics required it. "If war comes now," the *Tribune* asserted in February, 1938, "it will be because Great Britain and France will not return spoils to Germany or keep their word with Italy."[18]

The *Tribune* went so far as to compare the German position with that of the United States; both were, in its opinion, aggrieved have-not nations. Not only should the Allies give up some of their colonies to Germany, they should also give a choice one to the United States to pay their war debts! After all, Britain was so well off, according to McCormick, that it could support two kings. "Countries which can afford war, great world's fairs, shockingly extravagant coronations, and other shows can pay their honest debts." In the *Tribune*'s eyes, Britain was considerably more prosperous than the United States, and in lieu of an actual repayment of the debt, certainly could transfer to America its "offshore islands," including the British West Indies.[19]

The newspaper was intensely critical of those Americans who were most vehemently anti-Hitler, because it believed strong, open criticism of Germany increased the chances for American involvement in any future conflict. When, in March, 1937, Mayor La Guardia of New York lambasted Hitler to such a degree that the State Department made an apology to the German government, William Fulton, the *Tribune* correspondent in New York City, explained that the mayor was engaged in a "sly bid for votes in this city's mayoralty election this fall." Editorially the newspaper asserted that statements like those of La Guardia did nothing to aid the cause of the oppressed in Germany. But the *Tribune* went beyond the bounds of responsibility when it blasted another violently anti-Hitler administration leader:

> In some of his allusions to the United States, the Nazi leader was crafty and showed political sense, centering responsibility

for irrationality and irresponsibility in international affairs in Mr. Ickes, a job holder for whom few Americans can find a kind word. Herr Hitler's disagreeable characteristics are about evenly matched by Mr. Ickes' and an interchange between them would be mephitic.[20]

Despite having one of the most knowledgeable of all American correspondents in Berlin, Sigrid Schultz, the *Tribune* refused to take Hitler seriously. To take him seriously meant that the newspaper would be dangerously close to admitting that American security was at stake. Most of the correspondent's dispatches demonstrated a much deeper perception of European events than did the *Tribune's* editorial page. For example in August, 1938, she reported details of the rift between Hitler and his generals over how bellicose German policy should be. Even until the beginning of the war, Miss Schultz was able to send much material which was not censored. For instance, in July, 1939, she wrote that Hitler would never dream of taking a decisive step without consulting his astrologer.[21]

But editorially the *Tribune* disagreed with Miss Schultz's analysis. Although not liking his anti-Jewish policy, McCormick believed Hitler was basically not culpable for much more than "bad taste." Evil in Europe, he insisted, simply did not reside solely in Germany:

> Hitler's speech was in the bad taste for which allowance can be made as coming from an Austrian noncommissioned officer. His principal demands are entirely reasonable, including the colonies grabbed by the allies in the Treaty of Versailles and a square deal for Germans, separated from the fatherland through the hoggishness of other European powers.

The newspaper underestimated Hitler because it thought of him as an upstart, incapable of competing in the big leagues with experienced operators such as Britain and France:

> Either Hitler or Mussolini would give a month's pay to be invited to be the guest of King George and Queen Elizabeth. If Chamberlain wanted to get the Italians and Germans out of Spain to protect Czechoslovakia, and to make Europe as peaceful as a picnic ground in January, he would need only to ask the Furor [sic] and the Duce to pay a ceremonious visit to London and meet the royal family.

> The boys' chests would swell out so far their eyes would pop.[22]

Consequently when Chamberlain attempted to reach an accord with the Nazis, the *Tribune* was sympathetic. Czechoslovakia was expendable and, after all, was just the artificial creation of outside powers. In a series of powerful cartoons, John T. McCutcheon attempted to demonstrate that Czechoslovakia was merely a "Jig-Saw Nation," an unnatural product of the iniquitous Treaty of Versailles. One of his front-page cartoons asserted that if the world were saved from war, it would be because of "Chamberlain's unheroic, thankless courage." (Carey Orr, on the other hand, harped at Britain's willingness to sacrifice innocent victims to Hitler. Poor Albion almost always came off second best with *Tribune* cartoonists.)[23]

In late September, 1938, the crisis came to a head. On September 28, in type which must have been reserved especially for such an occasion, the *Tribune* announced: WAR! NAZIS SET HOUR.

The Colonel expected conflict.[24] This was the time Neville Chamberlain made his last, lonely trip to Munich to purchase peace. The *Tribune* was overjoyed at the results of the Munich conference. Since the ties which bound western Europe to the smaller military nations of the east had now been snapped, all grounds for conflict between Germany and France were cancelled. Hitler's work lay to the east, not to the west. The newspaper obviously hoped that Germany and the USSR would fight each other, while the western Allies did nothing. Russia, like Czechoslovakia, was expendable if it would keep Britain and France, and ultimately the United States, out of conflict.[25]

Since France and Great Britain now had "no reason" to fight Germany, the *Tribune* editorially attempted to shut its eyes to the war danger. To recognize the imminence of war would only have admitted the failure of the Munich conference. David Darrah, reporting from London, reinforced this attitude. On January 20, 1939, the following item under his name appeared in the paper:

> With war scares becoming more frequent and likely to continue during the coming year, suspicion is growing in circles

opposing the British government that the war scares are being consciously fomented here in order to extend the Fascist principle to this country and increase the power of Prime Minister Neville Chamberlain's government. . . .

European observers also are chortling over the way British propaganda is leading naive America by the nose in conjuring up a war bogey and inducing an increase of the military establishment. British publications are boasting that British propaganda has been responsible for making Germany a monster in American eyes and for persuading the American public to believe that Britain is a democracy.[26]

When it became evident in 1939 that the war scare indeed had some basis in fact, the *Tribune* announced, as it had for the previous two years, that the rivalry between Germany and the Allies was not simply over ideology, but for imperial gain. Since the British controlled fifty times as much area as did Germany, the *Tribune* implied that it should part with some of the territory. If war came, it would only be because of "empires unwilling to make a concession." Just before the actual fighting began, the *Tribune* went so far as to claim that if Germany had only been "better governed and therefore better behaved," it would have had justice on its side. Hitler was thus on "good ground" when he sought to bring the "German city of Danzig" under his rule.[27]

As late as the summer of 1939, the *Tribune* was sniping at the British far more than at the Germans. It manifested this attitude because there was imminent danger of the United States supporting the British, whereas there was no chance of America supporting Germany. At a time when Edmond Taylor, the newspaper's Paris correspondent, was thinking that "our private hope was America and Roosevelt," the Colonel abjured all sympathy for the Allies.[28]

In McCormick's mind the real threat to world security remained communism rather than Naziism, and the chief enemy the Soviet Union instead of Germany. The optimism that the *Tribune* had felt for the Soviet experiment in 1936, because of the new Soviet constitution, had disappeared by 1937. The Russian trials demonstrated anew how the regime was savagely bent on liquidating all opposition. As in the past, the *Tribune* believed that Moscow was fomenting plans to take over the American government. Consequently the newspaper continued to ascribe "most of the world's trouble" to communism. Donald Day, writing from Riga, continued to set forth his scathing indictments of Soviet exploitation of the people, with the same old, tired stories that the economy was going to collapse in the near future.[29]

It followed that France and Great Britain were foolish to ally themselves with the Soviet Union, and the newspaper further argued that the Soviet military machine was a second-rate instrument anyway, incapable of providing any substantial aid to the western democracies. With considerable foresight, it predicted that Stalin would be an unreliable ally and seek an accommodation with Hitler. "There is reason to believe," the *Tribune* argued in May, 1939, "that Stalin would welcome an understanding with Germany. It would pacify one front of the encirclement which Japan, Italy, and Germany are "drawing around him." So it would, and the *Tribune* was shrewd to perceive this. One reason the newspaper realized this was its underlying premise that the war was to be fought for imperial gain rather than for ideology. If one accepted the premise, what could be more natural than for Stalin to seek an accommodation with Hitler, since this would best serve his national interest? McCormick's premises often produced only blindness to world realities, but they also enabled him to look at certain events from a fresh viewpoint.[30]

Meanwhile the corrosive war in Spain persisted, a war which mirrored the greater rivalry between the democracies, the Rome-Berlin axis, and the communists. The *Tribune* continued during these years the difficult task of assembling the news from Spain—a Herculean chore since it was impossible to find a reporter without strong bias. At first, the reporters in Spain (e.g. Jay Allen and Edmond Taylor) had been staunchly pro-loyalist. After the first year, most *Tribune* reporters in Spain favored the rebel side.

Major General J. F. C. Fuller of the British army visited Spain in 1937 and reported his findings for the *Tribune*. He favored the Franco faction, admitting, however, that the struggle was infinitely complex. Nevertheless, he wrote glowingly that Spain, because of Franco, was "conquering the rottenness within herself" and predicted an eventual rebel victory in the war. David Darrah, who had been so violent in his hatred of Mussolini, found in July, 1937, that life was almost normal in rebel-held sections of Spain. Nine months later the same reporter testified that on General Franco's side of the lines, life was everywhere easy, there was no inflation, and shops were well stocked and filled with customers. Darrah predicted, however, that Franco would reorganize Spain on totalitarian lines if he won the war, and it was clear by the time he wrote that such would be the case.[31]

The *Tribune* was forced to gain most of its news from the rebel lines because, in its words, the "communist press censorship has been characteristically ruthless and 100 per cent effectual. Nothing but official handouts have been able to reach the newspapers for months." This influenced the paper's reporting which tended to be increasingly pro-Franco. But on the editorial page, the *Tribune* made a valiant effort to establish a balance. In September, 1937, the newspaper declared that neither side could be regarded as an attractive alternative. "Whether murderous Fascism or murderous communism wins the war," it predicted, "the losers will be the Spanish people." As late as January, 1939, it pointed out that the United States should never have embargoed arms to the loyalists:

> The embargo favors France. The lifting of it would favor Barcelona. If the United States had maintained its traditional attitude, the one which is the best for its own interests, it would have favored neither side. It would have taken no hand whatever in the war. In the name of neutrality it ceased to be neutral and now, no matter what it does, it cannot regain what it should have maintained. By laying on the embargo it intervened on one side. Now if it should remove the restraint, it intervenes on the other. The great mistake was made in taking any side at any time.[32]

In February, 1939, only a few days before the final victory, a front-page Parrish cartoon asserted that Franco was merely a puppet manipulated by Mussolini and Hitler. Certainly the newspaper recognized the failure of the Allied position in the Mediterranean, because of the Spanish Civil War. But it refused to be disturbed by the deterioration of loyalist fortunes because of its overriding fear of communism.[33]

Events on the other side of the world were also leading toward war. The Japanese army invaded China in 1937. As a result of this action, American public opinion turned against the Japanese government, but the *Tribune* refused to criticize the aggression. Its attitude was similar to that expressed over German advances in Europe. When the initial invasion occurred, the newspaper valiantly attempted to understand the underlying Japanese motives. What undoubtedly precipitated matters, the newspaper claimed, was the "communist coalition" with Chiang Kai-shek, with the Japanese figuring that time was working against them. "China has been the most fertile soil for communist activities ever since the Russian revolution." The *Tribune* believed that the Japanese had calculated the time was most opportune because of the flaccidity of the western power toward Italy and Germany—thus it would have nothing to worry about from England and France.[34]

John Powell was fired by McCormick in what turned out to be one of the Colonel's most unfortunate miscalculations. McCormick's personal emissary, Captain Maxwell Corpening, while on a tour of the world, visited Powell and told the correspondent that the Colonel no longer considered China an important source of news. According to McCormick's reasoning, China would soon be conquered by the Japanese and thus the *Tribune* would cover the Far East solely from Tokyo in the future. The firing came immediately after the *Panay* episode, just when Chinese news was assuming profound significance. Thus, from 1937 to 1941, the *Tribune* had only one correspondent in the Far East, Kimpei Sheba, a Japanese stationed in Tokyo! The newspaper was deprived of its eyes and ears in China and consequently its reporting of Far Eastern matters lacked the depth which Powell could have given. The basic problem of course was that McCormick was European-centered, and not particularly interested in Far Eastern affairs.[35]

As previously, the *Tribune* continued to view the Japanese attack on China as just another imperialistic war. The United States had only itself to blame in the first place for forcing the westernization of Japan, and for providing a bad example in such matters. The Japanese had modeled themselves after both Great Britain and the

United States. The *Tribune* reached the nub of the problem when it declared:

> We may protest against the violation of treaties. We may protest in the name of common humanity against the Japanese treatment of the Chinese. But can we question the Japanese contention that European imperialists, occupying positions of military importance at Japan's very door, are inimical to Japan's national security? Can we logically reject a Japanese restatement of Mr. Olney's sentences applicable to Asia, and are we prepared to go to war about it?[36]

The quarrel among Great Britain, the Soviet Union, and Japan was in fact over "spoils of conflict" and "spheres of influence." If Japan won in China, there was no difference between that and the British conquest of India and Burma, and the French of Indo-China.[37]

America's best bet was simply to sit back and smugly watch the belligerents devour each other. The newspaper chortled over Roosevelt's refusal to acknowledge the existence of the Japanese-Chinese war since, because of the provisions of the Neutrality Act, such acknowledgment would have deprived China of arms. To the *Tribune* this only pinpointed the absurdity of the Neutrality Act. What the newspaper most wanted the Roosevelt administration to do was pull all American troops out of China. Eight years previously, the *Tribune* had urged the United States to keep its extraterritorial privileges in China. Now it wanted the United States to withdraw as soon as possible, so it would be less likely to become involved in any conflict. The longer American military forces remained in China, the newspaper argued, "the more America is exposed to unforeseeable consequences, most of them appalling." This attitude corroborated the feelings of the American people, who, according to the Gallup poll, overwhelmingly favored the withdrawal of American troops from China. McCormick could not believe that American interests lay anywhere but in trying to accommodate themselves to Japanese expansion. If China were the price America paid for peace, so be it.[38]

When the *Panay,* an American vessel, was sunk by Japanese arms in the Yangtse River, the *Tribune* initially was concerned since it believed that American public opinion might work itself into a state of war. But the Japanese apology proved satisfactory to both McCormick and the administration, and the incident in the long run served only to reinforce the *Tribune*'s determination to withdraw United States military forces completely out of China. Who wanted to fight anyway on the slogan, "Make the World Safe for Americans in the War Zones?" That was what had embroiled the United States in World War I. "It has been a great life for the American resident in China, for soldiers and civilians alike," the paper declared. "Many of them will hate to abandon it, but the United States will be relieved of an anomalous situation."[39]

If any nation were dragging the United States into possible conflict with Japan, it was not China, however, but rather McCormick's old *bête noir,* Great Britain. The newspaper's greatest worry was that Roosevelt was conspiring with British leadership to save all English investments and interests, not only in Europe, but in the Far East. Britain had, so the argument ran, a much greater stake in China than did the United States, both financial and territorial. When some American naval vessels paid a call to Singapore, the *Tribune* was ready to believe the worst. "Is the United States in a secret alliance with Great Britain?" it asked. "The affair has a very serious appearance." The newspaper (on shaky historical grounds) accused Britain of consolidating Japan's position in the Pacific and reducing America's naval power at the Washington Naval Conference. Since the British created the difficulty, they should bear full responsibility. The *Tribune* refused to sympathize with the British predicament, since the United Kingdom only wished for the defeat of the Japanese in order to wipe out a commercial competitor. Great Britain, rather than China, furnished the most convenient scapegoat for McCormick's invective against American Far Eastern policy.[40]

The Roosevelt Quarantine speech of October, 1937, confirmed the worst fears of the *Tribune.* Two years later the newspaper claimed that the Roosevelt time schedule for war in the Far East was being followed faithfully. "We may be headed directly into an imperialistic war in which we have no proprietary stake. The portents indicate that the third term may require it." Later it declared, "Democracy does not fight imperialistic wars." The chances for peace were slim at best, however, since Roosevelt was, in the newspaper's words, "the most warlike head of government in any government today at peace."[41]

The way favored by the *Tribune* to prevent war with Japan would have been to sever all ties with the Philippines and allow the Japanese to conquer everything they wished in the western Pacific. The *Tribune* would have looked on with perfect equanimity if Japan seized the islands once they gained independence. In October, 1937, it urged the United States to withdraw by Christmas. It advised America to abrogate all defense obligations with the Philippines. "Our interest is purely academic. We will not be drawn into a great war across the Pacific by a people who have chosen to part from us." According to the newspaper's viewpoint, the strategic interests of the United States simply did not include the western Pacific.[42]

Nevertheless McCormick did not wish the United States to remain entirely supine. He asserted that American defenses had been neglected long enough. Specifically he believed the United States needed a fortified base in the Aleutians to command the area from Hawaii to Unalaska (in the Aleutians) to Sands Point (near Seattle). It would thus achieve unrivaled mastery in the eastern Pacific while Japan gained control in the west. In addition, the Colonel urged the fortification of Pago Pago in Samoa and declared that "Pearl Harbor should be made our chief air base and impregnable." With considerable foresight, the *Tribune* contended that no Japanese aviation should be permitted over Alaska. But McCormick was against fortifying Guam, which was 5,000 miles from Hawaii and only 1,300 from Japan, since that would stick a spear in Japan without defending anything. The idea of a fortified Guam, to his viewpoint, was an "insane notion" and a "crazy proposal." In short, McCormick wanted the United States to become impregnable where its strategic interests dictated, and reduce its forces elsewhere. As in the Atlantic theater, he envisaged a Fortress America, but deprived of the ability to fight offensive wars in far-off continents.[43]

It was unfortunate, to the Colonel's way of thinking, that Germany and Japan persisted in alienating American public opinion by their untactful behavior. The *Tribune* regretted the totalitarian nature of the Japanese government, and denied that Japan was acting in its

own best interest since that nation seemed anxious to take on all of
its opponents at once, instead of one at a time. The Empire was in
grave danger of overreaching itself.

> With heroic madness, Japan was taking on all comers, although
> its army of invasion in China is slugging away in the intermi-
> nable task of making the Chinese love their Japanese friends.
> For over two years this good neighbor policy has been eating up
> the resourses of the island and the love feast seems as far off as
> ever. It may be altogether too romantic an explanation of the
> Japanese belligerency toward the British and the Russians at
> this time to say that they have decided to be thoroughly licked
> by a combination of great powers rather than to be badly
> checked by the ill supplied Chinese.[44]

As prophecies go, this one turned out to be nearly correct.

When the first Neutrality Act passed congress in 1935 the *Tribune*
was skeptical about whether it would keep the United States out of
war, although it had been overwhelmingly endorsed by the Republicans in congress. Even though the isolationists generally were
pleased at the passage of the Neutrality Acts, perhaps the *Tribune*
was more prescient than most. It declared jeeringly that the act
would only please "such persons as think the munition maker's
daughter's diamond necklace is the chief cause of most conflicts."
Thus the newspaper disliked the anti-capitalistic premise of the law.
Furthermore, it asserted that the Neutrality Act was incapable of
preventing war and American involvement. It would only tie the
hands of the government and restrict freedom of diplomatic action.[45]

Nevertheless, by 1939 the *Tribune*'s viewpoint on this matter had
changed, for "cash and carry" appeared the only reasonable alternative, and that meant that the United States would furnish aid only
to Britain and France. By that time, although it believed the Neutrality Act was a "weak thing," the *Tribune* hoped that it could just
possibly prevent the American government from being caught in the
fatal chain of events leading to war. As in World War I, the United
States, if it adopted a "cash and carry" policy, would be a source
of supply only to those nations which had control of the sea. Thus,
a power like Germany, which would not maintain this control,
"probably would regard this as not a neutral but an unneutral act."[46]

More important than laws, however, would be the determination of the United States to keep out of the war, and here the newspaper lacked confidence. War could be prevented, but only if the president sincerely desired to avoid American involvement. A McCutcheon cartoon of May 4, 1939, illustrated this viewpoint. It portrayed "Uncle Sam" talking to Norway, Denmark, Sweden, Holland, and Switzerland—"experts who know that nations don't have to be drawn into wars unless they want to be drawn in." (Only the following year three of these five nations were to be overrun by the Nazi army.)[47]

The bulwark of a strong defense, the *Tribune* had argued for years, was a strong navy. But because of distrust of the administration, the newspaper began to shift its emphasis on naval matters. It became more interested in the acquisition by the United States of the "offshore islands" controlled by Britain, rather than the building of more ships. In fact it accused the administration of desiring to build up the navy for political ends. "Bases multiply ships," the *Tribune* argued in November, 1938. "To neglect our serious weakness [lack of bases] without effort to correct it, while expanding our responsibilities would be inexcusable." So long as the American navy confined its fighting to home waters—"so long as it waits to offer battle within air range of our own bases"—it could successfully defend the United States against any combination of foreign fleets.[48]

Thus McCormick wanted a navy strong enough to wage a purely defensive war, but not one mighty enough to go on the offensive. Then the administration would be less likely to enter a war if it did not have the means to do so. Chesly Manly, writing from Washington, criticized Roosevelt for attempting to build a "supernavy" as strong as that of Great Britain. This, Manly claimed, led to fears in Congress that the administration intended to police the world. Logical enough—but the Colonel's thinking was far different from what it had been ten years previously. The reason for this change was his deep-rooted distrust of Roosevelt and *any* policy which the president advocated, for he was ever ready to see sinister motives in the presidential mind.[49]

As for the army, McCormick insisted it should be built around artillery. He downgraded the value of bombing, arguing that its effects had been wildly exaggerated. It was natural for him to do so, because the interventionists only a year or two later were asserting that hordes of German planes were ready to cross the Atlantic and bomb New York City. And only two months before the war began he declared that conscription was useless for defensive purposes:

> Our regular army and National Guard, if properly equipped and trained, are sufficient to defend our coasts and the possessions that form their strategic outposts. We do not need conscription for defense, and we should not tolerate it for military adventures abroad.

Distrusting Roosevelt's motives, the *Tribune* feared that once a war broke out, "enterprise, industry, utility, and occupation in the country" would be put under conscription and dictatorship. The United States would go communist overnight." "That may be why a war is wanted," was the *Tribune*'s doleful conclusion. American participation in any conflict would thus mean only the destruction of the democratic way of life.[50]

NOTES

1.   *Chicago Tribune,* January 21, 1937, p. 1.

2.   *Ibid.,* April 17, 1937, 1:1; June 1, 1937, 1:8; Helen Murchie Costello, "Col. McCormick's Tribune, 1910–41," *New Republic,* CV (December 1, 1941), 725. A hostile view of the *Tribune*'s handling of the Republic Steel riots is expressed in Howard Fast, "An Occurrence at Republic Steel," *The Aspirin Age,* 1919–1941, ed. Isabel Leighton (New York: Simon and Schuster, Inc., 1963), pp. 383–402.

3.   *Chicago Tribune,* July 5, 1938, 12:1–2.

4.   *Ibid.,* January 25, 1938, p. 8; August 29, 1938, 10:2; Leo C. Rosten, *The Washington Correspondents* (New York: Harcourt, Brace and Company, 1937), p. 196; interview with Willard Edwards.

5.   *Chicago Tribune,* May 4, 1937, 12:1.

6. *Ibid.,* September 2, 1937, 12:2; September 15, 1937, 10:1; October 9, 1937, p. 1, Orr cartoon. The Quarantine speech was to be important in other ways, for this was the time when the *Tribune* became a violent opponent of the president's foreign as well as domestic policy.

7. *Ibid.,* September 2, 1937, 12:1; December 18, 1937, 1:7; November 24, 1938, 4:1; October 19, 1938, p. 1; July 5, 1939, 4:3; Tebbel, p. 241; *Editor and Publisher,* LXXI (April 16, 1938), 3.

8. *Chicago Tribune,* May 31, 1938, 10:1–2; November 9, 1938, p. 1; November 12, 1938, 10:1.

9. *Ibid.,* March 15, 1938, 8:1; March 20, 1939, 10:2; May 1, 1939, 12:1.

10. *Ibid.,* January 21, 1937, 12:1; March 12, 1937, 12:2; August 22, 1937, 1:1, p. 10.

11. *Ibid.,* November 15, 1937, 1:3.

12. *Ibid.,* November 19, 1937, 12:2.

13. *Ibid.,* April 28, 1937, 1:3.

14. *Ibid.,* April 29, 1937, 14:2; May 6, 1937, 14:1–2; May 14, 1937, 3:5.

15. *Ibid.,* May 15, 1937, 4:2; October 26, 1938, 1:4–5.

16. *Ibid.,* February 26, 1939, p. 1; May 18, 1939, 14:2; June 8, 1939, 16:2; June 9, 1939, p. 1.

17. *Ibid.,* February 17, 1938, 10:2; March 20, 1938, 15:1.

18. *Ibid.,* January 22, 1937, 10:2; January 29, 1937, 12:1–2; February 7, 1937, 12:2; February 11, 1937, 12:3; September 16, 1937, 14:1; February 6, 1938, 12:1; March 20, 1939, 10:1.

19. *Ibid.,* June 13, 1937, 15:1.

20. *Ibid.,* March 6, 1937, p. 1, 4:2; March 19, 1937, 16:2; February 1, 1939, 10:1.

21. *Ibid.,* December 28, 1937, 4:1–2; August 22, 1938, 5:4; July 14, 1939, 1:1.

22. *Ibid.,* February 23, 1938, 10:1; August 29, 1938, 10:2.

23. *Ibid.,* September 11, 1938, p. 1; September 20, 1938, p. 1; September 22, 1938, p. 1.

24. *Ibid.,* September 28, 1938, p. 1; Shirer, *Berlin Diary,* p. 129.

25. *Chicago Tribune,* October 2, 1938, p. 1; October 12, 1938, 14:2; December 8, 1938, 16:2.

26. *Ibid.,* January 20, 1939, 1:8.

27. *Ibid.,* July 3, 1939, 6:2; August 14, 1939, 10:1; August 29, 1939, 10:1.

28. Edmond Taylor, *The Strategy of Terror: Europe's Inner Front* (Boston: Houghton Mifflin Company, 1940), p. 81.

29. *Chicago Tribune,* January 26, 1937, 10:1–2; February 7, 1937, 16:2; March 3, 1937, 12:1–2; May 28, 1937, 12:2; November 29, 1937, 12:1–2; October 17, 1938, p. 1.

30. *Ibid.,* May 6, 1939, 12:2.

31. *Ibid.,* April 16, 1937, 1:1; July 22, 1937, 1:7; November 7, 1937, 1:7; February 12, 1938, 1:7; February 15, 1938, 5:3.

32. *Ibid.,* May 3, 1937, 10:2; September 13, 1937, 10:2; January 27, 1939, 12:2.

33. *Ibid.,* February 8, 1939, p. 1.

34. *Ibid.,* August 15, 1937, 12:2; August 31, 1937, p. 1; October 11, 1937, 12:2.

35. Powell, pp. 322–24; interview with Chesly Manly.

36. *Chicago Tribune,* August 9, 1939, 12:1.

37. *Ibid.,* August 15, 1939, 8:1.

38. *Ibid.,* August 17, 1937, 10:2; August 21, 1937, 8:1; August 31, 1937, 10:1; Walter Johnson, *The Battle against Isolation* (Chicago: The University of Chicago Press, 1944), p. 27.

39. *Chicago Tribune,* December 15, 1937, 12:1; December 16, 1937, p. 1; December 28, 1937, 8:2; February 27, 1938, 16:2.

40. *Ibid.,* October 6, 1937, 12:1; January 15, 1938, 12:1; January 30, 1938, 10:2; September 4, 1938, 1:2.

41. *Ibid.,* February 25, 1939, 10:1; August 11, 1939, 10:2.

42. *Ibid.,* February 20, 1937, 10:2; July 26, 1937, 10:1–2; October 21, 1937, 14:2; March 8, 1938, 10:2.

43. *Ibid.,* April 25, 1937, 16:1; January 5, 1938, 8:2; May 11, 1938, 12:1; February 7, 1939, 8:2.

44. *Ibid.,* May 8, 1937, 10:2; July 11, 1939, 8:1.

45. *Ibid.,* May 1, 1937, 10:1; August 3, 1937, 10:2; Walter Johnson, *The Battle against Isolation,* p. 23.

46. *Chicago Tribune,* June 19, 1939, 10:2.

47. *Ibid.,* March 22, 1937, 12:2; May 4, 1939, p. 1.

48. *Ibid.,* April 25, 1938, 10:2; November 20, 1938, 14:1.

49. *Ibid.,* October 2, 1938, 1:1.

50. *Ibid.,* September 25, 1937, 12:2; October 1, 1937, 14:1; September 6, 1938, 16:2; March 20, 1939, 10:2; July 9, 1939, 12:2; July 14, 1939, 10:1.

6

The Battle Against
Intervention, 1939–1941

reat Britain and France declared war on Germany on September 1, 1939, in retaliation for the Nazi advance into Poland. Philip Kinsley, who later was to write the official history of the *Tribune,* interviewed Chicago residents for three days and, not surprisingly, discovered that the vast majority of respondents thought America should stay out of the war. The *Tribune* agreed. On September 2, it announced its conviction that the war in Europe in no way impinged upon the vital interests of the United States. The tone of its warning was deadly serious, and a bit desperate:

> This is not our war. We did not create the Danzig situation. We did not sign the treaty of Versailles. The peace America made with Germany did not contain another war. The United States did not take spoils. It did not divide up colonies. . . .
> This is not our war. We should not make it ours. We should keep out of it.
> We may think their side is the better side. But it is their war. They are competent to fight it. . . . The frontiers of American democracy are not in Europe, Asia, or Africa.[1]

The newspaper had little confidence, however, that this plan would be heeded by the administration. Willard Edwards of the Washington Bureau predicted on the following day that President Roosevelt would almost certainly attempt to involve the United

States in the fighting within six months. Ominously he pointed out that the government held the names of forty million people who possessed social security numbers, although he failed to explain how the government would make use of those lists. The Colonel himself, in a speech delivered just prior to the beginning of the war, gave a long recital of European history, attempting to demonstrate that Europe's problems stemmed from complex racial and economic causes, and could not be rectified by the interposition of American military strength.[2]

The *Tribune* took it for granted that its readers were anti-German. They did not have to be reminded day after day that Hitler was a totalitarian dictator. Instead, the danger, to its way of thinking, was that Americans would be swayed by pro-Ally sentimentality into entering the war. Thus the newspaper spent much more space censuring the Allies than the Germans. The reasons, although purely tactical, were much misunderstood at the time, and perhaps maliciously so. Hence the opponents of the *Tribune* declared that McCormick was pro-fascist, more anti-English than anti-German, and a not-so-secret Nazi. These accusations had no basis in reality, but the weakness of the *Tribune* position was that it felt it constantly had to snipe at the popular side in order to prevent America's entry into the war.

Thus, after the war's beginning, France and Britain were usually called in news stories and headlines the "empires" rather than by the more commonly used names. The newspaper's somewhat disingenuous defense was to ask why "there should be any objection to the truthful description of what these powerful European nations have acquired? What," it asked, "suddenly has become disturbing, disagreeable, or even disreputable about the term?" What indeed— but the *Tribune* was brilliantly capable of squeezing various sinister connotations out of the word "empires." In depicting the Allies in an unfavorable light, it occasionally ignored the fact that it too had favored the policy of appeasement only the previous year.

> Mr. Chamberlain is the world's champion boob, with Earl Baldwin runner-up. Americans who may yet be asked to rescue Europe from Hitler may well meditate on the fact that Hitler is

> where he is because England and France let him get there. . . .
> It is their war, not ours, a war which would never have taken
> place if they had employed ordinary common sense at any one
> of a dozen critical junctures in the last twenty years.[3]

Although the *Tribune* had never been enthusiastic about the 1937
Neutrality Act, it now believed the law should remain on the books,
partly because the only alternative appeared to be a "cash and
carry" policy which would favor the Allies. Ironically, it now labeled
those who favored lifting the embargo on war materials (although
the *Tribune* itself had opposed such an embargo only two years
previously) as "the social climbers, the revolutionaries, and the
third termites." The newspaper urged congress to remain in session
during the fall of 1939 to serve as a brake upon the overly ambitious
Mr. Roosevelt.

Yet the *Tribune,* in its efforts to prevent the repeal of the Neutrality Act, did not display quite the vigor which would characterize
its efforts in later years. Perhaps this was because the war itself after
the fall of Poland failed to excite interest. None of the major powers
appeared determined to do much fighting. By November, 1939,
Tribune editors were shoving war news off the front page, and this
would have been unbelievable only three months previously. Consciousness of the war remained just under the surface, ever ready
to bob up at any time, but still not the all-pervading menace that it
would be seven months later.[4]

On the western front the war appeared to have reached a stale-
mate. Before April, 1940, Britain and France, although not notice-
ably improving their position, did not seem to be losing either. The
man in the street (and most experts) fully expected an eventual
Allied victory. This contributed to the general apathy, and thus
little pressure, either from abroad or internally, was directed at the
Roosevelt administration to give all-out aid to the western powers.
Since there was no pervasive sense of insecurity, the *Tribune* felt
free to step up its criticisms of Great Britain and France. In late
September, 1939, Chesly Manly asked why those two powers could
not pay their debts from World War I, since they were able to scrape
up the necessary cash for purchasing war supplies in the United
States. Editorially the newspaper demanded the immediate with-

drawal of English forces from the New World. It recommended that Newfoundland and Labrador be given to Canada, Jamaica and the other British West Indian islands to the United States, and the Falklands to Argentina.[5]

The *Tribune* also believed that America should take advantage of Britain's predicament. Since the United Kingdom was involved in war, neutral America could take the opportunity to increase its commercial profits. Thus in December, 1939, the newspaper suggested that since Great Britain was not buying pork from the United States, and Germany could not because of the blockade, American shippers should dump their excess pork in neutral countries, where Britain would be obliged to buy it. It urged American businessmen to go after increased Latin American trade and not permit "British competitors to take business which might come our way if it were energetically solicited." It also lambasted British interference with the mails. One eight-column banner headline in February, 1940, pointed up the *Tribune*'s irritation:

REVEAL BRITISH RAID ON MAIL

LETTERS SEIZED
AT POINT OF GUN
ON U.S. CLIPPER

A headline the previous month had screamed BRITAIN FLOUTS 21 REPUBLICS over the story about the English government's rejecting the protest of twenty-one American republics as a result of naval activity in the western hemisphere. All this emphasis on maritime rights served to bring back memories of British activities during World War I; the newspaper was implicitly criticizing the United States's entry into that war, an action which had become increasingly unpopular during the thirties. The *Tribune* even criticized the British for taking prisoners off the German ship *Altmark* in Norwegian waters, thus endangering Norweigan security.[6]

To bolster its thesis that the United States should not enter the war, nor provide military aid to the Allies, the newspaper argued that under the exigencies of war, the "empires" had become dictatorships. This, the *Tribune* claimed, was an object lesson for the United

THOSE BRITISH POSSESSIONS IN AMERICAN WATERS

March 5, 1940

States. Conversely it reiterated its old theme that Roosevelt was anxious for American entry into the war so he could become an autocratic dictator:

> The moment they entered the war the so-called democracies of Europe perforce abandoned all democracy. . . . It is not only state control of the economic system that has been copied from the totalitarian system. In Great Britain the rights of citizens that accrued from the struggles of centuries have been swept away for the duration of the war. . . . Liberty is often lightly yielded but always dearly won.[7]

The *Tribune* not only accused the administration of plotting to enter the war, but even of instigating it. The argument went this way: the Poles, facing the German army alone in September, 1939, relied upon help never given them. They had received promises of aid from the British and French, but no aid was given. The war, according to the *Tribune,* would never have occurred without that promise of aid from the western Allies. And back of the British and French determination were secret "assurances" from the American government, which thus bore the major responsibility for propping up the Allied resolution to fight. In the final analysis the war was caused by certain unpublicized commitments and promises from the American government.[8]

These were "commitments" which the *Tribune* was determined America would never fulfill. In its viewpoint the needs of the United States came before those of Britain and France, and all its energies had to be focused on its own rearmament. Since McCormick considered himself, and was regarded by many others, as a military expert, he felt free to argue what forms this rearmament should take. The newspaper urged the formation of a "mobile field army" like that of Germany, which had the added virtue of being small, precluding the need for conscription. A *Tribune* correspondent from Berlin perceptively described the strengths of the German army, and this presented a goal toward which the American army should work:

> The German army of today has changed its mode of warfare to a large extent. No longer do great masses of men roll across a field toward an objective, hoping to take it by sheer

strength of numbers. That's outdated. Field operations differ greatly from those of the world war.

Infantry tactics have been radically altered. The German army is free from the shackles of tradition. It has no compunctions in trying experiments and sticking to them until the best results are obtained.[9]

The war remained on the inside pages until the Russian invasion of Finland. At last here was an issue the *Tribune* could grapple with. The newspaper had not been too critical of Hitler's invasion of Poland, but now declared that the Russian attack on Finland posed a danger for all civilization:

> The invasion of Finland may present the greatest menace of this uncertain war. It may contain the beginning of the greatest catastrophe with which Europe has been threatened since the Hunnish invasion. Asiatic hordes are again crowding up on Europe's frontiers, under a leader whose personal history accepts no competition from any other terror that ever came out of the east.[10]

Three days after delivering this editorial, the *Tribune* published an even more vigorous one, urging that Germany and the Allies immediately make peace, unite their forces, and turn against the Soviet Union. "Western Europe needs a quick peace," it stated, "and a change of front from one which divides civilization against itself to one which again faces the Asiatic barbarism." Soviet fears that the British and French really wanted to fight the USSR rather than Nazi Germany were entirely valid as far as the wishes of the *Tribune* were concerned.

But the *Tribune* refused to face the implications of its anti-Soviet stand, and rejected any idea of American intervention. It had become truly isolationist. "If we let our natural and genuine sympathy for the Finns involve us in Europe again we shall have established a precedent for future action which in the long run must drain our country of its men, its wealth, and eventually its liberty." The *Tribune* was happy though that at last the "most brutal tyranny in the world" was recognized for what it was. Immodestly it noted that "some people, it is true, did not need the recent revelations."[11]

Donald Day reported the Finnish–Soviet Union war for the

Tribune. His dispatches continued in the same anti-communist vein as during the previous twenty years. Finnish leaders, recognizing a friendly correspondent, gave him every consideration, even allowing him to interview Soviet prisoners who blamed Stalin for their misery. After the Finnish resistance had proved unexpectedly durable, Donald Day's dispatches took on a more hopeful note—perhaps tiny Finland would be the force to end the Bolshevik stranglehold over the Soviet Union. But that, like many of Day's prognostications, was built more on fancy than fact.[12]

The *Tribune* could not help but suspect that Roosevelt was secretly plotting to aid the Russians. When the war ended (on terms not too unfavorable to the Finns) the *Tribune* blamed the whole thing on the president, thundering that the Soviet Union would never have had the power to invade Finland in any case except for Roosevelt's recognition of the regime in 1933. "It is difficult to avoid the conclusion," the newspaper pointed out, "that the administration which recognized Russia, congratulated it on numerous anniversaries, found its economic planning something to emulate, and placed Soviet sympathizers in many key positions in Washington still regards the Soviet regime as a model." Any New Deal claims of sympathy for the embattled Finns were discounted as hypocritical. Consequently, when Mrs. Franklin D. Roosevelt told the American Youth Congress convention that America's sympathies lay with Finland, the *Tribune* solemnly and irresponsibly headlined the event:

> MRS. ROOSEVELT
> DISAGREES WITH
> HER RED FRIENDS[13]

In April, 1940, the war broadened in scope and became more dangerous in its nature. Germany invaded Norway on April 6, 1940. Curiously, the *Tribune* commented on the aggression by blaming the British rather than the Germans for involving the Norwegians in the war. "The laying of mines," the newspaper declared, "was as much an invasion of Norway as the seizure of its ports or the landing of troops. It made the spread of the war unescapable." Donald Day, no longer stationed in Riga (Latvia having lost its national independence), reported on the progress of the Norwegian war from Stockholm. At first the *Tribune* believed the Germans had taken the short end of a very long gamble. It was difficult to lose the notion that the British were somehow infallible, militarily as well as diplomatically. By May 2, however, the character of the fighting had gone decisively against the British, and the newspaper, recognizing that the Allies, in Norway at least, were headed toward another Dardanelles-type debacle, vigorously denounced the English government for critically underestimating the German strength. The *Tribune* did not recognize that its criticism could have served as a self-indictment as well.[14]

With the British government reeling from the bad news from Norway, the Germans lunged into France and the low countries. On that crowded day of May 10, 1940, the British changed prime ministers, replacing Neville Chamberlain with Winston Churchill. The *Tribune* had always admired the strong-willed Churchill and declared that the British appeared to have picked their most capable man. Rather surprisingly, McCormick's paper had a few kind words for Chamberlain who had so futilely "tried to carry through a policy of good will and humanitarianism." It applauded "his part in trying to preserve the peace of Europe against the will of a man determined to have world war." The *Tribune,* however, refused to waste any editorial space bewailing the tragedy of France's quick defeat. Its attitude, instead of reflecting concern about American national security, was one of "I-told-you-so." French power, according to its point of view, had been sapped by the "New Deal" policies of Leon Blum, and its collapse should serve mainly as a lesson to the Democratic party. The newspaper steadfastly refused to display any emotion over the German victories. This lack of involvement was because of its arguments that American interests were not intertwined with European interests. Moreover, the paper did not agree with the idea that the United States had any moral stake in the battle then raging. Hence what happened in Europe was irrelevant to American policy decisions.[15]

The *Tribune* continued to insist that the British would be able to fight even without American aid. Anyway immediate military assistance would be "unable to change the course of events abroad."

> Nothing we gave the allies now could be sent overseas in time to affect the present battle. What action is to be taken can

better be determined when the outcome of that battle is known, for then we will have a clearer idea of our own defense responsibilities. Even in their present hard pressed situation the allies realize, probably more fully than some of their more excited partisans in Washington, that our first duty is the defense of the United States. That is not selfishness, but sanity.[16]

The newspaper denounced the opponents of its policies for being merely "excited partisans," and it characterized President Roosevelt as an overly-nervous charlatan—"hell-bent for war." By contrast the *Tribune* liked to picture itself as collected and calm in the middle of crisis. McCormick thought of himself as above the ephemeral emotions of the hour, capable of calmly and rationally analyzing world events. On June 17, 1940, the *Tribune* printed a speech which the Colonel had delivered the previous evening, introducing McCormick's words with this prefatory remark: "In an address delivered over WGN and the Mutual Broadcasting system on the Chicago Tribune Symphonic hour, Col. McCormick matched realities against hysteria." The Colonel's first words were soothing, like an all-wise father admonishing an hysterical child: "Last week at this hour," he declared, "I counseled calm in a troubled world." The *Tribune* was even capable of finding happy tidings in the French defeat, taking "comfort in the knowledge that now there is little prospect of another military adventure in Europe on our part." Not uncheerfully it pointed out that "there is no front in France to be defended by our men and guns." There was, after all, not so much to worry about. America could make an accommodation with Germany. Thus, appearing before the Republican platform committee on June 19, 1940, McCormick argued that the convention should not "heed the hysterical appeal for immediate conscription."[17]

The *Tribune* believed that the United States should mind its own business, prudently adding to its military forces, but not to such an extent that Roosevelt would have enough material on hand to indulge in aggressive warfare. No aid should be given England. Chesly Manly reported from Washington in early June, 1940, that any aid given the Allies would be "in the face of overwhelming senate opposition." Thank God, declared the *Tribune*, there was a Midwest to keep the United States on a pro-American policy:

> Inflamed by commercial radio commentators, the east has fallen into a complete state of hysteria. Old men who have avoided every war during their lifetime are screaming to send conscripted boys overseas to the shambles. Once staid newspapers are crying for conscription of manpower and capital. The mental confusion could hardly be worse if the enemy were in Long Island again.[18]

(One is tempted to think that if the enemy had been in control of Long Island, the *Tribune* would not have been overly distressed.)

The Colonel intended to be hopeful even if Germany were to defeat England. If Germany controlled all Europe, McCormick declared it would not be able to sink or capture the American fleet. As a precautionary measure, however, he urged the transferal of the fleet from the Pacific to the Atlantic, the fortification of the Pacific states, and the sending of two army divisions to the "outpost of Hawaii" to make it impregnable. That would be sufficient to guarantee American defense. If the necessary will were present, the United States need have no trouble coexisting with Germany. He reiterated his stand against conscription, declaring that the army did not have the weapons with which to equip the draftees. In June, 1940, the *Tribune* asserted that since Roosevelt was a "panty-waist Hitler" he had "apparently" borrowed the idea of conscription from Hitler's youth movement. When the administration, almost a month later, requested equipment for a large army, the newspaper objected in characteristic fashion.

> If we are not going to fight in Europe we have no need of 1,200,000 soldiers or of equipment for an army of even greater size. Either Mr. Roosevelt is concealing his real purpose to send an expeditionary force abroad or he is asking congress to appropriate far more money than is needed for defense.

What was necessary, McCormick held, was not an army on the European scale but one "of moderate size, highly mobile, and possessed of the most modern of equipment." However, if conscription were to be put into effect, McCormick believed that the "idlers" should be first called. "The CCC enrollee and the WPA worker are logical military material, not because of their economic status but because they are not contributing anything to industry and all too frequently lack the training to be useful in industry."[19]

It must have surprised many *Tribune* readers when the newspaper proved fairly receptive to the bases-for-destroyers trade consummated with Great Britain in September, 1940. This was not inconsistency. In May of that year, the *Tribune* had suggested that England could give the United States four battleships in exchange for forty destroyers—a rather harsh deal for the British. On July 22, 1940, the newspaper had argued that the United States would be stronger if it controlled adequate bases away from its shores; a day later specifically naming Bermuda as a "dagger pointed at the United States." However the *Tribune* had insinuated that Pershing must have been senile when the venerable World War I general pleaded that fifty destroyers be made available to Great Britain. Yet, when the terms of the trade were hammered out and announced, the *Tribune* was content, even taking credit for them:

WE GET THE BASES

THE TRIBUNE rejoices to make this announcement which fulfills a policy advocated by this newspaper since 1922. In spite of much discouragement, THE TRIBUNE persisted, month by month and year by year, in calling for these additions to the national defense. It may be found, as we think it will be, that this is the greatest contribution of this newspaper to the country's history since the nomination of Lincoln.

The agreement is not in terms THE TRIBUNE would have preferred. Nevertheless, any arrangement which gives the United States naval and air bases in regions which must be brought within the American defense zone is to be accepted as a triumph.[20]

The *Tribune* also praised the Roosevelt administration for its alliance with Canada, made effective in the Ogdensburg agreement of August, 1940. It hoped that Canada and the United States together could keep the hopes of mankind alive.[21]

But 1940 was a presidential election year and McCormick fought it in as partisan a spirit as he had in 1936. Although it managed (barely) to hide its disappointment for the duration of the campaign, the *Tribune* was unhappy over the selection of Wendell Willkie as the Republican candidate. Even during the campaign, McCormick had little use for Willkie, and the Colonel had warned in the pre-convention period that the Willkie candidacy was being backed mainly by those forces interested in sabotaging the Republican party. In fact on June 22, 1940, the newspaper had come out for Thomas E. Dewey for the nomination. According to the *Tribune*, the New Yorker's credentials were impressive: Dewey had been defeated two years previously for the New York governorship "only by a few thousand communist votes" and seemed a young, fresh face in politics. Furthermore, he had overwhelmingly won the Illinois primary with an impressive total of 911,000 votes. When the Republicans decided to nominate Willkie instead, the *Tribune* was caught by surprise and withheld editorial comment for a few days. As a delegate to the convention, McCormick had persisted in his support of Dewey even until the seventh and last ballot, the only holdout in the Illinois delegation. Finally on June 30 the *Tribune* mentioned Willkie by name on its editorial page and then only in the most guarded terms, declaring that the candidate had a "good public reputation and a strong personality." Naturally McCormick had no choice but to support him.[22]

If the *Tribune* was lukewarm to Willkie, it could comfort itself by attacking the Democrats at their convention. When Speaker of the House William B. Bankhead delivered the keynote address at the Democratic convention, the *Tribune* chortled that the delegates "cheered politely but without conviction. . . . They knew it was hopeless to persuade the voters that Mr. Roosevelt is trying to keep us out of war." As it had done with Landon, the newspaper never admitted the slightest doubt over Willkie's chances, and its reporters wrote with determined optimism. Thus Arthur Sears Henning (who had seen into the glass darkly before) wrote on July 29 that either Roosevelt would be reelected by a "narrow margin" or Wendell Willkie would triumph "by anything from a handful of electoral votes to a landslide." His conclusion of course was that Willkie would win.[23]

The *Chicago Tribune*'s campaign coverage was as one-sided in 1940 as it had been in previous years, with the significant exception that it ran a battle page, which presented both sides of the political dispute. The *Tribune*'s sister paper, the *New York Daily News* had pioneered this technique four years before with good results. Except for the battle page, however, and the constant scolding of the Democrats on the editorial page, it must have been difficult for a casual reader of the *Tribune* to tell whether anyone were opposing Willkie for the presidency, since he was regularly given all the available front-page space. Rarely, for example, during the month of October, 1940, did Roosevelt's name appear on the front-page banner headline. Harold Ickes calculated that the *Tribune* devoted twenty-four times as much news space to Willkie as it did to Roosevelt during that month. Although Ickes was a biased researcher, the statistics could not have been far wrong.[24]

The following is a listing of all the front-page banner headlines in the *Chicago Tribune* dealing with the political situation, from October 1 to the election:

October 1, 1940	WOMEN CHEER WILLKIE "CREED"
October 5, 1940	HALT DRIFT TO WAR—WILLKIE
October 8, 1940	"PUNY HITLERS" HIT BY WILLKIE
October 10, 1940	HOW TVA WAS WHITEWASHED!
October 13, 1940	POLL REVEALS GAIN FOR G.O.P.
October 15, 1940	HITS "3D TERM DICTATOR"
October 17, 1940	WILLKIE: "FREE RELIEF SLAVES"
October 21, 1940	WILLKIE TO F.D.R.—DEBATE!
October 22, 1940	CHICAGO HAILS WILLKIE TODAY
October 23, 1940	WILLKIE CLASHES WITH F.D.R.
October 31, 1940	WILLKIE TELLS DEFENSE PLAN
November 1, 1940	STRIKE AT VOTE THIEF DRIVE
November 3, 1940	NAB GUNMAN NEAR WILLKIE!
November 4, 1940	WILLKIE PLEA: BAR 3D TERMS
November 5, 1940	PROSPERITY! NO WAR! WILLKIE

The news was regularly slanted in an anti-Roosevelt direction. Arthur Sears Henning, for example, pointed out on October 5 that Elliott Roosevelt's "draft dodging" was shoving Colorado into the Republican column. (It went for Roosevelt a month later.) On October 21 the newspaper began to serialize John T. Flynn's book, *Country Squire in the White House,* which spoke of Roosevelt's fiscal

THE PRICE OF A "THIRD TERM"

April 14, 1939

irresponsibility and economic ineptitude. Only a few days later the newspaper was delighted with the news that John L. Lewis had declared for Willkie—the same Lewis whom the *Tribune* had in less propitious moments called a communist. On October 28 the *Tribune* poll of the state of Illinois indicated that Willkie would win by a slim margin of 50.7 percent of the vote, while C. Wayland Brooks and Dwight Green, both McCormick protégés, would respectively gain the senatorial seat and the governorship by more substantial margins. Walter Trohan, who covered the Roosevelt campaign, always referred to the president's audiences as "partisan." A classic example of a slanted *Tribune* story was written around an incident in which Stephen Early, Roosevelt's press secretary, allegedly kicked a Negro while the presidential party was in New York City. The story appeared in the newspaper in the following way:

> Stephen Early, President Roosevelt's Virginia born secretary who admitted kicking a colored policeman in New York Monday night, apologized to the injured man by telegraph tonight— and denied kicking him. Early, a kinsman of Jubal Early, noted confederate general, added he did not believe he had done anything wrong.[25]

On November 3, 1940, readers of the *Tribune* read of the "probable election of Mr. Willkie" over their breakfast coffee. On Tuesday, the day of the election, they were confronted with the giant, banner headline: PROSPERITY! NO WAR! WILLKIE! But these great halcyon hopes soon faded. Willkie only managed to muster 45 percent of the popular vote and eighty-two electoral votes. The *Tribune* was not slow in finding where to cast the blame—predictably on Wendell Willkie himself. The antipathy manifested toward the Republican standard bearer before the party convention immediately reasserted itself. He was not, the newspaper claimed, enough different from Roosevelt to have waged a meaningful campaign. For example, he erred in supporting conscription. The Republican party, it maintained, made an even greater error in failing to nominate Thomas E. Dewey. As usual the New Deal victory was also ascribed to the "profitseekers, illiterates, radicals, and political bosses," since the "great bulk of the intelligent people" had obviously voted Repub-

2 CENTS PAY NO MORE!

Chicago Daily Tribune

THE WORLD'S GREATEST NEWSPAPER

FINAL ★★★

VOLUME XCIX—NO. 266 C   TUESDAY, NOVEMBER 5, 1940.—28 PAGES   PRICE TWO CENTS

PROSPERITY! NO WAR! WILLKIE

10 Die in Air Liner's Mountain Crash

MISHAP IN UTAH LAID TO FAILURE OF RANGE BEAM

Peak Hit by Plane in Snowstorm.

VOTE TODAY THE WAY THE ONES WHO PRESERVED OUR NATION WOULD VOTE

Jail the Crooks on Spot! Vote Army Is Told

BY WAYNE THOMIS

SHARON, N. H., FIRST TO REPORT ELECTION, 24 TO 7 FOR WILLKIE

Here's What to Do Today if You Encounter Obstacles at Polls

VOTE
—Or Lose It!

1. Vote early.
2. Vote your personal wishes.

NEW YORK CROWD SINGS ITSELF OUT OF CAMPAIGN RIOT

ROOSEVELT ENDS CAMPAIGN WITH PLEA FOR UNITY

Closes Address on Prayerful Note.

BY WALTER TROHAN

50 Millions Go to Polls Today in Record Vote

Election Facts

G. O. P. NOMINEE TELLS AIMS IN FINAL APPEAL

He Urges All to Get Out and Vote.

Willkie's Stand

BY ARTHUR SEARS HENNING

BY PHILIP KINSLEY

THE WEATHER

TUESDAY, NOVEMBER 5, 1940.

November 5, 1940

lican. The *Tribune* would have much more to say about Mr. Willkie in the future![26]

Since Roosevelt was so determined to enter the war, a key question for McCormick was whether America would be able to defeat Germany militarily. The Colonel repeatedly emphasized the high price the United States would pay if it succumbed to the war fever. In October, 1940, in a radio address, he gave his expert opinion that it would indeed be possible for an American army to defeat the Germans and land successfully in Europe, but the burden of such a victory would be heavy: twenty million men conscripted, four hundred billion dollars spent, and one million lives lost. It would be by far the most costly and desperate war the United States had ever fought. To avoid this unnecessary and prolonged conflict, the Colonel urged the United States to adopt as neutral a course as possible.[27]

Unlike most opponents of the Roosevelt foreign policy, McCormick was against *all* aid to Great Britain. A November, 1940, *Tribune* editorial criticized administration policy in sending B–17s to Europe on the ground that if England suddenly negotiated a peace with Germany while the United States was still unarmed, America would be in a desperate plight. An enraged Germany could then turn on the United States without any fear of reprisals from the English. A month later, John T. McCutcheon beat the drums for a negotiated peace. He portrayed a boy telling his parents (in unlikely language), "And now, if there was a chance of a negotiated peace today—knowing, as we do, about how the other peace worked out—would or wouldn't it be better for everybody than an indefinite prolongation of the war and another dictated peace such as in 1918."

Instead of aiding Great Britain, said the newspaper, the United States should use its considerable influence to force the British to negotiate. An editorial of December 8, 1940, declared that if the United States were to refuse all aid to Britain, this might be the means for forcing the English to negotiate such a peace, saving the world much slaughter. Giving aid to Britain only served to prolong the carnage.[28]

Implicit in the *Tribune* argument was the belief that World War II was basically the same type of conflict as World War I. The present was only a reflection of what had occurred twenty-five years previously.

> America would like to help Great Britain to a peace which would leave it, its dominions, and its empire intact and safe. That this peace should impose other conditions upon Europe is not within our sphere. Europe has been in many forms and in many convulsions. This is only another. We cannot assume that the United States is its guardian. Time has always been the greatest conqueror in Europe. It will take charge again.[29]

Hitler was not the demonic conqueror that some contemporaries made him out to be; instead he was rather like Franklin D. Roosevelt. "They think alike, and given a free hand would reach much the same goal." Presumably, a Hitler with those characteristics, unlikeable as he might be, could be amenable to negotiation. Peace, in the Colonel's viewpoint, was far more important than any "crusade" to defeat Naziism. Implicitly the newspaper believed that perhaps then the nations of Europe could unite and turn on Soviet communism, the real foe of western civilization.[30]

By far the most important issue facing congress in the first part of 1941 was lend-lease. Of all newspapers opposing the measure, the *Tribune* was easily the most powerful, and the loudest in voicing its dissatisfaction. The *New York Daily News,* which also opposed lend-lease, had a greater circulation than the *Tribune* but comparatively little editorial influence. To McCormick the stakes were vital. If the lend-lease bill could be defeated, the United States probably would not enter the war; if it were passed, war was inevitable. When President Roosevelt initially took up the matter with congress, the *Tribune* blared in a front-page banner headline:

SENATORS TO FIGHT F.D.R. BILL

DEMAND FOR UNLIMITED POWER OVER ARMS STUNS CONGRESS.

This headline indicated a genuine weakness in the *Tribune* style of reporting. The implication of the headline was of course that the bill would be defeated in congress. The trouble was that Roosevelt's bills were always being defeated on the pages of the *Tribune*—until the final roll call was taken. Then they always seemed to be passed—although the newspaper seldom prepared its readers for such an eventuality. The *Tribune's* lack of realism hurt the integrity of its reporting.[31]

The *Tribune* fervently believed that the lend-lease bill was expressly designed to destroy the Republic and give Roosevelt the dictatorship for which he had so long thirsted. Beginning from this premise, the newspaper stressed the domestic implications of the bill (dictatorship) far more than it did the implications for foreign policy (war). Therefore it believed that it was the patriotic duty of all sincere Americans to oppose lend-lease by any means at their command. This was true particularly for the Republican party, and the *Tribune* consequently read out of the party all those who supported Roosevelt's foreign policy, for such a person according to its lights was simply not a sincere American.

McCormick did not visualize the Republican party as a group of coalitions, but rather as a tightly unified organization of all patriotic Americans, facing the Democratic party which was controlled by foreign "isms." Thus, as conceived by McCormick, the Republican party was the bailiwick of American ideals. (The fact that making the GOP into a narrowly "American" party or closed corporation might alienate the majority of voters never occurred to him.) The Republican party was thus obligated by its traditions to oppose whatever the president proposed, and those who supported any Roosevelt measure had to be expelled as forcefully as possible.[32]

Not surprisingly the Republican who most aroused the Colonel's displeasure was Wendell Willkie, since he was one of the most articulate supporters of lend-lease. In a series of unusually vigorous editorials, the *Tribune* dramatically threw Willkie out of the Republican party. "He should no longer be consulted in the national party organization, should have no place in its councils, and should neither give nor be asked advice." Fervently denouncing the New York leader, the newspaper urged the party to "take leave of the late standard bearer with the hope that it will never again see him or he it." Willkie, according to the *Tribune,* had been nominated in the first place only because of "an audacious and unscrupulous conspiracy of Wall Street bankers and the New Deal." To a slightly less vigorous extent, Thomas E. Dewey was also cast out of the party. Although once McCormick's darling, Dewey's advocacy of lend-lease constituted too grave a heresy. "If the Republican party remains an American party," the *Tribune* solemnly declared, "it will not make Mr. Dewey a candidate for President of the United States." Prominent columnists such as Dorothy Thompson and Claire Boothe were villified for wishing to annex the United States to the British Empire. Lend-lease thus afforded the *Tribune* the self-appointed opportunity of purging the party of its enemies.[33]

Perhaps the greatest villains of all were the Wall Street bankers. Five years before, the *Tribune* had denounced those historians who had found the money-power instrumental in pushing the United States into World War I. It was indicative of the newspaper's growing extremism that by 1941 it was espousing much the same point of view, openly asserting that Wall Street in collusion with the president was dragging a reluctant nation into war. Instead of regarding the eastern financial leadership as the bulwark of American free enterprise, the newspaper increasingly regarded it as the prisoner of foreign interests. The *Tribune* centered its hate upon New York City (somehow Chicago's La Salle Street was absolved of complicity) and day after day heaped scorn upon the "colonials of Wall Street and Park Avenue and the theatrical pets of Broadway." The big Wall Street bankers were nothing more than British lackeys and if the United States were to enter the war, disaster would be their lot. In an editorial which contained some overtones of anti-Semitism (almost unprecedented for the *Tribune*) the newspaper pointed out what their fate would be:

> What shift may they [the Wall Street bankers] expect from the millions upon whom they bring the war? Given a terrible injury, the American people, we may fear, *will yield to that instinct of intolerance for minorities* that had bred a series of disasters throughout all history. The stage is being set by its inevitable victims. [Emphasis added.]

Illustrative of the paper's growing extremism was the headline: U.S. DRIVE FOR DICTATORSHIP AMAZES FRENCH. Thus, even Vichy French officials were enlisted in McCormick's cause, to be quoted as authorities on what course American policy should follow.[34]

The assault against lend-lease absorbed McCormick's fullest

energies. It was one of the three great, sustained crusades the newspaper had enlisted in: the two others being the elections of 1936
and 1940. Other news was cast into the shade. Roosevelt's third
inaugural address, for example, was barely mentioned on the front
page of January 21, 1941; the newspaper was too busy filling its
pages with antiadministration material to concern itself unduly about
such an event as an inaugural address. On February 1, 1941, Dalton
Trumbo (later to be denounced by the *Tribune* as a communist)
gave some critical imaginary comments of what Andrew Jackson
would have thought about lend-lease and the Roosevelt administration. In its fight against the bill, the *Tribune* furnished effective aid
to the America First Committee. It urged all persons who opposed
lend-lease to writ or telephone America First headquarters in Chicago. As a result, by March, the Chicago chapter of the organization
had gathered 700,000 signatures and 328,000 telephone calls, an
indication of the newspaper's power.[35]

In February, 1941, Colonel McCormick appeared before the
Senate Foreign Relations Committee to give his views on lend-lease.
Charles Lindbergh appeared immediately after him. In response to
questioning by Senator Tom Connolly of Texas, McCormick reiterated his belief that the United States should not adopt a crash program to build up its defenses, and that America did not need a
two-ocean navy, because of the Panama Canal. He had an interesting
exchange with Senator Claude Pepper of Florida.

> Q.   What would be your attitude as to the policy of this
> country if Hitler should conquer England and proceed to take
> over and occupy the British bases in what is regarded as this
> hemisphere?
> A.   I would not let him do it.
> Q.   What would you do to prevent it?
> A.   Attack him. . . .
> Q.   You said England was not going to be conquered. Do
> you think she has the means of producing enough materials of
> war to continue to defend herself against Hitler without aid
> from this country?
> A.   I am certain of it. . . . If Britain were in any serious
> danger of invasion, can you imagine her sending a huge motor-

ized army corps to Libya. Would she not keep those machines in England? That is evidence to me.

Q. So you think it would be all right for us to cut now the arteries of supply to England?

A. If there is to be an invasion of the continent she will need many munitions from this country and several million men . . . and I am against that. I am willing to furnish material to Britain for her own defense, but not to carry a great and terrible war to the continent of Europe. She should have whatever she needs for defense—and I do not think she needs anything.

McCormick's appearance actually did very little good for the isolationist cause, and certain proadministration journals made fun of the way the Colonel handled himself. A certain egocentricity (and fatuousness) antagonized and amused opponents. The Colonel did not seem realistic even to his political allies. Senator Carter Glass of Virginia summed up best what many proadministration minds were thinking when he said, "I think that if things are as serene as Col. McCormick imagines the congress ought to pass the normal appropriations and go home."[36] McCormick was obviously not as formidable working alone as he was surrounded by a corps of very able editorial writers.

One of the most arresting aspects of the Colonel's testimony pointed up the differences between him and such conservative leaders as Senator Robert Taft of Ohio and former President Herbert Hoover. Hoover openly and proudly supported "maximum aid" to Great Britain. He suggested that as the United States was unprepared for war, it was to the United Kingdom's interest for America to remain neutral. If the United States joined the war, Hoover asserted, it would have to join in earnest and consequently would be forced to use a larger portion of its production to supply its own army. This would hurt Britain during "her most critical period." Senator Robert Taft held to a similar viewpoint, arguing that the United States should give RFC loans of one billion dollars to England and one half billion to Canada, both of which could be increased if that should prove necessary. House Minority Leader Joseph Martin agreed with this viewpoint, often privately supporting President Roosevelt, although publicly opposing him for reasons of partisanship. This was apparently true of many of the Republicans in congress, who dutifully voted against the president in full realization that their votes would be on the losing side, secretly hoping to be on the losing side. McCormick, by comparison, isolated himself from the Republican leadership by denying Britain's need for aid, and even refusing to admit that a crisis existed. His attitudes were closer to those of Charles Lindbergh and Democratic Senator Burton Wheeler, than to Hoover's and Taft's.[37]

The main tie uniting all these divergent viewpoints was common distrust of Roosevelt's motives. Even Hoover and Taft opposed lend-lease because they believed it would allow the president to create a dictatorship. The conservative opposition to the administration's foreign policy was worried that the nation would be subjected to more "New Deal" measures because of war conditions. By contrast liberal opponents of lend-lease, men such as Robert Hutchins, Norman Thomas, and Charles Beard felt that Roosevelt's "obsession" with foreign policy indicated that he would neglect needed domestic reform. A seemingly valid generalization can be made that most "isolationists," liberal or conservative, opposed lend-lease because of its domestic implications.[38]

The great majority of the conservative "isolationists" would have agreed that the president had singled out the wrong enemy. Supporters of the administration agreed that Hitler's Germany constituted the worst menace to United States security, and indeed to world civilization. Most conservative opponents of Roosevelt believed instead that Stalin's nation posed the chief threat to western civilization, and that communism was, if anything, more evil than fascism and probably would be the end result of a war. Perhaps, so the wistful thoughts ran, if Britain negotiated peace, Germany could be induced to turn on the arch-enemy Russia.

With the passage of the lend-lease bill, the *Tribune*'s tone grew more harsh and strident. Probably it realized that the fight was lost. It became increasingly sensitive to the jibes of its opponents, whereas earlier it had wisely chosen to ignore them as if they were not worthy of its measured attention. When the afternoon *Chicago Times* and *Chicago Daily News* began to criticize *Tribune* policies for being soft on Hitlerism, the *Tribune* retorted in a scathing editorial head-

lined THESE JACKALS GROW TOO BOLD. It declared, "these newspapers are so deeply in debt that whoever may be held up as the
editor or manager is little more than an office boy for the creditors."
More to the point perhaps, it lambasted Hitler's system of government: "We hate it in Italy, we hate it in Russia, and we hate it in
the United States." Along the same line, a few days later the *Tribune*
announced that the Democratic party had become the fascist party
in the United States. Harold Ickes, always a convenient whipping
boy, was especially singled out for his devotion to Nazi methods.
"Mr. Ickes has some of the physical as well as mental characteristics
of Herr Goebbels, the Nazi minister of propaganda." The only difference between the two, so far as the *Tribune* could see, was that
Ickes, "that nasty old man," lacked "only opportunity to deal with
victims summarily."

The attacks on other administration leaders were on an equal
level. The newspaper described the "warmongers" as "fat old men,
senile hysterics, and able bodied men in bombproof public positions
who devote their every energy to stirring up wars for other men to
fight." It concluded, "They are pathological cases, men with the
psychology of women" (with implications of homosexuality), and
the policies they advocated could "carry little weight with normal
men or women." The attacks rose as a crescendo upon the president.
According to the *Tribune,* during the American Revolution all the
Roosevelts had been Tories and disloyal to the patriot cause. "The
President's branch of the Roosevelt family," it thundered, "has yet
to put a man in uniform on a firing line in the whole history of the
country." Perhaps these were the reasons Franklin Roosevelt gravi-
tated toward London as if it were the center of the universe. The
infuriating attacks only demonstrated the *Tribune*'s sense of defeat
after lend-lease.[39]

But the German invasion of the USSR brought a new element into
the war, and a renewal of hope to the Colonel. The *Tribune* had
consistently asserted that Stalin was worse than Hitler and Mussolini,
and that his acts had "a cruelty and a callousness which even the
others could not equal." As mentioned, one of the chief differences
between the interventionists and most "isolationists" appeared to
be that the former thought Hitler was the worst menace facing the

United States whereas the latter tended to think Stalin earned that dubious honor. It was to the credit of the perspicacity of the *Tribune's* foreign correspondents that Germany's attack on the Soviet Union came as no surprise. Neither did the high quality of the Russian resistance. As early as April, 1941, Donald Day had reported that Germans in Finland and Sweden were whispering about an imminent attack on the Soviet Union and that the German high command had virtually completed its plans. If the newspaper had emphasized this story more it might have been one of the most famous scoops in journalism. But the tendency at the *Tribune* by 1941 was to be skeptical of much of Day's reporting. McCormick's personal aide, Captain Maxwell Corpening, had visited the USSR in early 1941 and found that it was the most underrated of all the great powers. The Soviets, he asserted, had used inferior troops in Finland. (Corpening also contended that Japan was the most overrated power, and that Germany was being weakened because of the poor state of its railroads.)[40]

On June 15, 1941, an eight-column front-page headline featured the news: HITLER–STALIN CRISIS NEAR. (The *Tribune*, however, was not alone among American newspapers in sniffing trouble.) Seven days later, an editorial pointed out that war between the Soviet Union and Germany would be a blessing to mankind. This was printed before the editors knew of the attack by German troops on Russian soil. When the news was announced, the *Tribune* was jubilant. It thought that the attack completely undercut all the arguments of the interventionists that Great Britain was in danger of being defeated.

> The German declaration of war against Russia has cut the ground from under the war party in this country.
> They said they must go to war to save Britain from invasion. Britain is no longer threatened with invasion. German air power must be concentrated against the new enemy. So must German land power. . . .
> The news is hardly less welcome in this country than in Britain, for it means that if there ever was any justification for our intervention in arms that justification no longer exists. The heat is off. The pressure upon us is relaxed. . . .[41]

Hopes for American neutrality which had disappeared after lend-lease, now revived.

The *Tribune* believed that the best way for peace would be for Stalin and Hitler to destroy each other. The entry of the Soviet Union into the war only strengthened the newspaper's conviction that this was a war for nothing but empire, a "struggle for the keys to world domination" (hence presumably a threat to United States security), and not a fight for the four freedoms or "for anything that could be called democracy." The newspaper was realistic enough to anticipate the strength of Soviet resistance. Colonel McCormick, leaning on his experience as an observer of the Russian military forces in 1915, declared over the radio in July, 1941, that the Russians had fought well in World War I and could be expected to do so again. Captain Corpening, in analyzing the strength of the Soviet army, pointed out its excellent equipment and the good physical condition of the troops.[42]

To McCormick, the invasion of the USSR changed the whole complexion of the fighting and brought hope for the eventual defeat of communism. More than ever the time was now propitious for Great Britain to make peace with Hitler's Germany, so the Nazi troops could invade the USSR without a strong enemy at their back. Donald Day, reporting from Helsinki in August, 1941 declared that Churchill was in trouble with British Catholic leaders for carrying on the war and accepting communism as an ally. The *Tribune* asserted that if peace could be made between Britain and Germany, few tears would be shed as long as Hitler was bought off "at the expense of Russia." By August, 1941, McCormick believed (prematurely) that the Germans had won their fight. At last, according to the Colonel, Hitler had succeeded in accomplishing one great task: he had "destroyed Stalin and communism" and wiped out the Bolshevik menace. Naturally the *Tribune* was shocked when Roosevelt moved to extend aid to the beleaguered Soviet leaders—aid which could only improve communism's chances for survival—and thus it supported Illinois congressman Stephen Day's resolution which would have barred sending lend-lease supplies to the Soviet Union.[43]

If McCormick had nothing good to say about the Soviet resistance

September 30, 1941

to Germany, Britain came off little better, although by July, 1941, he was shifting his grounds of attack. Ironically the exigencies of war required the newspaper to adopt a position rather similar to Stalin's. According to the Colonel, Britain was contributing nothing to the fighting and desired American intervention just so the English would not need to fight any longer and could continue their war profiteering. The newspaper denounced a British editor for speaking of "pouring blood down a common drain" and overlooking "the fact that the British have done precious little pouring themselves." It taunted the Churchill government for refusing to open a second front, and also for not permitting food shipments to slip through the blockade resulting in the "slaughter of the babies in France and the other conquered countries." By following such a policy Churchill was "blinded by partisanship."[44]

Since Roosevelt continued issuing aid to Great Britain and the USSR, the *Tribune* asserted that he must really be a communist. Somewhat inconsistently, and passing beyond rational criticism, it claimed he was also helping the Allies because of his insatiable desire to be surrounded by European kings and queens, fawning for his favor. A McCutcheon cartoon sadly noted that the only royalty not yet entertained or getting an audience at the White House was Jesus—"The Prince of Peace." An editorial commented:

> A photograph reproduced on page 5 of the picture section of this morning's TRIBUNE tells a story the importance of which can hardly be exaggerated. The photograph shows Crown Princess Juliana of the Netherlands bending the knees in greeting to Mrs. Roosevelt. Mrs. Roosevelt is obviously enjoying the experience. Evidently those in the White House take great satisfaction in having a deferential royalty around for hardly a week goes by without a visit from one or another of the crowned heads. That is one reason, and in our judgment a most important one, for the hysterical attitude of the Roosevelts in the world crisis.[45]

As time passed, the *Tribune* lost the flicker of hope it had sustained after the Nazi invasion of the USSR. The newspaper now urged the president to ask congress for a declaration of war (so he would be defeated), but obviously Roosevelt was not to fall into such an evident political trap. It continued to support America First, but even this organization produced disillusionment. The newspaper's great hero had been Colonel Charles Lindbergh, but when Lindbergh untactfully asserted in Des Moines, Iowa, that the Jewish people were leading the United States to war, the *Tribune* regretfully was forced to disavow him:

> Attention has already been called in these columns to the impropriety of Col. Lindbergh's reference to the Jews in his Des Moines speech. The remark was ill-considered in several senses. Every one will agree that it violated a cardinal principal of public discussion in this country; and every one who is aware of the facts will reject the inference that all Jews, or most Jews, in this country are citizens whose loyalty is divided. That is not true and it should not have been said or suggested.

The *Tribune* staff feared that Lindbergh's unfortunate remarks would discredit the entire movement. Thus the newspaper criticized the America First Committee for not having examined the address in advance. After that debacle the paper discontinued its practice of reporting Lindbergh's speeches in full.[46]

Tribune hopes were to rise once more—when it managed to unearth one of the most famous scoops in newspaper history, a scoop which it believed would finally discredit the administration's influence in Congress and among the American people. On December 4, 1941, its banner headline screamed—with the largest print ever used by the newspaper: F.D.R.'S WAR PLANS! What the *Tribune* printed was a strategic plan framed by the War Department to be used in case the United States should declare war against Germany. The plan was made at the order of President Roosevelt who, on July 9, 1941, charged Secretary Stimson with the responsibility of "exploring at once the over-all production requirements required to defeat our potential enemies." The plan called for the drafting of over ten million men into the armed forces, and a joint American-British invasion of the European continent on July 1, 1943, with a force of five million men in 215 divisions. The authors of the document were "convinced that the first major objective of the United States and its associates should be the complete military defeat of Germany." Thus they anticipated the policy of unconditional sur-

2 CENTS PAY NO MORE!

Chicago Daily Tribune

THE WORLD'S GREATEST NEWSPAPER

FINAL ★★

VOLUME C—NO. 290 C

THURSDAY, DECEMBER 4, 1941.—46 PAGES

PRICE TWO CENTS

F.D.R.'S WAR PLANS!

REDS BEGIN NEW DRIVE TO BREAK VISE ON MOSCOW

Strike at Nazi Line South of Leningrad.

BULLETIN.
BERNE, Switzerland, Dec 4

LEIBER TRADED TO GIANTS; CUBS GET BOWMAN

The Chicago Cubs early this morning traded Outfielder Hank Leiber to the New York Giants for Pitcher Bob Bowman and an unannounced sum of cash.

HOUSE ADOPTS DRASTIC BILL TO BLOCK STRIKES

Goes to Senate on 252-136 Vote.

BY WILLIAM STRAND

NEWS SUMMARY
of The Tribune

WAR SITUATION.

THE STRONGHOLD OF PEACE

GOAL IS 10 MILLION ARMED MEN; HALF TO FIGHT IN AEF

Proposes Land Drive by July 1, 1943, to Smash Nazis; President Told of Equipment Shortage.

BY CHESLY MANLY

REVEAL TURKEY GETS LEND-LEASE GOODS SINCE MAY

BY WALTER TROHAN

Woman Slays Insane Brother as 'Mercy' Act

"YOU KNOW BETTER"

Country Kids Prove Smart as Quiz Kind

SCIENCE PINCHES HALF OF AN INCH OFF CLOTHESPINS

New York, Dec. 3 (Special)

BLIND DOG PLUNGES FROM RISING BRIDGE INTO RIVER; RESCUED

British Return 17 More Oil Ships, Ickes Reports

Engineers Award Medal to Garand, Rifle Inventor

THE WEATHER

OCTOBER. 1941
1,000,000
THE CHICAGO TRIBUNE

Only **18** Shopping days till Christmas

December 4, 1941

render long before such a policy was officially announced. The document revealed for the first time the strategy of the American-British leadership which sought the defeat of Germany first "while holding Japan in check." It significantly stated that Great Britain and the Soviet Union alone could not defeat Germany and that an American expeditionary force would be required to accomplish that task. To the administration's discomfort the document was authentic. Chesly Manly was the *Tribune* reporter responsible for the story. In a congratulatory wire to Manly, McCormick rejoiced that it was "perhaps the greatest scoop in the history of journalism." That praise may have been too generous, but the story sorely embarrassed the administration.[47]

At his news conference the following day, President Roosevelt referred the reporters to the Secretary of War. Stimson in turn was sulphuric. He stated that the "war plans" document was merely a study formulated for the fighting of a potential war (although the plan itself referred to United States entry into the war as necessary to the defeat of Germany). "What would you think," he asked, "of an American General Staff which in the present condition of the world did not investigate and study every conceivable type of emergency which may confront this country and every possible method of meeting the emergency?" He heaped scorn upon McCormick. "What do you think," he queried again, "of the patriotism of a man or a newspaper that would take those confidential studies and make them public to the enemies of this country? Doubtless," he continued, "the publication of the papers would be a gratification to our potential enemies." In his diary, Harold Ickes voiced the belief that the charge of treason should be hurled immediately at McCormick. Attorney General Francis Biddle menacingly stated that it was his considered opinion that the *Tribune* had violated the Espionage Act.[48]

Government officials searched tirelessly for the leak but never found it. The full story has not been told even today. Albert C. Wedemeyer, who was responsible for formulating the army sections of the plan, was repeatedly questioned. John J. McCloy warned Wedemeyer, "Wedemeyer, there's blood on the fingers of the man who leaked the information about our war plans." One copy of the document had been sent to the secretary of war (Stimson), one to the assistant secretary of war (McCloy), one to the chief of staff (Marshall), one to the chief of war plans division (General Leonard T. Gerow), and one copy had been retained by Wedemeyer. The questioning did not stop with the hapless Wedemeyer. Senator Walsh of Massachusetts told Senator Wheeler of Montana that he was trailed by government agents for several days. Chesly Manly naturally was questioned but maintained, quite properly, that as a reporter he could not disclose his source.[49]

Not until 1962 were some of the facts released. Burton K. Wheeler in his autobiography published that year announced that it was he who gave the document to Manly. A "worried army captain" who had access to the plan delivered it to Wheeler on December 3, 1941. The senator decided to disclose its contents to Manly since in his estimation its publication would not aid the Axis—it was a set of estimates or a prospectus rather than an actual operational war plan. But it was based "on the conclusion that the United States would soon have to wage a global war if Germany and Japan were to be defeated." It was political dynamite, perhaps just the information the isolationists needed to defeat Roosevelt in his seemingly inexorable drive toward war. Wheeler did not take the document to the Senate Foreign Relations Committee because he was sure it would bury it. Instead he wanted publicity. Thus he sought out Manly whom he knew and liked, and who worked for a newspaper which would give the plan the kind of attention it deserved. Wheeler said:

> Manly was as startled and fascinated as I was by the report, I arranged for him to come to my home that evening to make extracts. There for several hours we selected the most important selections and had them copied in shorthand by one of my secretaries. The document had to be back in the hands of the army officer by early morning so it could be returned to its niche in the War Department.[50]

Unfortunately for the dramatic value of the scoop, Pearl Harbor intervened in three days. But the *Tribune* milked it for all it was worth in the few days it had at its disposal.

Mr. Manly's great scoop has brought the discussion of national policy down to earth. There can no longer be any doubt what the administration intends. . . . Mr. Roosevelt and those about him think that the preservation of the British empire and the four freedoms for Chinamen are worth the lives of a million American boys and a couple of hundred billion dollars to boot. He didn't talk that way when he was a candidate for the third term, just a little more than a year ago. If he had he would have been defeated as a madman.[51]

The German leaders read the *Tribune* scoop carefully, apparently taking it at face value. When Hitler declared war upon the United States on December 11, one of his stated reasons was this "war plan." "Thus," the Führer thundered, "our patience has come to the breaking point." Ironically, the *Tribune* scoop, instead of accomplishing its aim of discrediting Roosevelt, simply became a convenient scapegoat for the German dictator.[52]

With the European war dominating the daily news, the *Tribune* tended to forget about the Japanese. The newspaper inexplicably failed to replace John Powell whom it had summarily fired in 1937. Kempei Sheba, a Nisei, reported news from Tokyo but his reports were rarely used by the home office. Thus, the *Chicago Tribune,* in reporting news from the Pacific had to depend upon outside news services. It was reporting blindly and resolved the problem in the worst possible fashion by almost totally neglecting the Sino-Japanese War and its implications for American security.

From 1939 to 1941 the *Tribune* hewed closely to the viewpoint it had espoused in the previous decade: reduce the areas of contention with Japan, halt all aid to China, get out of the Philippines, remove all marines from China, and do nothing to provoke the Japanese. "Japan's policy in China is an asiatic question. It does not affect this hemisphere. It does not fall within the police duties of the United States." Since the fate of China should not be the concern of American statesmanship, the China trade was not worth the life of a single United States marine. This line thus reversed the *Tribune* policy of some years past. The *Tribune* could not understand why Roosevelt had adopted such stern policies toward the Japanese government—except on the grounds that he was trying to

1939, 1940, 1941

protect British, French, and Dutch interests in the Far East. In a prescient editorial, the *Tribune* in September, 1940, warned that the Far East would prove a morass for American fighting power.

> If we prevent Japan from taking Indo-China from the French, the East Indies from the Dutch, etc., we have solved no problems. We have only assumed a responsibility for the future of those territories. We don't want them and whoever has them, whether native governments or someone else, will hold them thanks to our power to maintain the status quo which we shall have created. That means a continuing liability. It means that we must, at any moment, be ready to defend these places,' 6,000 miles and more from our shores, against any nation or combination of nations which may court them.[53]

Not so presciently the *Tribune* entirely dismissed the possibility of war with Japan. "Is the badly shaken Japan about to assault Hawaii or even the Philippines?" it asked rhetorically in July, 1941. The implied answer of course was no. As late as the end of November, 1941, the *Tribune* optimistically claimed: "The only person or body which does not seem to think that we are about to go to war with Japan is also the only body that can sanction such a war. That is the congress of the United States."[54]

The *Tribune* continued to argue that if anybody were the aggressor in the Pacific it was the American government. This was to anticipate a trend of historiography which appeared after 1945. It urged the government not to fortify Guam, for this would be equivalent to the Japanese fortifying a Japanese island in American waters. In its opinion American gasoline only served to drive the Japanese government further into the open arms of Hitler. Arthur Sears Henning, in late October, 1941, argued that the American viewpoint was too unyielding; indeed he speculated that Japan had offered great concessions to the United States. The concessions included an offer to withdraw from the Axis, to withdraw from China (except for two air bases to be retained on Chinese soil), and to make no further moves toward the British and Dutch colonies in the East Indies. This story was inaccurate, but it is characteristic that the *Tribune* accepted it as truth, taking the mendacity of the

United States government for granted. Above all an American war against Japan would be unjust and inhumane.

> In these circumstances we are facing the possibility that the American navy will come to grips with the Japanese in the far east and American bombers will be destroying the populous Japanese cities, whose flimsy construction would invite disaster. No doubt there are many people who would think this a just retaliation for the fury the Japanese have expended on China, but some undoubtedly will not regard it as the noblest work of American military power, even if it visits on Japan what the Japanese people have permitted their military to do to the Chinese.[55]

Basically, however, the *Tribune* was surprised by Pearl Harbor. It had become so preoccupied with the war in Europe and with domestic politics that it had not devoted much attention to the worsening relations between Japan and the United States. An analysis of sixteen Canadian and United States papers demonstrates that the *Tribune* devoted less headline space to the crisis than any other newspaper.[56] For three days before Pearl Harbor, December 5, 6, and 7, respectively, the *New York Times*'s headlines emphasized Far Eastern news.

> TOKYO REPORTS HULL PLAN IMPOSSIBLE;
> JAPANESE HAND IN THEIR REPLY TODAY;
> RUSSIANS PRESS THE RETREATING NAZIS
>
> ARMY SENT SOUTH ONLY TO CHECK CHINA,
> TOKYO REPLIES TO ROOSEVELT INQUIRY;
> BRITAIN DECLARES WAR ON 3 NAZI ALLIES
>
> ROOSEVELT APPEALS TO HIROHITO
> AFTER NEW THREAT IN INDO–CHINA
> GERMANS TRAPPED AT TAGANROG

The *New York Herald Tribune* also played up the Japanese crisis on December 5, 6, and 7:

> U.S. GETS JAPAN'S ANSWER TODAY;
> REJECTION OF HULL TERMS REPORTED;
> BREAKDOWN OF PARLEYS FORECAST

JAPAN TELLS U.S. INDO–CHINA ARMY
IS JUST A DEFENSE AGAINST CHINESE;
FAILS TO REPLY TO HULL PEACE TERMS

ROOSEVELT SENDS MESSAGE DIRECT TO EMPEROR OF JAPAN
TOKYO TROOP CONVOYS SIGHTED ON WAY TO GULF OF SIAM

Obviously a reader after perusing the front pages of the *New York Times* and the *New York Herald Tribune* would gain the accurate impression that a crisis was developing in the Far East. The *Chicago Tribune* failed to demonstrate the same news sense. Its banner headlines for December 5, 6, and 7 concentrated on items closer to McCormick's heart:

NATION STIRRED BY AEF PLAN

Nothing concerning the Japanese appeared on page one. Rather, the *Tribune* devoted most of its front-page space to congratulating itself on its "War Plans Scoop" of the previous day.

WAR ON FINNS! BRITISH ORDER

Still nothing on the front page regarding the Far Eastern crisis.

U.S. NAVY SEIZES FINN SHIPS

A subheadline on December 7 took note of the Japanese deployment of troops to Indo-China, but the emphasis still lay with British and U.S. mistreatment of Finland. Another subheadline on page one told of how the United States acted as BRITISH OPEN WAR ON LITTLE COUNTRY.

The *Tribune* had become so completely tied to certain pet ideas that it failed to notice where the real news stories were occurring. As a result the newspaper was caught off guard by Pearl Harbor—so surprised that it reversed its editorial position on December 8 and completely supported the administration in its new battle to win the war:

War has been forced on America by an insane clique of Japanese militarists who apparently see the desperate conflict into which they have led their country as the only thing that can prolong their power.

Thus the thing that we all feared, that so many of us have worked with all our hearts to avert, has happened. That is all that counts. It has happened. America faces war thru no volition of any American.

Recriminations are useless and we doubt that they will be indulged in. Certainly not by us. All that matters today is that we are in the war and the nation must face that simple fact. All of us, from this day forth, have only one task. That is to strike with all our might to protect and preserve the American freedom that we all hold dear.[57]

Although revisionist historians were later to blame Roosevelt for adopting a "back-door-to-war" policy which attempted to goad the Japanese into attacking, contemporary issues of the *Tribune* did not raise the accusation. In November and December of 1941, the newspaper took it for granted that war, if it came, could only be from Europe. It had forgotten the Far East, a commentary on the sad state of *Tribune* reporting from that area.

In any study of the *Tribune,* one wonders to what degree the newspaper spoke for its readers. The paper thrived by taking positions seemingly at complete variance with the majority of public opinion. Nowhere was this more true than during the controversy about whether the United States should have furnished aid to the Allies.

According to a Gallup poll, by December, 1941, 68 percent of the American people believed it was more important that Germany be defeated than that the United States stay out of the war. This figure had remained fairly constant throughout 1941. The polls by Gallup consistently found American public opinion to be traveling ahead of the president, leading him in his interventionist course, rather than the other way around. The Roper polls arrived at similar conclusions.[58]

On the other hand, the *Chicago Tribune* always argued that public opinion was far less belligerent than the president. To buttress this claim, it conducted an independent poll in the summer of 1941 which asked this question: "Shall the United States enter the war to help Britain defeat Hitler?" The paper sent a postcard to every tenth voter on the Chicago registration lists, the rest of Cook County, and the downstate cities of Cairo, Bloomington, Springfield, Rockford, Aurora, Peoria, East St. Louis, Danville, and Galesburg. The results demonstrated that 80.8 percent of the respondents were *opposed* to United States involvement in the war. The *New York Daily News,* the *Tribune*'s sister newspaper, conducted an identical poll which arrived at a similar conclusion—70.5 percent of the 174,000 people sending in a postcard declared against war. According to these polls (or at least the way they were interpreted by the two newspapers), American public opinion was strongly opposed to the Roosevelt foreign policy. The *Tribune* always claimed that the majority of the American public supported its viewpoint. It liked nothing better than to send out reporters interviewing the man-in-the-street, who somehow always turned out to be antagonistic to the president.[59]

Much of the discrepancy of course lay in the way each side worded its polls, and both the Gallup and *Tribune* samplings had their inherent bias. A person could very well believe that it was more important that Germany be defeated than that the United States remain out of the war (Gallup) and at the same time believe that it was not yet propitious to enter the war to help Britain defeat Hitler (*Tribune*); the two polls were asking different questions, but they were asking them in such a way as to force a yes answer.

Comparison of the Gallup and *Tribune* samplings demonstrates, if nothing else, that people's minds were inconsistent and confused on the basic question of whether America should enter the war. Thus interventionists could quote Gallup to their hearts' content, and isolationists complacently repeated the latest findings of the *Chicago Tribune,* both confident in the belief that they had the most up-to-date scientific polling techniques on their side. And the *Tribune* could make a deep imprint, even among pro-Roosevelt, Democratic voters, with its distrust of Britain and of communism, and its arguments that the president's actions were leading toward war. These assertions struck sensitive nerves in 1940–1941.

Although its opposition at times was carried to the point of irresponsibility, the *Tribune* in a way fulfilled a valuable function

December 31, 1940

in society—that of the gadfly always stinging away at the established order. This accorded with McCormick's views on the proper function of the press. In a speech before the Chicago Church Federation in 1924, the Colonel gave his "final definition" of the newspaper. "The newspaper," he asserted, "is an institution developed by modern civilization to present the news of the day, to foster commerce and industry through widely circulated advertisements, and to furnish that check upon government which no constitution has ever been able to provide."[60] Implicit in this definition was his idea that government and newspapers were natural enemies and the proper role of the press was to oppose the spread of government. Something was wrong with a newspaper which inordinately supported the government, *any* government. He proved faithful to this idea as long as he lived.

In spite of the fact that newspapers for the most part opposed the president, especially on domestic policy, Roosevelt was not entirely lacking in devices of his own to counteract this opposition. As Daniel Boorstin has noted, FDR was our "first nationally advertised President." Through masterly use of the radio and the press conference, Roosevelt was able to defy the opposition of the newspapers. And through occasional manipulation of the news, as in the *Greer* incident, the administration could blunt criticism.[61]

Many historians accept this manipulation. Thomas A. Bailey wrote in his *Man in the Street*:

> A president who cannot entrust the people with the truth betrays a certain lack of faith in the basic tenets of democracy. But because the masses are notoriously shortsighted, and generally cannot see danger until it is at their throats, our statesmen are forced to deceive them into an awareness of their own long-run interests. This is clearly what Roosevelt had to do, and who shall say that posterity will not thank him for it?[62]

In the context of World War II, posterity may very well give Roosevelt its thanks, but the implications of the policy are dangerous. It was newspapers like the *Tribune* which kept alive the American tradition of press freedom, and the right to ferret out the mistakes of the administration. The *Tribune* often used the right unwisely, and it certainly lacked responsibility in certain of its criticisms. But it did keep the tradition of free speech active, both in and out of wartime conditions, and probably also forced the Roosevelt administration to move more warily than it might otherwise have done.

One encounters difficulty in assessing the influence of the *Chicago Tribune*. Critics of the newspaper discounted its power, and often cited presidential election statistics which showed that Chicago voted consistently for Roosevelt by overwhelming margins. Obviously, they asserted, the *Tribune* could not even carry its own bailiwick. On the other hand, a considerable proportion of *Tribune* readers lived in the Chicago suburbs and the surrounding rural areas. In these places, consistent Republican majorities were reported.

In fact, the newspaper represented a wide spectrum of midwestern political sentiment. This can be seen most readily by analyzing the votes in the House of Representatives on crucial issues of the period 1939 to 1941. In November, 1938, the states of Illinois, Wisconsin, Iowa, and Indiana—areas where the *Tribune* had a wide distribution—elected thirty-two Republicans, twenty-four Democrats, and two Progressives. Two years later the Republicans increased their strength to thirty-seven, Democrats fell to eighteen, and Progressive representation rose to three.[63]

In analyzing the votes, one finds that the Republicans from these four states were almost unanimous in their disapproval of Roosevelt measures, whereas the Democrats were badly split. Some illustrations will suffice:

	Vote on the Fourth Neutrality Bill[64]			Renewal of the Reciprocal Trade Agreements Act[65]	
	Yes	*No*		*Yes*	*No*
Rep.	1	29	Rep.	0	30
Dem.	20	4	Dem.	22	0
Prog.	0	2	Prog.	0	1

	Selective Service Act[66]			Lend-Lease[67]	
	Yes	*No*		*Yes*	*No*
Rep.	0	32	Rep.	1	35
Dem.	16	5	Dem.	14	3
Prog.	0	2	Prog.	0	3

	Selective Service Extension[68]			Repeal of the Neutrality Acts[69]	
	Yes	No		Yes	No
Rep.	0	36	Rep.	2	35
Dem.	9	6	Dem.	12	4
Prog.	0	3	Prog.	0	3

An examination of these congressional votes indicates that the Republicans from "Chicagoland" (these four states) voted as a solid bloc (against Roosevelt 98 percent of the time) which the Democrats failed to do (only supporting Roosevelt 80 percent of the time). Furthermore the absentee rate among the Democrats (average—9 percent) was consistently higher than among the Republicans (average—3 percent). Thus the Republicans from this area were far more united against the president's foreign policy than the Democrats were for it. It was entirely possible the *Chicago Tribune* helped create the climate of opinion which solidified the Republicans and divided the Democrats.

A Gallup poll, released in the early days of 1941, showed that 58 percent of the American people favored lend-lease. Yet in the east central portion of the United States, comprising Illinois, Indiana, Michigan, and Ohio, only 39 percent were in favor of the bill. The *Tribune* undoubtedly contributed to this unfavorable result. People were not simply divided between "interventionists" and "isolationists." There was a complex of factors pulling them each way. As a result it was possible for the *Tribune* editorial views to appeal to a wider clientele than just the narrow "isolationist" group. The mere fact that so many liberals were vehement in their criticisms of the newspaper would indicate a fear of its influence. Although they claimed otherwise, they obviously did not believe they were fighting an impotent force.[70]

Even if the *Tribune* did not convert Democrats, which is difficult to prove or disprove, it certainly reinforced the intransigence of midwestern Republicanism. Robert R. McCormick was indisputably the most powerful Republican in Illinois, and after the defeat of William Hale Thompson in 1931, had little opposition in state party circles. Surely he was partly responsible for imparting the strongly isolationist tone that midwestern Republicanism had at the time.

$\mathfrak{N}$OTES

1. *Chicago Tribune,* September 2, 1939, 10:2.

2. *Ibid.,* September 3, 1939, 1:1; Robert R. McCormick, *An Address Delivered at the University of Notre Dame, July 29, 1939* (Chicago: The Tribune Company, 1939), p. 30.

3. *Chicago Tribune,* October 2, 1939, 12:2; October 18, 1939, 16:2.

4. *Ibid.,* September 26, 1939, 10:1; October 1, 1939, 16:2.

5. *Ibid.,* December 1, 1939, 18:1.

6. *Ibid.,* December 20, 1939, 18:1; December 28, 1939, 12:2; December 29, 1939, 8:2.

7. *Ibid.,* January 12, 1940, 1:7; January 14, 1940, 3:2; *Editor and Publisher,* LXXIII (January 13, 1940), 4.

8. *Chicago Tribune,* February 12, 1940, 1:7; February 22, 1940, 14:1; March 6, 1940, 14:1.

9. *Ibid.,* September 27, 1939, 2:2; October 22, 1939, 16:1.

10. *Ibid.,* December 7, 1939, 14:2; December 30, 1939, 6:2; January 16, 1940, p. 1; February 21, 1940, 12:2; February 22, 1940, p. 1.

11. *Ibid.,* September 26, 1939, 10:2.

12. *Ibid.,* April 6, 1940, 12:1–2; April 22, 1940, 12:1. This is also the thesis advanced in Chesly Manly, *The Twenty-Year Revolution from Roosevelt to Eisenhower* (Chicago: Henry Regnery Company, 1954), p. 76.

13. *Chicago Tribune,* March 24, 1940, 14:3; June 8, 1940, 12:1.

14. *Ibid.,* April 10, 1940, 18:1; May 2, 1940, 14:1.

15. *Ibid.,* May 12, 1940, 16:2; June 14, 1940, 14:1; interview with Chesly Manly.

16. *Chicago Tribune,* May 23, 1940, 16:2.

17. *Ibid.,* June 13, 1940, 16:1; June 17, 1940, 1:4; June 18, 1940, 12:1; June 20, 1940, 12:2–3.

18. *Ibid.,* June 7, 1940, 1:6; June 8, 1940, 12:1; Walter Johnson, *The Battle against Isolation,* p. 2.

19. *Ibid.,* June 10, 1940, 3:4; June 21, 1940, 14:1; July 8, 1940, 3:4; July 11, 1940, 12:1; July 22, 1940, 10:2; Walter Johnson, *The Battle against Isolation,* p. 2.

20. *Chicago Tribune,* May 27, 1940, 10:1; July 22, 1940, 10:2; July 23, 1940, 10:1; August 6, 1940, 10:1; September 4, 1940, 14:1.

21. *Ibid.,* September 5, 1940, 16:1.

22. *Ibid.*, June 14, 1940, 14:2; June 23, 1940, 16:2; June 30, 1940, 10:2; Jack Alexander, "The World's Greatest Newspaper," *The Saturday Evening Post*, CCXIV (July 26, 1941), 88; Donald Bruce Johnson, *The Republican Party and Wendell Willkie* (Urbana: The University of Illinois Press, 1960), pp. 111, 117; Mary Earhart Dillon, *Wendell Willkie* (Philadelphia: J. B. Lippincott Company, 1952), pp. 161–63.

23. *Chicago Tribune*, July 17, 1940, 12:1; July 29, 1940, 1:8.

24. Harold L. Ickes, *Freedom of the Press Today: a Clinical Examination by 28 Specialists* (New York: The Vanguard Press, 1941), p. 9.

25. *Chicago Tribune*, October 5, 1940, 7:1; October 21, 1940, 1:1; October 28, 1940, p. 8; October 29, 1940, 12:1; October 31, 1940, 1:6; November 1, 1940, 1:3; Grace Tully, *F.D.R., My Boss* (New York: C. Scribner's Sons, 1949), pp. 152–53.

26. *Chicago Tribune*, November 3, 1940, 1:7; November 5, 1940, p. 1; November 7, 1940, 14:2; December 10, 1940, 16:2.

27. *Ibid.*, October 7, 1940, p. 3; Porter Sargent, *Getting Us into War* (Boston: Porter Sargent, 1941), pp. 414, 431; Robert R. McCormick, "Can America Fight in Europe," *Scribner's Commentator*, IX (January, 1941), 90.

28. *Chicago Tribune*, November 25, 1940, 14:1; December 5, 1940, p. 1; December 8, 1940, 26:2.

29. *Ibid.*, December 9, 1940, 14:1.

30. *Ibid.*, December 11, 1940, 16:2; December 15, 1940, 18:1–2; Robert R. McCormick, "Our Republic Is at Stake, Heed Well the Warning," *Vital Speeches of the Day*, VI (March 15, 1940), 330.

31. *Chicago Tribune*, January 11, 1941, p. 1.

32. *Ibid.*, January 15, 1941, 12:1.

33. *Ibid.*, January 18, 1941, 8:1; February 15, 1941; February 17, 1941, 1:1; Sargent, p. 423; Joseph Barnes, *Willkie* (New York: Simon and Schuster, 1952), p. 256.

34. *Chicago Tribune*, February 17, 1941, 10:1; February 25, 1941, 4:3, 10:1–2.

35. *Ibid.*, January 21, 1941, 1:8; February 1, 1941, 1:1; March 10, 1941; Wayne S. Cole, *America First: The Battle against Intervention, 1940–1941* (Madison: The University of Wisconsin Press, 1953), p. 49.

36. *Chicago Tribune*, February 7, 1941, p. 6. The *Tribune* was not overly appreciative of Senator Pepper's questioning and in May, 1941, called him the "spotted screamer of the Everglades," *Chicago Tribune*, May 12, 1941. United States Senate, *Hearings before the Committee on Foreign Relations, United States Senate, Seventy-Seventh Congress, First*

Session on S. 275. A Bill Further to Promote the Defense of the United States and for Other Purposes, Part 2. February 4 to February 10, 1941.

37.   Nancy Schoonmaker and Doris Fielding Reid (eds.), *We Testify* (New York: Smith & Durrell, Inc., 1941), pp. 3–12, 215–29; John Paul Armstrong, "Senator Taft and American Foreign Policy: The Period of Opposition" (unpublished Ph.D. dissertation, University of Chicago, 1953), p. 27; Joseph Martin, pp. 96–98.

38.   Herbert Hoover, *Addresses upon the American Road, 1940–1941* (New York: Charles Scribner's Sons, 1941), p. 50; Schoonmaker and Reid, pp. 37–45, 63–81, 151–65, 187–96, 199–211, 215–29.

39.   *Chicago Tribune,* March 22, 1941, 10:1; April 15, 1941, 14:2; May 13, 1941, 12:1; May 15, 1941, 12:1; May 18, 1941, 16:2.

40.   *Ibid.,* April 10, 1941, 1:5; April 15, 1941, 14:1; May 8, 1941, 12:2.

41.   *Ibid.,* June 15, 1941, p. 1; June 22, 1941, 14:1; June 23, 1941, 10:1.

42.   *Ibid.,* July 12, 1941, 6:1; July 20, 1941; July 27, 1941, 1:1; Raymond H. Dawson, *The Decision to Aid Russia, 1941: Foreign Policy and Domestic Politics* (Chapel Hill: The University of North Carolina Press, 1959), pp. 80–81; Robert R. McCormick, "The Lessons of This War, The Appalling Cost of Ignorance," *Vital Speeches of the Day,* VII (August 15, 1941), 645; James MacGregor Burns, *Roosevelt: The Soldier of Freedom* (New York: Harcourt Brace Jovanovich, 1970), pp. 111–12.

43.   *Chicago Tribune,* August 9, 1941, 6:1; August 24, 1941; August 28, 1941, 4:5; September 21, 1941, p. 3; Dawson, p. 281; William Cecil Rogers, "Isolationist Propaganda, September 1, 1939 to December 7, 1941" (unpublished Ph.D. dissertation, University of Chicago, 1943), p. 49.

44.   *Chicago Tribune,* July 6, 1941, 8:1; October 27, 1941, 12:1; October 31, 1941, 14:2; November 4, 1941, p. 1, 12:1.

45.   *Ibid.,* June 29, 1941, 12:1; June 30, 1941, 10:1; September 24, 1941, 16:1; October 26, 1941, p. 1.

46.   *Ibid.,* August 24, 1941, 14:2; September 20, 1941, 10:2; September 24, 1941, 16:1; October 4, 1941, p. 31; October 24, 1941, 14:1; Helen Murchie Costello, "Col. McCormick's Tribune: 1910–41," *New Republic,* CV (December 1, 1941), 724–27; Cole, *America First,* p. 251; interview with a *Tribune* executive; *New York Times,* September 12, 1941, 2:7, 3:8; Charles Lindbergh, *The Wartime Journals of Charles A. Lindbergh* (New York: Harcourt Brace Jovanovich, 1970), pp. 536–42.

47.   *Chicago Tribune,* December 4, 1941, p. 1; *Congressional Record, Appendix,* LXXXVII, Part 14 (Washington: Government Printing Office,

1942), A5448–51; Burton K. Wheeler, *Yankee from the West* (Garden City, N.Y.: Doubleday & Company, Inc., 1962), p. 34; William L. Langer and S. Everett Gleason, *The Undeclared War, 1940–1941* (New York: Harper & Brothers Publishers, 1953), p. 923.

48.   *New York Times*, December 6, 1941, 3:1; Ickes, III, 659; Andrews, p. 295; Seldes, *Facts and Fascism*, p. 86.

49.   Interview with Chesly Manly; Wheeler, p. 36; Albert C. Wedemeyer, *Wedemeyer Reports* (New York: Henry Holt & Company, 1958), p. 21.

50.   Wheeler, p. 3.

51.   *Chicago Tribune*, December 5, 1941, 18:2.

52.   *New York Times*, December 12, 1941, 4:8; Seldes, *Facts and Fascism*, p. 215; John L. Balderston, *Chicago Blueprint* (New York: Alfred A. Knopf, 1943), pp. 5, 90. The Nazi leaders paid considerable heed to the attacks of the *Chicago Tribune* hoping that they would encourage the growth of "the little plant of Anglo-American enmity," *The Goebbels Diaries*, ed. and trans. Louis P. Lochner (New York: Popular Library, Inc., 1948), pp. 261–62.

53.   *Chicago Tribune*, September 1, 1939, 14:1; September 23, 1939, 10:2; September 28, 1940, 10:1; Langer and Gleason, *The Challenge to Isolation*, p. 601.

54.   *Chicago Tribune*, July 21, 1941, p. 1; November 29, 1941, 12:1.

55.   *Ibid.*, April 20, 1940, 10:1; June 13, 1941, 10:1; October 27, 1941, 12:2; December 2, 1941, 14:1; George Morgenstern, *Pearl Harbor: The Story of the Secret War* (New York: The Devin-Adair Company, 947), p. 104; Walter Johnson, *William Allen White's America* (New York: Henry Holt and Company, 1947), pp. 534–35.

56.   The newspapers were *New York Times, New York Herald Tribune, Globe and Mail* (Toronto), *PM* (New York), *St. Louis Post Dispatch, Atlanta Constitution, Chicago Daily News, Chicago Tribune, Chicago Sun, Courier-Journal* (Louisville), *Detroit News, Des Moines Register, Winnipeg Free Press, Washington Post,* and *Daily Worker.*

57.   *Chicago Tribune*, December 8, 1941, quoted in Chicago Tribune, *A Century of Tribune Editorials*, p. 131.

58.   William A. Lydgate, *What America Thinks* (New York: Thomas Y. Crowell Company, 1944), pp. 32–36; Elmo Roper, *You and Your Leaders: Their Actions and Your Reactions, 1936–1956* (New York: William Morrow and Company, 1957), pp. 49–50.

59.   *Chicago Tribune*, June 28, 1941, 1:7; July 15, 1941; August 25, 1941, 1:1; Rogers, p. 50.

60.   Robert R. McCormick, *What Is a Newspaper: A Talk before the*

Chicago Church Federation at the Hotel Morrison, October 27, 1924 (Chicago: The Tribune Company, 1927).

61.   Daniel J. Boorstin, "Selling the President to the People," Commentary, XX (November, 1955), 421. A more sympathetic view of Roosevelt's selling techniques is given by Walter Johnson, *1600 Pennsylvania Avenue: Presidents and the People* (Boston: Little, Brown and Company, 1960), pp. 189–91.

62.   Thomas A. Bailey, *The Man in the Street* (New York: The Macmillan Company, 1948), p. 13.

63.   In 1938 in these four states the Republican candidates for the House received a plurality of approximately 125,000; in 1940 this increased to 250,000. Roosevelt on the other hand carried the area by 50,000 votes. See U.S., *Congressional Directory,* 78th Cong., 1st Sess., 1942, p. 252.

64.   This was the "Cash and Carry" Bill, passed November 3, 1939, U.S., *Congressional Record,* 76th Cong., 2nd Sess., 1939, LXXXV, Part 2, 1389.

65.   Passed February 23, 1940. U.S., *Congressional Record,* 76th Cong., 3d Sess., 1940, LXXXVI, Part 3, 1936.

66.   Act of September 7, 1940. U.S., *Congressional Record,* 76th Cong., 3d Sess., 1940, LXXXVI, Part 11, 11754–55.

67.   Act of February 8, 1941. U.S., *Congressional Record,* 77th Cong., 1st Sess., 1941, LXXXVII, Part 1, 815.

68.   Act of August 12, 1941. U.S., *Congressional Record,* 77th Cong., 1st Sess., 1941, LXXXVII, Part 7, 7074–75.

69.   Act of November 13, 1941. U.S., *Congressional Record,* 77th Cong., 1st Sess., 1941, LXXXVII, Part 8, 8891.

70.   *Public Opinion Quarterly,* V (June, 1941), 322–24.

7

The Founding of the Sun, 1941

The *Chicago Tribune*'s stand on the European war produced mounting criticism. Attacks on the newspaper's editorial policy arose in Canada, where the *Tribune* had numerous forest holdings, and thus where it was economically vulnerable. In referring to the *Tribune,* the *Ottawa Journal* ominously pointed out in January, 1941, that it was well Canada should know who its enemies were. The *Montreal Star,* the chief English-language daily of that city, had a series of editorials violently against the Chicago newspaper, in one editorial comparing McCormick to Laval and Quisling, in another asserting that the Colonel was an "utterly unscrupulous journalist" who put "Benedict Arnold in the shade," in bringing out his "particularly nauseating" paper. The Conservative leader of the Canadian Senate, Arthur Meighan, went so far as to voice strong objections to permitting the sale and distribution of the *Tribune* in Canada. He argued its circulation would weaken popular enthusiasm for the war. There was a precedent for such an action; in World War I the Hearst newspapers had been forbidden in Canada.[1]

But the main problem for the *Tribune,* as the *Toronto Globe and Mail* aptly noted, was that it imported paper made in Canada from Canadian pulpwood (and had $40 million invested in its paper mill). Some Canadians suggested that there should be economic reprisals against the *Tribune,* that paper at the *Tribune* mills be rationed as a punitive measure. This proposal got nowhere, although it created considerable discussion. McCormick refused to be coerced. He stated that no threats of any kind "from any source" would ever have the slightest effect on the *Tribune*'s editorial policy. And there the matter rested.[2]

Potentially more dangerous, however, was the explosive situation in Chicago which developed eventually into the founding of an opposition morning newspaper. The *Tribune* had retained its morning monopoly since August, 1939, and growing resentment manifested itself in the nation's second city because there was not more editorial flexibility. The year 1941 witnessed the culmination of anti-*Tribune* activity. Under the aegis of the Chicago chapter of the Fight For Freedom Committee (which was founded nationally in April, 1941), a rallying point was established for those who wished to combat the influence of McCormick and his newspaper. This local chapter, headed by Courtenay Barber, Jr. and Albert Parry, was officially launched in July with advertisements in the Chicago papers. It immediately aroused interest. For example, Mrs. Emmons Blaine, a prominent Chicago liberal and socialite, sent a check for $500 to help further the operations of the group.[3]

On July 29, 1941, the Fight For Freedom Committee sponsored a large rally at Orchestra Hall. Featured speaker at the meeting was Edmond Taylor, formerly a foreign correspondent for McCormick, who addressed the gathering on the subject, "What's Wrong with the Chicago Tribune?" According to one of the movement's leaders, three thousand people jammed into the hall to hear Taylor, and a thousand others had to be turned away for lack of seating space. They had been lured to the gathering by advertisements reading:

HEAR THE TRUTH
about
COL. McCORMICK
"Duke of Chicago"
(HITLER LIKES HIM)

Four days before the meeting Courtenay Barber had sent out a press release promising that Taylor would "show why Hitler and Mussolini approve of the Chicago Tribune so highly."[4]

Taylor's address was more temperate than the advertising brochures. He praised McCormick for his sense of fairness as an employer and described him as a "man of integrity and high character." His criticisms of the Colonel were based mainly on the thesis that the *Tribune* was a "dirty fighter," whose editorials concerning American foreign policy went beyond the realm of fair politics.

> Of course Hitler is not interested in teaching Americans how to regenerate themselves by revolution. For one thing he is too well informed to believe for a minute that a fascist revolution could succeed in this country. All he wants and all he needs is to stir up enough disunity in America to cripple our defenses while he gets in position to deal us a knockout blow. The Chicago Tribune along with Wheeler and Lindbergh and a few others is helping to create this kind of disunity.[5]

Reacting enthusiastically to Taylor's remarks, the crowd proceeded to tear up and burn copies of the *Chicago Tribune* on Michigan Avenue after the meeting—one of the few times in the twentieth century when copies of an American daily newspaper have been publicly burned in the streets. The only drawback to the festivities was that Orchestra Hall's cooling system broke down, which the Fight For Freedom leaders characterized as "pro-Nazi" sabotage.[6]

But the most important outcome of the meeting was to prepare the way for the establishment of a new morning newspaper. A petition which circulated during and after the meeting read as follows:

> We the undersigned heartily agree with the resolution adopted at the Orchestra Hall rally of July 29, 1941, in which the people of Chicago condemned the CHICAGO TRIBUNE for its attacks on our national policy of defense. We also agree to give our support to a new morning newspaper.
>
> We are against the CHICAGO TRIBUNE. We want a new morning newspaper which will oppose Hitler, expose un-Americanism, support our government. . . .[7]

Other rallies were held to intensify public reaction against the *Tribune*. On October 3, 1941, a Fight For Freedom rally was held at Orchestra Hall with speeches by Stanley High, Augustus F. Lindbergh, and Rex Stout. Stout, the main speaker, addressed himself to the topic, "Hitler and the Chicago Tribune or Let Me Call You Sweetheart." "I say," he thundered, "it is irresponsible to the point of lunacy, utterly shameless, utterly without scruples, and beneath contempt." Stout also denounced the "nasty little men" who ran the newspaper. The *Chicago Daily News* reporter at the scene noted that the crowd roared its approval. In reply the *Tribune* somewhat ungraciously denounced Stout's chief fictional character, Nero Wolfe, as "gross, gluttonous, drunk, and bestial."[8]

On November 19 the Fight For Freedom group held another rally with Dorothy Thompson and Jan Masaryk as chief speakers. The *Tribune* concentrated its attack on Miss Thompson (Masaryk was a relatively invulnerable figure), running several editorials and cartoons ridiculing this journalist.[9]

The slugging was low and vigorous on both sides. Many liberals who were to be most critical of Senator Joseph McCarthy's methods a decade later were among the most active in affixing the charge of "pro-Hitler" and "Nazi" upon McCormick. Courtenay Barber, in a letter dated September 27, 1941, declared that the *Tribune* "exemplifies to the nth degree everything that Hitler and America First stand for," suggesting the German dictator and the American anti-war organization were somehow identical in their aims. Albert Parry wrote cavalierly about "the Tribune and other pro-Nazis." Cards were sent out stating that "Chicago needs a Non-Nazi Morning Paper!" and one letter to the *Chicago Daily News* asserted that the *Tribune* should change its name to *Der Fuehrer Hitler's Daily Blitz.* Even other newspapers joined the fray, the Madison *Capital Times,* for instance, calling the *Tribune* "The No. 1 fifth columnist in the United States." One correspondent advised Barber that "using fair and square methods to fight the Tribune avails nothing. . . . The only answer is to use the *Tribune*'s own insidious methods. Undermine the *Tribune* in the same way they seek to undermine our Government." These "insidious methods" were in fact used by the opponents of the *Tribune* to create a climate favorable to the establishment of a rival newspaper.[10]

The opaque vision of the FFF leaders is illustrated by a letter Barber wrote to McCormick demanding that the *Tribune* mention the German composition of the crowds which greeted Lindbergh. In reply, the *Tribune* forwarded to Barber a letter from reporter William

Fulton addressed to McCormick, stating that the Lindbergh crowds looked typically American to him. "If one was to say there were German elements in Lindbergh's crowds, one should point out the large number of Jews who frequented the meetings of the pro-ally groups." Barber replied to McCormick that the Fulton letter only demonstrated to him how pro-Nazi and anti-Semitic the *Tribune* really was![11]

The *Tribune* replied in kind. Both sides lost their heads, although admittedly the issue was a great one. In fact, McCormick's newspaper can be blamed for creating the super-heated atmosphere of the Chicago of 1941. It could never believe that its opponents were working from honest motives; instead it charged that they were bought. Immediately after the formation of the Fight For Freedom Committee the *Tribune* accused its leaders of being draft dodgers:

> Many of the members doubtless can find no inner peace in war except vicariously. They will not seek release from inner turmoil by stopping a bullet or a bomb fragment, although even for the most infirm of them some service might be found in bombed areas, in carrying consolation if not stretchers.[12]

A more specific, serious charge was that brought against the Episcopal Bishop of Cincinnati, Bishop Hobson, who spoke with Edmond Taylor at the first Fight For Freedom rally:

> . . . If he were a sensitive man he would have seen the necessity of choosing between Christianity and blood lust.
>
> It would be unfair to the bishop to suggest that he has not resigned [as a church leader], because of a desire to retain his source of income. He can have no worries on that account. He knows there is plenty of money in the lend-lease funds to support him in great comfort for the rest of his life.[13]

The *Tribune,* wittily if not entirely accurately, characterized its opponents as "a popular front lineup of communists, cookie pushers, and fighters of the marshmallow set." In the battle of wits, the *Tribune* was by no means outclassed by its enemies.[14]

The most devastating criticism of the *Tribune* that this researcher could find was not made by the FFF, or by any journalism magazine, but by an obscure Ohio weekly, the *Bryan Democrat.* In September,

September 6, 1941

1941, it printed the "Folklore of the Tribune" which is worth quoting in full. Unlike the Fight For Freedom leaders, the *Bryan Democrat* managed to catch the tone and spirit of the *Tribune* editorial page in its satirization:

FOLKLORE OF THE TRIBUNE

When a man commits a despicable crime he is a goon or a moron.

The Gallup poll is all wet.

Public ownership is immoral; it does not work anywhere.

There is a personal Devil; his name is Harold Ickes.

When a strike takes place it is the result of Communist leadership, and the strikers are always wrong.

It really doesn't matter much to the United States whether England or Germany wins this war.

When the nations of Europe wanted to have a war they called in the American ambassadors, and after receiving assurance that this country would support such a war, and enter it eventually, they went ahead.

Roosevelt has been trying his best to get this country into war for the last two years, but has failed largely because of the Chicago Tribune.

If the people had known how Roosevelt stood, before the election, he would have been defeated, two to one.

Newspapers that disagree with the Tribune have been bought up; individuals who disagree are war mongers, communists, pinks or traitors.

Wendell Willkie was nominated by international bankers and other war mongers, as a Charlie McCarthy to Roosevelt. He is a traitor and a low down skunk.

The Tribune is the only paper that prints the truth, fearlessly and honestly, respecting national and international affairs.

Roosevelt would be happy to see this country in war because it would give him a greater opportunity to mingle with kings and queens.

Every other bill, introduced in Congress, has back of it the purpose of making Roosevelt a dictator.

There are no shortages of aluminum, steel and gasoline; talk of such shortages is by officials who want to be dictators and ruin private business.

Freedom of the press would have been wiped out long ago by this administration, if it had not been for the Tribune.[15]

One of the more unusual aspects of this supercharged atmosphere was the manner in which the newspapers jumped to the attack. Newspapers are normally hesitant to criticize one another or to print attacks on the competition. A letter from Paul Scott Mowrer, editor of the *Chicago Daily News,* to Albert Parry in August, 1941, indicated that it was "contrary to established newspaper custom" to criticize one's competitors. But both the *Daily News* and *Daily Times,* perhaps smarting under *Tribune* criticism that they had been "bought" up by lend-lease money, gave the Fight For Freedom group considerable publicity.[16]

The *Chicago Daily Times,* in March, 1941, carried a long news story with the headline: AXIS PRESS PRAISES TRIBUNE. Both Italian and German newspapers were quoted to support the contention that the *Tribune* was held in high favor among Axis notables. *Editor and Publisher,* the trade weekly, took the unusual step of criticizing the *Daily Times* for this supposed breach of journalistic decorum. Both that newspaper and the *Daily News* gave extensive coverage to the anti-*Tribune* rallies sponsored by the Fight For Freedom movement. Vaughn Shoemaker, the *Daily News*'s chief cartoonist, drew a cartoon in August entitled "ORGAN RECITAL," showing Hitler playing at an organ—"Sleep America SLE-E-E-P." The organ was shaped like the Tribune Tower. A month later another Shoemaker cartoon had Hitler again at the *Tribune* organ, singing "Let me call you sweetheart." Knox's paper went so far as to print a letter on its editorial page which claimed that the *Tribune* "with its un-American hatred of the President, would rather see Hitler and his gang of cutthroats take over our beloved country than to give our government the support it so urgently needs." By November, 1941, the *Daily News* was running a daily feature entitled "Famous Sayings of History," which consisted entirely of quotes of Colonel McCormick. One "saying" reproduced by the newspaper was "People of inherited wealth are not admired here." The *Daily News*'s comment was, "—Col. Robert R. McCormick—son of Robert S. McCormick, grandson of William McCormick, great-grandson of Robert McCormick."[17]

Adlai Stevenson was to recall later how this newspaper antagonism worked. "The *Tribune* used to send photographers to photo-

graph all empty seats, if any, in halls where we presented programs—
and the *News* photographers photographed all the full ones."
Stevenson would be a "dirty dog" in the *Tribune* in the morning and
a "shining hero" in the *News* at night. An example of this newspaper rivalry is seen in the reporting of Wendell Willkie's address
to a Chicago crowd in which he urged all-out aid to the British. The
Tribune buried the story on page three and remarked that "The
crowd gathered slowly for the meeting." The *Daily News* emblazoned
the Willkie speech on page one and estimated the crowd at an
overflowing 24,000.[18]

Conditions were obviously propitious for the founding of an
opposition newspaper. Ever since Hearst's *Herald-Examiner* had
expired in August, 1939, the *Tribune* had enjoyed a morning
monopoly in the nation's second largest city. By November, 1941,
the situation appeared ideal for the anti-McCormick faction.

It looked even better when Marshall Field III, grandson and heir
of the merchant prince and backer of the newly established *PM* of
New York City, agreed to raise the money for the new Chicago daily
which took the name, the *Sun*. Its supporters were more than a little
optimistic (and a bit impractical) about the newspaper's chance for
survival. One contemporary article claimed that the times could
not be "more auspicious" for the founding of a new morning newspaper, and actually went so far as to predict that *Tribune* circulation
would be cut in half. L. M. Birkhead, a long-time antagonist to the
Colonel, wrote Courtenay Barber, in *late 1942* that he was under
the impression that Field still believed the *Chicago Sun* would "put
the *Chicago Tribune* out of business eventually or at least give Col.
McCormick a run for his money." George Seldes, always a foe of
the *Tribune,* was also optimistic about the *Sun*'s chances for survival: "Never in American history have so many people hated a
newspaper as much as Chicago hates the *Tribune*."[19]

In an interview reported in *Editor and Publisher,* Field stated his
reasons for backing the *Sun*. He did so because of the one-sided
emphasis of the *Tribune,* and contended there was "room for the
other point of view which people would like to see presented editorially." This statement suggests that if McCormick had been less
biased in the way he presented the news and less opposed to the

Roosevelt administration, he might well have retained his morning monopoly.[20]

First indications looked favorable. On the initial day of publication, December 4, 1941, the presses ran ten hours and the *Sun* sold 896,000 copies. The seventy-two-page first edition was heavy with advertising. The following Sunday a million copies were issued. These figures almost equalled *Tribune* circulation. But the founding of the *Sun* was attended by more than its share of bad luck, and the newspaper could not compete with the *Tribune* in editorial skill. It was also badly hurt because it lacked an Associated Press franchise. On the first day of publication the *Sun* had to compete with the *Tribune*'s tremendous scoop on F.D.R.'s war plans. And only three days later came Pearl Harbor, which submerged the whole isolationist-interventionist controversy. Now the *Tribune* was able to put on the ever popular mantle of patriotism and thunder that the Roosevelt administration was not doing enough to win the war. Consequently the *Sun*'s circulation dipped to 275,000 in 1942, an ignominious last in the Chicago field and a bare 30 percent of the *Tribune*'s circulation, which was hardly affected at all. Field was to lose many millions of dollars before the *Sun* was to make money.[21]

OTES

1.   *The Evening Telegram* (Toronto), September 4, 1941, 6:2; *Montreal Daily Star,* January 10, 1941, October 30, 1941, 10:1; *Ottawa Journal,* January 9, 1941; *New York Times,* July 19, 1940, 8:2.

2.   *Editor and Publisher,* LXXIV (February 8, 1941), 12; Philip Kinsley, *Liberty and the Press; A History of the Chicago Tribune's Fight to Preserve a Free Press for the American People* (Chicago: The Tribune Company, 1944), pp. 84–88; Tobin Creeley, "Promoting a Newsprint Crisis," *The Canadian Forum,* XXI (May, 1941), 47–48; *Chicago Tribune,* June 10, 1947, Section C, 23:8.

3.   Walter Johnson, *The Battle against Isolation,* p. 225; letter of Mrs.

Emmons Blaine to Courtenay Barber, Jr., July 24, 1941, Fight For Freedom Committee papers, University of Chicago Library.

4. Walter Johnson, *The Battle against Isolation,* pp. 225–26; Helen Murchie Costello, "Col. McCormick's Tribune: 1910–1941," *New Republic,* CV (December 1, 1941), 724–27; form letter sent out by Denison B. Hull, July 30, 1941; press release written by Courtenay Barber, Jr., July 25, 1941, Fight For Freedom papers, University of Chicago Library.

5. Edmond Taylor, "What Is Wrong with the Chicago Tribune?"; speech delivered July 29, 1941, Fight For Freedom Committee papers, University of Chicago Library.

6. Albert Parry to Gifford A. Cochran, July 31, 1941, Fight For Freedom papers, University of Chicago Library.

7. Petition distributed by Fight For Freedom Committee, Fight For Freedom papers, University of Chicago Library.

8. Poster for October 3, 1941, Fight For Freedom Rally, and Resolution adopted by October 3, 1941, Fight For Freedom Rally, Fight For Freedom Committee papers, University of Chicago Library; *Chicago Daily News,* October 4, 1941; John J. McPhaul, *Deadlines and Monkeyshines: The Fabled World of Chicago Journalism* (New York: Prentice-Hall, Inc., 1962), pp. 290–91.

9. *Chicago Tribune,* November 20, 24, 26, 1941.

10. Courtenay Barber, Jr., to Fred H. Knowles, September 27, 1941, University of Chicago Library; letter of Hamlet C. Ridgway to the Chicago press, August, 1941; Albert Parry to Milton G. Patrick, August 20, 1941; Leonard Rosenthal to Courtenay Barber, Jr., August 30, 1941, University of Chicago Library; *Fight For Freedom,* I, No. 10; *The Capital Times* (Madison), August 22, 1941, Fight For Freedom Committee papers, University of Chicago Library.

11. Barber to McCormick, April 28, 1941, May 19, 1941; William Fulton to McCormick, May 6, 1941. Papers of the Fight For Freedom Committee, University of Chicago Library.

12. *The South Works Bulletin,* I (November 7, 1941), 1; quoted from *Chicago Tribune,* April or May, 1941, Fight For Freedom Committee papers, University of Chicago Library; *Chicago Tribune,* August 4, 1941, 12:1.

13. *Chicago Tribune,* July 31, 1941, 10:1.

14. *Ibid.,* August 15, 1941.

15. *Bryan Democrat,* September 2, 1941 (Cass Cullis, editor); Fight For Freedom Committee papers, University of Chicago Library.

16. Paul Scott Mowrer to Albert Parry, August 21, 1941, Fight For

Freedom Committee papers, University of Chicago Library. The *Tribune* often accused other papers of "being bought or bought up by lend-lease or other money to have American boys sent to Europe to die for un-American objects." *Chicago Tribune,* August 4, 1941, 12:1.

17.   *Chicago Daily Times,* March 20, 1941; *Editor and Publisher,* LXXIV (March 29, 1941), 26; *Chicago Daily News,* August 20, 1941, September 13, 1941, September 16, 1941, November 25, 1941.

18.   Kenneth S. Davis, *A Prophet in His Own Country: The Triumphs and Defeats of Adlai E. Stevenson* (Garden City, N.Y.: Doubleday & Company, Inc., 1957), p. 217; *Chicago Tribune,* June 7, 1941, 3:2; *Chicago Daily News,* June 7, 1941, p. 1.

19.   Costello, pp. 724, 727; L. M. Birkhead to Courtenay Barber, December 7, 1942, Fight For Freedom Committee papers, University of Chicago Library; *In Fact,* IV (November 24, 1941), 2.

20.   *Editor and Publisher,* LXXIV (October 4, 1941), 4.

21.   *Chicago Sun,* December 5, 1941; *Editor and Publisher,* LXXIV (December 6, 1941), 3; LXXIV (December 13, 1941), 16; Oswald Garrison Villard, *The Disappearing Daily: Chapters in American Newspaper Evolution* (New York: Alfred A. Knopf, 1944), p. 150; Stephen Becker, *Marshall Field III* (New York: Simon and Schuster, 1964), pp. 282–302. McCormick once told Kent Cooper, the head of the Associated Press, that if Field had personally asked him for the AP franchise, he would have been glad to waive his rights. As it was there was litigation extending to the Supreme Court, which Field won. Kent Cooper, *Kent Cooper and the Associated Press: An Autobiography* (New York: Random House, 1959), p. 280.

Epilogue

Although the *Tribune* changed a few of its attitudes toward foreign policy from 1929 to 1941, its fundamental concepts remained the same. The newspaper continued to emphasize its belief in the superiority of the United States over any other nation, and the superiority of Midwestern culture over that of the Eastern seaboard. Chicago still survived as the apex of civilization. The United States continued to be played for an international sucker by the brilliance of European diplomacy. America, said the newspaper, was always being duped into strange foreign adventures. For various reasons, United States leadership, in McCormick's view, never measured up to the quality of American life.

The Colonel never could understand why the various administrations followed the foreign policies they did, and this was true for Republicans as well as Democrats. Everyone seemed out of step, except him. His answer was that these presidents and the State Department were joined in a gigantic conspiracy to subvert the American way of life as he interpreted it. For reasons of social prestige, and an insatiable desire to meet and bow down to royalty, American leaders consistently knuckled under to foreign diplomacy. Franklin Roosevelt's motives were declared even more serious; he wished nothing less than to establish a personal dictatorship by getting the nation into a war.

This twelve-year period did witness, however, a transformation in the Colonel's attitude toward certain elements of foreign policy. In 1929 he was a militarist, and advocated universal military training, a large navy, and a bellicose foreign policy. This had all changed by 1941, because he came to believe that the Roosevelt administration would use universal military training and a large navy to push America into war, and thus be in a position to establish a dictatorship. As a consequence McCormick accused Roosevelt of being a "warmonger" for even considering these policies, policies which he himself had supported in previous years. The Colonel changed some aspects of his foreign policy because he doubted the credibility and motives of the president who would implement it. In the final analysis, McCormick's change in foreign attitudes was his reaction to the domestic aspects of the New Deal. This reaction was to change him from a "nationalist" in 1929 to an "isolationist" by 1941.

His ideas on the Far East also reveal an interesting evolution. In 1929 the Colonel's policy was pro-Chinese; by 1941 it was, if not actually pro-Japanese, frantically attempting to prevent war with Japan. By 1941 he was perfectly willing to allow China to be swallowed up if that was the only way the United States could avoid conflict. Destroy Japan, he asked, and what would the Americans have in the Far East? A resurgent communism.

The Colonel thought little of President Hoover, tried to dump him in favor of Calvin Coolidge in 1932, and only lukewarmly supported the president against Governor Roosevelt of New York. At first McCormick was enthusiastic about the Roosevelt administration for the courageous actions it took during the Hundred Days, but in a few months he moved into opposition because of the N.R.A. ("Dictatorship Bill") and the New Deal's heavy spending. By 1934 the *Chicago Tribune* was irreconcilably opposed to the Roosevelt administration and all its domestic policies. The break in foreign policy occurred in October, 1937, when the president delivered his famous Quarantine speech in Chicago.

The *Tribune* used every journalistic trick it knew to defeat Roosevelt and his measures, particularly during the presidential elections of 1936 and 1940 and the battle over lend-lease. Its efforts, however, were by no means confined to these periods. It regularly suppressed news sympathetic to the New Deal, played up the opposition to

Roosevelt, and generally used every possible weapon to oust "that man in the White House." By no means least in its arsenal was its cleverly written editorial page.

The vehemence of the Colonel undoubtedly derogated the national political tone. He could not fight for anything moderately, and if he turned against a politician he would oppose him by the most ill-mannered means possible. Many of his devices anticipated those of Senator Joseph McCarthy a decade later. He fought, however, in full sincerity, most likely not even aware that he was falsifying and oversimplifying the issues. Certainly, if he had been less artless, he would not have resisted the New Deal so violently, and he could have headed off the challenge of Marshall Field's *Chicago Sun,* thus retaining a morning monopoly. With McCormick reading the most sinister motives into the minds of his opponents, they retaliated by calling him a Nazi. For this decline in tone, the Colonel was to a large degree responsible.

After Pearl Harbor, the *Tribune* continued its fiery attacks on everything connected with Roosevelt and the Democrats. The administration on its part kept a tight surveillance on the activities of the newspaper. The government came close to prosecuting the *Tribune* after its correspondent at the Battle of Midway had written that the Navy had known that the attack was to take place and, in his story, gave the position of the Japanese ships. This implied, correctly, that the U.S. Navy had broken the Japanese code. One admiral was so apoplectic over the incident that he threatened to send in marines to take over Tribune Tower, but the matter was dropped after considerable publicity. The *Tribune* invited further trouble from the government by refusing to waive certain prohibitive payments which the *Sun* would have had to pay in order to obtain an Associated Press franchise. The government, siding with the pro-administration *Sun,* began action in 1942 against the Associated Press for violation of the Sherman Anti-Trust Act. The case was appealed all the way to the Supreme Court, which in 1945 decided in favor of the *Sun,* which then received its franchise. Throughout the remainder of McCormick's life, the *Tribune* continued to blend its editorial position into its news reporting. As an example of this, perhaps the most famous photograph associated with the election of 1948 was that of President Truman, the morning after election, gleefully holding the *Chicago Tribune*'s early edition which contained the resounding, banner headline: DEWEY DEFEATS TRUMAN.[1]

After the death of Eleanor Patterson in 1948, Colonel McCormick took over the management of the *Washington Times-Herald*. The formula which had proven so successful in Chicago did not work in Washington, D.C., and in 1954, an increasingly weary McCormick sold the newspaper to Eugene Meyer, publisher of the liberal *Washington Post*. Although Meyer's political views were completely opposed to those of McCormick, the Colonel respected his ability as a newspaperman. The *Times-Herald* was immediately merged into the *Post*.[2]

In 1952, disgusted at the continued domination of the Republican party in national conventions by its moderate, eastern-based wing, and by the nomination of Dwight D. Eisenhower over Robert A. Taft, McCormick broke for the second time with the party of his birth. On August 23, 1952, speaking over the Mutual Broadcasting System, the Colonel issued a call for a new "American Party." In his words,

> I swallowed Willkie in '40, Dewey twice in '44 and '48, candidates foisted upon the majority by sharp practice, but now that the Democrats have taken over our party by voting in Republican primaries by the ruse of falsehood and corruption and can be expected to do it again four years from now, I will be imposed upon no longer.

He then went on to endorse 15 Senate candidates (11 were elected) and 197 House candidates (185 won election). The attempt, however, to build a new third party proved a failure, and McCormick's work on the project was halted by his death on April 1, 1955. Rarely had a single individual imprinted his personality so deeply upon a major American newspaper; this in an age when newspapers were increasingly evolving into faceless business enterprises.[3]

The *Tribune* reached its greatest circulation in 1947, with 1,031,-851 copies printed daily and 1,544,770 on Sunday. For the six months ending September 30, 1969, daily circulation sagged badly to 775,416 and Sunday circulation to 1,045,176, although the newspaper has attained record prosperity from increased advertising. Its circulation, however, is now less than forty years ago, and instead of being first in the nation among standard sized dailies, is now only fourth—after the *Los Angeles Times, New York Times,* and *Wall Street Journal.* Although difficult to assess, the probability is that the *Tribune*'s editorial influence has declined since the Colonel's death.

The fall in circulation reflects a major shrinkage of the Chicago newspaper market, which has declined approximately 30 percent from 1947 to 1969. Accompanying this drop, the *Tribune* is faced with a much more competitive situation than had been the case during the Colonel's lifetime, and Chicago has become quite possibly the most competitive newspaper town in the United States. There are only two newspaper ownerships remaining in the city, but they operate on far more equal terms than in the past. The Tribune Company operates the *Tribune* and *Chicago Today* (formerly the Hearst *American*) and Field Enterprises runs the *Sun Times* (which has become a profitable, entrenched morning rival to the *Tribune*) and the *Daily News* (which leads the evening field). The *Tribune* remains by far the most profitable newspaper in Chicago, but is working within what has been a shrinking market and amid more balanced competition.[4]

NOTES

1. *Christian Century,* LIX (August 19, 1942), 997; *Time Magazine,* XL (August 17, 1942), 42; *Newsweek,* XX (August 17, 1942), 64; XX (August 31, 1942), 65; Waldrop, picture opposite p. 142, 251–263; Becker, 302–310; Cooper, pp. 278–282.

2. Waldrop, pp. 276–279.

3. Waldrop, pp. 298–303.

4. Standard Rate and Data Service, Inc., *Newspaper Rates and Data, June 12, 1970* (Skokie, Ill.: Standard Rate and Data Service, Inc., 1970), p. 226.

₿IBLIOGRAPHY

BOOKS

Adler, Selig. *The Isolationist Impulse*. London and New York: Abelard-Schuman, 1957.

Allen, Jay; Paul, Elliot; and Quintanilla, Luis. *All the Brave*. New York: Modern Age Books, 1939.

Allen, Jay; Wallace, Henry; and Mumford, Lewis. *New World Theme*. Palo Alto, Calif.: James Ladd Delkin, 1943.

Allen, Robert S. *Washington Merry-Go-Round*. New York: Horace Liveright, Inc., 1931.

Andrews, Wayne. *Battle for Chicago*. New York: Harcourt, Brace & Company, Inc., 1946.

Ashburn, Frank D. *Peabody of Groton*. New York: Coward-McCann, Inc., 1944.

Bailey, Thomas A. *The Man in the Street: The Impact of American Public Opinion on Foreign Policy*. New York: The Macmillan Company, 1948.

Balderston, John L. *Chicago Blueprint. Translated by John L. Balderston from Papers Submitted to the Fuehrer by Supreme High Control Board Sector America with Marginal Comments and Inserts, Many Initialed "A.H."* New York: Alfred A. Knopf, 1943.

Barnes, Joseph. *Willkie*. New York: Simon and Schuster, 1952.

Beard, Charles A. *American Foreign Policy in the Making, 1932–1940: A Study in Responsibilities*. New Haven: Yale University Press, 1946.

.... *Giddy Minds and Foreign Quarrels*. New York: The Macmillan Co., 1939.

Becker, Stephen. *Marshall Field III*. New York: Simon and Schuster, 1964.

Bird, George L., and Merwin, Frederic E. (eds.). *The Newspaper and Society: A Book of Readings*. New York: Prentice-Hall, Inc., 1942.

Browder, Earl. *The Way Out*. New York: International Publishers, 1941.

Burns, James MacGregor. *Roosevelt: The Soldier of Freedom*. New York: Harcourt Brace Jovanovich, 1970.

Cantril, Hadley (ed.). *Public Opinion, 1935–1946*. Princeton, N. J.: Princeton University Press, 1951.

Carlson, John Roy. *Under Cover*. New York: E. P. Dutton & Co., Inc., 1943.

Chicago Tribune. *Book of Facts, 1931*. Chicago: The Tribune Company, 1932.

.... *A Century of Tribune Editorials*. Chicago: The Tribune Company, 1947.

.... *Pictured Encyclopedia of the World's Greatest Newspaper*. Chicago: The Tribune Company, 1928.

.... *The W–G–N*. Chicago: The Tribune Company, 1922.

Childs, Marquis W. *I Write from Washington*. New York: Harper & Brothers, 1942.

Cohen, Bernard C. *The Press and Foreign Policy*. Princeton: Princeton University Press, 1963.

Cole, Wayne S. *America First: The Battle against Intervention, 1940–1941*. Madison: The University of Wisconsin Press, 1953.

.... *Senator Gerald P. Nye and American Foreign Relations*. Minneapolis: University of Minnesota Press, 1962.

Cooper, Kent. *Kent Cooper and the Associated Press: An Autobiography*. New York: Random House, 1959.

Cutler, John Levi. *Gilbert Patten and His Frank Meriwell Saga: A Study in Sub-Literary Fiction, 1896–1913*. Orono, Maine: University Press, 1934.

Darrah, David. *Hail Caesar!* Boston: Hale, Cushman & Flint, 1936.

Davids, Jules. *America and the World of Our Times: United States Diplomacy in the Twentieth Century*. New York: Random House, 1960.

Davis, Kenneth S. *A Prophet in His Own Country: The Triumphs and Defeats of Adlai E. Stevenson*. Garden City, N. Y.: Doubleday & Company, Inc., 1957.

Dawes, Charles G. *Notes as Vice-President, 1928–1929*. Boston: Little, Brown and Company, 1935.

Dawson, Raymond H. *The Decision to Aid Russia, 1941: Foreign Policy and Domestic Politics*. Chapel Hill: The University of North Carolina Press, 1959.

DeConde, Alexander (ed.). *Isolation and Security*. Durham, N. C.: Duke University Press, 1957.

Dennis, Charles H. *Victor Lawson, His Time and His Work*. Chicago: The University of Chicago Press, 1935.

Desmond, Robert W. *The Press and World Affairs*. New York: D. Appleton-Century Company, 1937.

Dilling, Elizabeth. *The Red Network: A "Who's Who" and Handbook of Radicalism for Patriots*. Chicago: Published by the Author, 1934.

Dillon, Mary Earhart. *Wendell Willkie*. Philadelphia: J. B. Lippincott Company, 1952.

Duranty, Walter. *I Write as I Please*. New York: Simon & Schuster, 1935.

Ferrell, Robert H. *American Diplomacy in the Great Depression: Hoover-Stimson Foreign Policy, 1929–1933*. New Haven: Yale University Press, 1957.

.... *Frank B. Kellogg, Henry L. Stimson*, Vol. XI of *American Secretaries of State and Their Diplomacy*. New York: Cooper Square Publishers, Inc., 1963.

Flannery, Harry W. *Assignment to Berlin*. New York: Alfred A. Knopf, 1942.

Ford, Edwin H., and Emery, Edwin. *Highlights in the History of the American Press*. Minneapolis: University of Minnesota Press, 1954.

Freidel, Frank. *Franklin D. Roosevelt*, Vol. I. *The Apprenticeship*. Boston: Little, Brown and Company, 1952.

Gibbons, Edward. *Floyd Gibbons, Your Headline Hunter*. New York: Exposition Press, 1953.

Gosnell, Harold F. *Machine Politics: Chicago Model*. Chicago: The University of Chicago Press, 1937.

Gunther, John. *Inside U.S.A.* New York: Harper & Brothers, 1947.

.... *Taken at the Flood: The Story of Albert D. Lasker*. New York: Harper & Brothers, 1960.

Hallgren, Mauritz A. *Seeds of Revolt: A Study of American Life and the Temper of the American People during the Depression*. New York: Alfred A. Knopf, 1933.

Hanighen, Frank C. (ed.). *Nothing But Danger: Thrilling Adventures of Ten Newspaper Correspondents in the Spanish War*. London: George G. Harrap & Co., Ltd., 1939.

Healy, Paul F. *Cissy*. Garden City: Doubleday & Company, Inc., 1966.

Hohenberg, John. *Foreign Correspondence: The Great Reporters and Their Times*. New York: Columbia University Press, 1964.

Hogue, Alice Albright. *Cissy Patterson*. New York: Random House, 1966.

Hoover, Herbert. *Addresses upon the American Road, 1940–1941*. New York: Charles Scribner's Sons, 1941.

.... *The Memoirs of Herbert Hoover*. Vol. II: *The Cabinet and the Presidency, 1920–1933*. New York: The Macmillan Company, 1952.

Hoyt, Edwin P. *The Tempering Years*. New York: Charles Scribner's Sons, 1963.

Ickes, Harold L. *America's House of Lords: An Inquiry into the Freedom of the Press*. New York: Harcourt, Brace and Company, 1939.

.... *Freedom of the Press Today: A Clinical Examination by 28 Specialists*. New York: The Vanguard Press, 1941.

.... *The Secret Diary of Harold Ickes*. 3 vols. New York: Simon and Schuster, 1953–54.

Jackson, Gabriel. *The Spanish Republic and the Civil War.* Princeton: Princeton University Press, 1965.

Johnson, Donald Bruce. *The Republican Party and Wendell Willkie.* Urbana: The University of Illinois Press, 1960.

Johnson, Walter. *The Battle against Isolation.* Chicago: The University of Chicago Press, 1944.

.... *1600 Pennsylvania Avenue: Presidents and the People.* Boston: Little, Brown and Company, 1960.

.... *William Allen White's America.* New York: Henry Holt and Company, 1947.

Kingdon, Frank. *That Man in the White House: You and Your President.* New York: Arco Publishing Co., 1944.

Kingsbury, Susan M.; Hart, Hornell, and Associates. *Newspapers and the News.* (Bryn Mawr College Series in Social Economy, No. 1.) New York: G. P. Putnam's Sons, 1937.

Kinsley, Philip. *Liberty and the Press: A History of the Chicago Tribune's Fight to Preserve a Free Press for the American People.* Chicago: The Tribune Company, 1944.

Langer, William L., and Gleason, S. Everett. *The Undeclared War, 1940–1941.* New York: Harper & Brothers, 1953.

.... *The Challenge to Isolation.* New York: Harper & Brothers, 1952.

Lindbergh, Charles A. *The Wartime Journals of Charles A. Lindbergh.* New York: Harcourt Brace Jovanovich, 1970.

Linn, James Weber. *James Keeley, Newspaperman.* Indianapolis: The Bobbs-Merrill Company, 1937.

Lochner, Louis P. (ed. and trans.). *The Goebbels Diaries.* New York: Popular Library, Inc., 1948.

Lydgate, William A. *What Our People Think.* New York: Thomas Y. Crowell Company, 1944.

Manly, Chesly. *The Twenty-Year Revolution from Roosevelt to Eisenhower.* Chicago: Henry Regnery Company, 1954.

Martin, Joseph. *My First Fifty Years in Politics.* New York: McGraw-Hill Book Co., Inc., 1960.

Matthews, Herbert L. *The Education of a Correspondent.* New York: Harcourt, Brace and Company, 1946.

.... *Two Wars and More to Come.* New York: Carrick & Evans, Inc., 1938.

McCormick, Robert R. *Addresses by Colonel Robert R. McCormick Broadcast over WGN and the Mutual Broadcasting System, 1940–1941.* 5 vols. Chicago: The Tribune Company, 1941.

.... *The American Revolution and its Influence on World Civilization.* Chicago: The Tribune Company, 1945.

.... *The Army of 1918.* New York: Harcourt, Brace and House, 1920.

.... *The Freedom of the Press: A History and an Argument Compiled from Speeches on this Subject Delivered over a Period of Fifteen Years.* New York: D. Appleton-Century Company, 1936.

.... *How We Acquired Our National Territory.* Chicago: The Tribune Company, 1942.

.... *Ulysses S. Grant: The Great Soldier of America.* New York: D. Appleton-Century Company, Inc., 1934.

.... *With the Russian Army, Being the Experiences of a National Guardsman.* New York: The Macmillan Company, 1915.

McCoy, Donald R. *Landon of Kansas.* Lincoln: University of Nebraska Press, 1966.

McCutcheon, John T. *Drawn from Memory.* Indianapolis: The Bobbs-Merrill Company, Inc., 1950.

McPhaul, John J. *Deadlines & Monkeyshines: The Fabled World of Chicago Journalism.* New York: Prentice-Hall, Inc., 1962.

Mencken, Henry L. *Making a President: A Footnote to the Sage of Democracy.* New York: Alfred A. Knopf, 1932.

Morgenstern, George. *Pearl Harbor: The Story of the Secret War.* New York: The Devin-Adair Company, 1947.

Morison, Elting E. *Turmoil and Tradition; A Study of the Life and Times of Henry L. Stimson.* Boston: Houghton Mifflin Company, 1960.

Mott, Thomas Bentley. *Twenty Years as Military Attaché.* New York: Oxford University Press, 1937.

Myers, William Starr. *The Foreign Policies of Herbert Hoover, 1929–1933.* New York: Charles Scribner's Sons, 1940.

Osgood, Robert Endicott. *Ideals and Self-Interest in America's Foreign Relations.* Chicago: The University of Chicago Press, 1953.

Patterson, Joseph Medill. *The Notebook of a Neutral.* New York: Duffield and Company, 1916.

Pearson, Drew, and Brown, Constantine. *The American Diplomatic Game.* Garden City, N. Y.: Doubleday, Doran & Company, Inc., 1935.

Pierson, George Wilson. *Yale College, An Educational History, 1871–1921.* New Haven: Yale University Press, 1952.

Powell, John B. *My Twenty-Five Years in China.* New York: The Macmillan Company, 1945.

Presbrey, Frank. *The History and Development of Advertising.* Garden City, N. Y.: Doubleday, Doran & Company, 1929.

Rascoe, Burton. *Before I Forget.* New York: The Literary Guild of America, Inc., 1937.

Reilly, Michael F. (as told to William J. Slocum). *Reilly of the White House.* New York: Simon and Schuster, 1947.

Roper, Elmo. *You and Your Leaders: Their Actions and Your Reactions, 1936–1956.* New York: William Morrow and Company, 1957.

Rosten, Leo C. *The Washington Correspondents.* New York: Harcourt, Brace and Company, 1937.

Rue, Larry. *I Fly for News.* New York: Albert and Charles Boni, Inc., 1932.

Sargent, Porter. *Getting Us into War.* Boston: Porter Sargent, 1941.

Saunders, Hilary St. George. *Pioneers! O Pioneers!* New York: The Macmillan Company, 1944.

Sayers, Michael, and Kahn, Albert E. *Sabotage! The Secret War against America.* New York: Harper & Brothers Publishers, 1942.

Schlesinger, Arthur, Jr. *The Coming of the New Deal.* Boston: Houghton Mifflin Company, 1959.

.... *The Crisis of the Old Order.* Boston: Houghton Mifflin Company, 1957.

.... *The Politics of Unheaval.* Boston: Houghton Mifflin Company, 1960.

Schoonmaker, Nancy, and Reid, Doris Fielding (eds.). *We Testify.* New York: Smith & Durrell, Inc., 1941.

Schultz, Sigrid. *Germany Will Try it Again.* New York: Reynal & Hitchcock, 1944.

Seldes, George. *Facts and Fascism.* New York: In Fact, Inc., 1943.

.... *Lords of the Press.* New York: Julian Messner, Inc., 1938.

.... *One Thousand Americans.* New York: Boni & Gair, 1947.

.... *Tell the Truth and Run.* New York: Greenberg, 1953.

Shannon, David A. *Between the Wars: America, 1919–1941.* Boston: Houghton Mifflin Company, 1965.

Shirer, William. *Berlin Diary.* New York: Alfred A. Knopf, 1941.

.... *End of a Berlin Diary.* New York: Alfred A. Knopf, 1947.

Smith, Howard K. *Last Train from Berlin.* New York: Alfred A. Knopf, 1947.

Stokes, Thomas L. *Chip off My Shoulder.* Princeton: Princeton University Press, 1940.

Taylor, Edmond. *The Strategy of Terror: Europe's Inner Front.* Boston: Houghton Mifflin Company, 1940.

Taylor, Edmond; Snow, Edgar; and Janeway, Eliot. *Smash Hitler's International: The Strategy of a Political Offensive against the Axis.* New York: The Greystoke Press, 1941.

Tebbel, John. *An American Dynasty.* Garden City, N. Y.: Doubleday & Company, Inc., 1947.

Tupper, Eleanor, and McReynolds, George E. *Japan in American Public Opinion.* New York: The Macmillan Company, 1937.

Turner, Frederick Jackson. *The Frontier in American History.* New York: Henry Holt and Company, 1921.

Vandenburg, Arthur H., Jr. *The Private Papers of Senator Vandenburg.* Boston: Houghton Mifflin Company, 1952.

Villard, Oswald Garrison. *The Disappearing Daily: Chapters in American Newspaper Evolution.* New York: Alfred A. Knopf, 1944.

Waldrop, Frank C. *McCormick of Chicago: An Unconventional Portrait of a Controversial Figure.* Englewood Cliffs, N. J.: Prentice-Hall, Inc., 1966.

Wedemeyer, Albert C. *Wedemeyer Reports.* New York: Henry Holt & Company, 1958.

Welch, Lewis Sheldon, and Camp, Walter. *Yale: Her Campus, Class-Rooms and Athletics.* Boston: L. C. Page and Company, 1899.

What America Thinks: Editorials and Cartoons, Reproduced, with Permission, from American Newspapers. Chicago: What America Thinks, Inc., 1941.

Wheeler, Burton K. (with Paul F. Healy). *Yankee from the West.* Garden City, N. Y.: Doubleday & Company, Inc., 1962.

Wiegman, Carl. *Trees to News: A Chronicle of the Ontario Paper Company's Origin and Development.* Toronto: McClelland & Stewart Limited, 1953.

Yale University, Class of 1903. *Class Book, 1903.* New Haven: n.p., 1903.

.... *History of the Class of 1903. Vol. II. Trennial.* New Haven: Yale University, 1906.

.... *History of the Class of 1903. Vol. III. Sexennial.* New Haven: Yale University, 1906.

.... *History of the Class of 1903. Vol. IV. Decennial.* New Haven: Yale University, 1913.

PAMPHLETS

America First. *To Enter the Wars Now Raging in Europe, Asia and Africa Would Be an Act of National Folly from Which Our Country Must Be Spared!* N.p., n.d.

Chicago Citizen's Committee on Press and Radio. *The Chicago Tribune— Poison.* Chicago: n.p., n.d.

Chicago Tribune. *The Destiny of Chicago—Reprinted from the Sunday Chicago Tribune, September, 1929.* Chicago: The Tribune Company, 1929.

.... *The First Hundred Years: Some Highlights of the First Century of the Publication of the Chicago Tribune, 1847–1947.* Chicago: The Tribune Company, 1947.

.... *From Paper to Papers: How the Titanic Task of Producing over 800,000 Tribunes Every Night is Accomplished.* Chicago: The Tribune Company, 1936.

.... *In Furtherance of the Movement for International Peace and for Closer Relations of Italy and America.* Edited by Mary Howell. Chicago: The Tribune Company, 1933.

.... *Thunderer of the Prairies: A Selection of Wartime Editorials and Cartoons, 1941–1944.* Chicago: The Tribune Company, 1944.

.... *Trees to Tribunes.* Chicago: The Tribune Company, 1951.

McCormick, Robert R. *An Address . . . at Yale University, November 18, 1930 under the Auspices of the Paul Block Foundation of Journalism.* Chicago: The Tribune Company, 1931.

.... *An Address by Colonel Robert R. McCormick at a Dinner Given in His Honor on His Sixty-fifth Birthday, Chicago, Illinois—July 30, 1945.* Chicago: The Tribune Company, 1945.

.... *An Address by Robert R. McCormick at the Annual Banquet of the Advertising Department of the Chicago Tribune, January 2, 1932, Drake Hotel, Chicago.* Chicago: The Chicago Tribune, 1932.

.... *An Address by Col. Robert R. McCormick at the Annual Dinner of the Chicago Better Business Bureau, March 16, 1932.* Chicago: The Chicago Tribune, 1932.

.... *An Address by Col. Robert R. McCormick before the Chicago Association of Commerce, April 6, 1932.* Chicago: The Tribune Company, 1932.

.... *An Address by Colonel Robert R. McCormick before the Foreign Policy Association, New York City, November 17, 1945.* Chicago: The Tribune Company, 1945.

.... *An Address by Col. Robert R. McCormick, Civic Opera House, Chicago, February 12, 1936.* Chicago: The Tribune Company, 1936.

.... *An Address by Colonel Robert R. McCormick, Delivered at the Dinner Following the Twenty-fifth Semi-Annual Convention of the Advertising Department of the Chicago Tribune, December 29, 1932.* Chicago: The Tribune Company, 1932.

.... *An Address by Colonel Robert R. McCormick to the Annual Banquet of the Chicago Tribune Advertising Department, December 10, 1942.* Chicago: The Tribune Company, 1942.

.... *An American's Creed, Delivered before the Detroit Athletic Club, December 15, 1943.* Chicago: The Tribune Company, 1943.

.... *Another Voyage to Three Continents, Based on a Series of Addresses Broadcast over WGN, WGNB and the Mutual Broadcasting System, February 16–March 29, 1952.* Chicago: The Tribune Company, 1952.

.... *The Cost of Government: An Address Delivered before the Chicago Assembly of the Hamilton Club, Chicago, February 18, 1932.* Chicago: The Tribune Company, 1932.

.... *Europe from Afar: An Address Delivered at the University of Notre Dame, July 29, 1939.* Chicago: The Tribune Company, 1939.

.... *An Exchange of Views Regarding America and the War between Colonel Robert R. McCormick and Lord Kemsley. Reprinted from the Chicago Tribune, November 19 and 21, 1941.* Chicago: The Tribune Company, 1941.

.... *The Fall of Liberty: An Address Written by Col. Robert R. McCormick for the District Conference of the Wisconsin State Chamber of Commerce, Madison, May 11, 1932.* Chicago: The Tribune Company, 1941.

.... *Help Save Your Country: An Address by Col. Robert R. McCormick for the District Conference of the Wisconsin State Chamber of Commerce, Madison, May 11, 1932.* Chicago: The Tribune Company, 1932.

.... *How the Tax Cancer Was Started: An Address Delivered before the Chicago Assembly of the Hamilton Club, Chicago, February 19, 1932.* Chicago: The Tribune Company, 1932.

.... *Mussolini, Moscow or America: An Address by Col. Robert R. McCormick.* Chicago: The Tribune Company, 1932.

.... *The National Peril: An Address by Col. Robert R. McCormick, April 16, 1932.* Chicago: The Tribune Company, 1932.

.... *The Rise and Fall of the Third Estate: An Address by Col. Robert R. McCormick, April 16, 1932 before the Chicago Bar Association.* Chicago: The Tribune Company, 1932.

.... *The Sack of Rome and the Sacking of America: An Address by Col. Robert R. McCormick before the Kansas City Branch of the Federation of American Business, Kansas City, Missouri, July 7, 1932.* Chicago: The Tribune Company, 1932.

.... *Save the Republic: An Address Delivered at Mount Carroll, Illinois, August 1, 1935.* Chicago: The Tribune Company, 1935.

.... *What is a Newspaper: A Talk before the Chicago Church Federation at the Hotel Morrison, October 27, 1924.* Chicago: The Tribune Company, 1927.

Ontario Paper Company. *Fair Play: Published in the Interests of Better Understanding between Canada and the United States.* Thorold, Ontario and Montreal: Ontario Paper Company Limited and North Shore Paper Company, Ltd., 1940.

Thomason, S. E. *The Low Down on Our Slogan.* Chicago: The Tribune Company, n.d.

Union for Democratic Action [Elmer Gertz]. *The People vs. the Chicago Tribune.* Chicago: Union for Democratic Action, 1942.

The War Record of the Chicago Tribune, Submitted to the People of Illinois, Indiana, Iowa, Wisconsin and Michigan . . . Compiled for Henry Ford. N.p., n.d. (probably 1919).

ARTICLES AND PERIODICALS

Alexander, Jack. "The Duke of Chicago." *Saturday Evening Post* CCXIV (July 19, 1941), 10–11, 70–75.

.... "The World's Greatest Newspaper." *Saturday Evening Post* CCXIV (July 26, 1941), 27, 80–89.

Atlanta Constitution, December, 1941.

The Beacon, 1937–1938.

Billington, Ray A. "The Origins of Middle Western Isolationism." *Political Science Quarterly* LX (March, 1945), 44–64.

Boorstin, Daniel J. "Selling the President to the People." *Commentary* XX (November, 1955), 421–24.

Bryan Democrat, September 2, 1941.

Capital Times (Madison), August 22, 1941.

Carlson, John Roy. "Inside the America First Movement." *American Mercury* LIV (January, 1942), 9–25.

"Censorship," *Fortune Magazine* XXIII (June, 1941), 88, 153–54, 158, 160.

Chicago Daily News, 1940–1942.

Chicago Daily News Almanac and Year Book.

Chicago Record Herald, 1905–1912.

Chicago Sun, December, 1941.

Chicago Times, October–November, 1936; 1940–1941.

Chicago Tribune, 1929–1941.

"Chicago Tribune," *Fortune Magazine* IX (May, 1934), 101–13, 180–88, 201–11.

Chicago, *Proceedings of the City Council,* 1904–1906.

Chicago Sanitary District, *Proceedings of the Board of Trustees,* 1906–1910.

Creeley, Tobin. "Promoting a Newsprint 'Crisis.'" *Canadian Forum* XXI (May, 1941), 47–48.

Daily Worker, December, 1941.

Des Moines Register, December, 1941.

Detroit News, December, 1941.

Editor and Publisher, 1929–1941.

Editor and Publisher, International Year Book, 1929–1941.

Fast, Howard. "An Occurrence at Republic Steel." *The Aspirin Age,* 1919–1941. Edited by Isabel Leighton. New York: Simon and Schuster, Inc., 1963. Pp. 383–402.

Fight For Freedom Committee, Bulletins, 1941–1942.

Friends of Democracy, Press Releases, 1942.

Friends of Democracy's Battle, November 15, 1947.

"Gallup and Fortune Polls." *Public Opinion Quarterly* V (June, 1941), 322–24.

Gertz, Elmer. "Chicago's Adult Delinquent: The Tribune." *Public Opinion Quarterly* VIII (Fall, 1944), 415–24.

.... "Eccentric Titan: McCormick of the Tribune." *The Nation* CLXXX (April 30, 1955), 362–64.

Gertz, Elmer, and Tebbel, John. "The Chicago Tribune." *American Mercury* LVIII (March, 1944), 299–307.

Gunther, John. "Funneling the European News." *Harper's Monthly* CLX (April, 1930), 635–47.

Hallgren, Mauritz A. "Chicago Goes Tammany." *The Nation* CXXII (April 22, 1931), 446–48.

In Fact, July 1, 1940–1942.

Jacob, Philip E. "Influences of World Events on U.S. 'Neutrality' Opinion." *Public Opinion Quarterly* IV (March, 1940), 48–65.

Lasch, Robert. "Chicago Patriot 'The World's Greatest Newspaper,'" *Atlantic Monthly* CLXIX (June, 1942), 691–95.

Louisville Courier-Journal, December, 1941.

Markey, Morris. "Land of the Pilgrim's, Pride the Urgent City." *McCalls* LIX (March, 1932), 67.

Martin, John Bartlow. "Colonel McCormick of the Tribune." *Harper's Magazine* CLXXXIX (October, 1944), 404–13.

Mayer, Milton. "The Siege of Idiot's Tower." *Common Sense* (March, 1944), pp. 110–11.

McCormick, Robert R. "Can America Fight in Europe." *Scribner's Commentator* IX (January, 1941), 88–90.

.... "Lessons of Military History: Our Army and Modern Warfare." *Vital Speeches of the Day* VII (October 1, 1941), 753–55.

.... "The Lessons of this War: The Appalling Cost of Ignorance." *Vital Speeches of the Day* VII (August 15, 1941), 644–46.

.... "Our Republic Is at Stake, Heed Well the Warning." *Vital Speeches of the Day* VI (March 15, 1940), 327–32.

.... "Tanks and Wartime Defense." *Scribner's Commentator* X (October, 1941), 91–94.

.... "The Torch of Liberty." *Vital Speeches of the Day* I (May 20, 1935), 524–26.

Montreal Daily Star, October 30, 1941.

New York Herald Tribune, December, 1941.

New York Times, 1931–1941.

New Yorker Magazine, XXIII (August 2, 1947), 30.

P.M. (New York), December, 1941.

"The Press and the Public." *New Republic* XC (March 17, 1937), 178–91.

Review of Reviews, XCIII (February, 1936), 42.

St. Louis Post-Dispatch, December, 1941.

San Francisco Chronicle, December, 1941.

Sargent, S. S. "Emotional Stereotypes in the Chicago Tribune." *Sociometry* II (April, 1939), 69–75.

Seldes, George. "The Men Who Fake the News." *New Masses* XXXIV (January 30, 1940), 14–17.

Shebs, Robert L. "What's Happening at the Tribune." *Chicago* I (December, 1954), 20–25.

Smuckler, Ralph A. "The Region of Isolationism." *American Political Science Review* XLVII (June, 1953), 386–401.

The South Works Bulletin, I (November 7, 1941), 1.

Time Magazine, 1929–1941.

Toronto Evening Telegram, September 4, 1941.

Toronto Globe and Mail, December, 1941.

The Trib, 1929–1941.

Trohan, Walter. "My Life with the Colonel." *Journal of the Illinois State Historical Society* LII (Winter, 1959), 477–502.

Twohey, James S. "An Analysis of Newspaper Opinion on War Issues." *Public Opinion Quarterly* V (Fall, 1941), 448–55.

Villard, Oswald Garrison. "Red Menace and Yellow Journalism." *The Nation* CXXXII (June 3, 1931), 602–603.

Washington Post, December, 1941.

Williams, Greer. "I Worked for McCormick." *The Nation* CLV (October 10, 1942), 348–49.

Winnipeg Free Press, December, 1941.

UNPUBLISHED MATERIAL

Armstrong, John Paul. "Senator Taft and American Foreign Policy: The Period of Opposition." Ph.D. dissertation, University of Chicago, 1953.

Barber, Courtenay. Miscellaneous material given to the University of Chicago Library.

.... "The Enigma of One Robert Rutherford McCormick: The Internationalization of a Super-Nationalist or Watta Scholar!" Speech, November 8, 1943. University of Chicago Library.

Basich, George. "The Opinion of the Chicago Tribune Concerning Internationalism in 1939 and 1946." Master's dissertation, University of Chicago, 1947.

Beck, Edward Scott. Collection. Chicago Historical Society.

Briscoe, Jerry Bowles. "A Study of the Chicago Council on Foreign Relations." Master's dissertation, University of Chicago, 1949.

Carlson, Ronald E. "Organization and Activities of the Chicago Chapter of the Fight for Freedom Committee." Master's dissertation, University of Chicago, 1961.

Dawes, Charles. Papers. Northwestern University Library.

Faw, Volney. "The Chicago Tribune and its Control." Master's dissertation, University of Chicago, 1940.

Fight For Freedom Committee. Papers. University of Chicago Library.

Gunther, John. Papers. University of Chicago Library.

Harrison, Carter H. Papers. Newberry Library.

Henson, Corwin Edward. "Crusade in 1940, The Foreign Policy of Wendell Willkie in the Presidential Campaign." Master's dissertation, University of Chicago, 1960.

Jenkins, Warren Gard. "The Foreign Policy of the Chicago Tribune, 1914–1917: A Program of National Self-Interest." Ph.D. dissertation, University of Wisconsin, 1943.

Johns, Elizabeth Dewey. "Chicago's Newspapers and the News: A Study of Public Communication in a Metropolis." Ph.D. dissertation, University of Chicago, 1942.

Landon, Alf. Letter to author. December, 1967.

McCormick, Chauncey. Papers. Newberry Library.

McCormick, Robert R. "Memoirs." Unpublished Ms. Latest revision, July 22, 1954. Chicago Tribune Library.

.... "Why I Broke with F.D.R." 4 parts. WGN Speeches, August 7, 14, 28, September 4, 1954. Unpublished Ms. Chicago Tribune Library.

McCutcheon Papers. Newberry Library.

McMahon, James J. "A Study of the Effect of Newspaper Partisanship and the Correlation of Votes to Circulation." Burgess Papers. University of Chicago Library.

O'Reilly, Alice M. "Colonel Robert Rutherford McCormick: His Tribune and Mayor William Hale Thompson." Master's dissertation, University of Chicago, 1963.

Rogers, William Cecil. "Isolationist Propaganda, September 1, 1939, to December 7, 1941." Ph.D. dissertation, University of Chicago, 1943.

Schultz, Sigrid. Letter to author. March, 1968.

Taylor, Edmond. "What is Wrong with the Chicago Tribune." Speech delivered July 29, 1941. University of Chicago Library.

Wheeler, Burton K. Letter to author. February, 1968.

OTHER MATERIAL

Cleveland, Charles. Personal interview. July 1, 1967.

Dirksen, Everett. Personal interview. July 27, 1967.

Edwards, Willard. Personal interview. July 24, 1967.

Hughes, Frank. Personal interview. August 10, 1965.

Manly, Chesly. Personal interview. June 14, 1965.

McCormick, Maryland. Personal interview. July 25, 1967.

Strand, William. Personal interview. July 25, 1967.

Tribune Executive. Personal interview. July 14, 1965. Name withheld by request.

Trohan, Walter. Personal interview. December 30, 1964.

PUBLIC DOCUMENTS

U.S. *Congressional Directory.* 78th Cong., 1st Sess., 1942.

U.S. *Congressional Record.* Vols. LXXXV–LXXXVII.

U.S. House of Representatives. *Hearings before the Committee on Foreign Affairs, House of Representatives, Seventy-Seventh Congress, First Session on H.R. 1776, A Bill to Promote the Defense of the United States, and for Other Purposes, January 15–29, 1941.* 77th Cong., 1st Sess., 1941.

U.S. Senate. *Hearings before the Committee on Foreign Relations, United States Senate, Seventy-Seventh Congress, First Session on S. 275, A Bill Further to Promote the Defense of the United States and for Other Purposes, Part 2, February 4, to February 10, 1941.* 77th Cong., 1st Sess., 1941.

INDEX

SPO, CARSON CITY, NEVADA, 1971